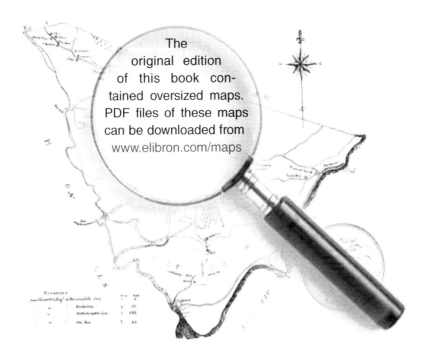

The
original edition
of this book con-
tained oversized maps.
PDF files of these maps
can be downloaded from
www.elibron.com/maps

EDWARD AUGUSTUS FREEMAN

THE

OTTOMAN POWER
IN EUROPE

ITS NATURE, ITS GROWTH, AND ITS DECLINE

Elibron Classics
www.elibron.com

Elibron Classics series.

© 2005 Adamant Media Corporation.

ISBN 1-4021-4428-8 (paperback)
ISBN 1-4021-5485-2 (hardcover)

This Elibron Classics Replica Edition is an unabridged facsimile
of the edition published in 1877 by Macmillan and Co.,
London.

Elibron and Elibron Classics are trademarks of
Adamant Media Corporation. All rights reserved.

This book is an accurate reproduction of the original. Any marks, names, colophons, imprints, logos or other symbols or identifiers that appear on or in this book, except for those of Adamant Media Corporation and BookSurge, LLC, are used only for historical reference and accuracy and are not meant to designate origin or imply any sponsorship by or license from any third party.

THE

OTTOMAN POWER IN EUROPE.

a

" Illi vero nihilominus bellum quam pacem elegerant, omnem miseriam caræ libertati postponentes. Est namque hujuscemodi genus hominum, durum et laboris patiens, victa levissimo assuetum, et quod nostris gravi oneri esse solet, Slavi pro quadam voluptate ducunt. Transeunt sane dies plurimi, his pro gloria et pro magno latoque imperio, illis pro libertate ac ultima e servitute, varie certantibus."

WIDUKIND, ii. 20.

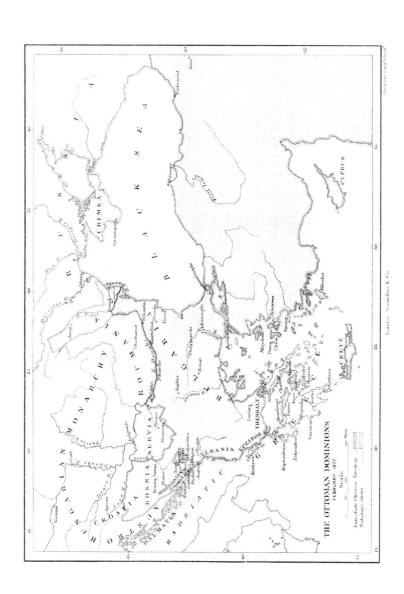

THE OTTOMAN DOMINIONS
FEBRUARY 1877

Scale

Immediate Ottoman Territory
Tributary States

London, Macmillan & Co.

THE

OTTOMAN POWER

IN EUROPE,

ITS NATURE, ITS GROWTH, AND ITS DECLINE.

BY

EDWARD A. FREEMAN, D.C.L., LL.D.,

KNIGHT COMMANDER OF THE GREEK ORDER OF THE SAVIOR,
AND OF THE SERVIAN ORDER OF TAKOVA,
CORRESPONDING MEMBER OF THE IMPERIAL ACADEMY OF SCIENCES
OF SAINT PETERSBURG.

Ἐν τούτῳ νίκα.
Deus id vult.

WITH THREE COLOURED MAPS.

London:

MACMILLAN AND CO.

1877.

[*The Right of Translation and Reproduction is Reserved.*]

INVICTAE · GENTIS · INVICTO   PRINCIPI ·

FIDEI · AC · LIBERTATIS · VNICO · PROPVGNATORI ·

IN · CIVES   AMABILI · IN · BARBAROS   TERRIBILI ·

N I C O L A O ·

DEI · GRATIA ·

MONTIS   NIGRI · ET · BERDAE · PRINCIPI

VICINARVM · GENTIVM · DEO · IVVANTE · LIBERATORI · FVTVRO

VITA ET VICTORIA.

PREFACE.

I should wish this little book to be taken as in some sort a companion to my lately reprinted History and Conquests of the Saracens. I there, while speaking of most of the other chief Mahometan nations, had no opportunity of speaking at all at length of the Ottoman Turks. That lack is here supplied, supplied that is in the same general way in which the whole subject of Mahometan history was treated in the earlier volume. Neither pretends to be at all a full account of any branch of the subject; in both I deal with Eastern and Mahometan affairs mainly in their reference to Western and Christian affairs. The Ottoman Turks have had, at least for some centuries past, a greater influence on Western and Christian affairs than any other Eastern and Mahometan people. Their history, from the point of view in which I look at it, is therefore the natural completion of my former subject.

But there is one wide difference between the two books, a difference wide at least in appearance, though I believe that the difference is in appearance only.

In ordinary language, my former book would be
said to be primarily historical; it would be called
political, only secondarily and to a very small extent.
My present book may be thought to be—in the
eyes of those who draw a distinction between history
and politics it will rightly be thought to be—
political rather than historical. But between history
and politics I can draw no distinction. History is
the politics of the past; politics are the history of
the present. The same rules of criticism apply to
judging alike of distant and of recent facts. The
same eternal laws of right and wrong are to be
applied in forming our estimate of the actors in either
case. The championship of right and the championship of wrong bear exactly the same character in any
age. A Montfort and a Gladstone, a Flambard and a
Beaconsfield, must stand or fall together. It shews
the low view that some men take of politics that they
can conceive the word only as meaning a struggle to
support some and upset others among the momentary
candidates for office. Men who have no higher notion
of politics than this seem unable to understand that
there are those who support or oppose this or that
minister, because he follows or does not follow a
certain line of policy, who do not follow or oppose a
certain line of policy because it is or is not the policy
of this or that minister. Politics, the science of Aris-
totle, the science of the right ruling of men and
nations, means something higher than this. It teaches
us how to judge of causes and their effects; it teaches

us how to judge of the character of acts, whether done yesterday or thousands of years ago. The past is studied in vain, unless it gives us lessons for the present ; the present will be very imperfectly understood, unless the light of the past is brought to bear upon it. In this way, history and politics are one. In my former little book, consisting of lectures read before a certain society at its own request, it would have been obviously out of place to do more than point the political moral of the story in a general way. The subject naturally led me to shew that the pretended reforms of the Turk were in their own nature good-for-nothing. Two and twenty years ago, I drew that inference from the general current of Mahometan history ; and I think that the two and twenty years of Mahometan history which have passed since then, have more than borne out what I then said. My present business is to work out the same position more fully, from a survey of that particular part of Mahometan history which bears most directly on that position, and on the immediate practical application of that position. I use the past history of the Ottoman Turks to shew what is the one way which, according to the light of reason and experience, can be of any use in dealing with the Ottoman Turks of the present day.

In this way then my book is at once political and historical. That is, it deals with the politics or the history — I use those words as words of the same meaning—both of past and of present times. In opposition to all theoretical and sentimental ways of looking at things, I argue from what has happened to what is likely to happen. I argue that what has been done already can be done again. As every land that has been set free from the Turk has gained by its freedom—as every land which remains under the Turk has but one wish, namely to get rid of the Turk —as the lands which are set free do not envy the bondage of their enslaved neighbours, while the lands which remain enslaved do envy the freedom of their liberated neighbours—I therefore argue from all this that the one work to be done is to put the enslaved lands on the same level as the liberated lands. So to do is the dictate of right; so to do is the dictate of interest. As long as any Christian land remains under the Turk, there will be discontents and disturbances and revolts and massacres; there will be diplomatic difficulties and complications; in a word, the "eternal Eastern Question" will remain eternal. From the experience of the past I infer that the only way to settle that question is to get rid of the standing difficulty, the standing complication, the standing cause of discontent and revolt and massacre, namely the rule of the Turk. And I further infer from the experience of the past that the rule of the Turk can be got rid of, because, wherever men have thoroughly had the will to get rid of him, he has been got rid of. He has been got rid of in Hungary, in Servia, in the liberated part of Greece. With the same hearty will and zealous effort, he may be got rid of in all the other lands where he still does his work of evil. By the policy of Canning backed by the sword of Sobieski, perhaps by the policy of Canning without the sword of Sobieski, the Eastern Question may be solved. But, as long as there is neither sword nor policy, but only the helpless babble of a man who can never make up his mind, the Eastern Question will go on for ever.

Since my last chapter was written, the long talked-of Protocol has been signed. I do not pretend to know what can be the object of Russia or of any other power in proposing or signing it. The one practical thing about it is that it does not bind Russia to disarm. That is, it does not take away from the South-eastern nations the last hope of deliverance that is left to them. It is with a blush that an Englishman writes such words as these. It is with shame and sorrow that an Englishman has to confess that, when another nation undertakes the work which should above all things have been the work of England, the utmost that he can dare to hope for is that England may not be a hinderer in that work. We have no wish for Russian aggrandizement, for Russian ascendency, for Russian influence in any form. We believe that the exclusive ascendency of Russia in the South-eastern lands would be an evil; only we do not hold it to be the greatest of evils. We would fain see England, Russia, any other civilized power, have its fair share of influence in those lands. But, if we are reduced to a choice between Russia

and the Turk, then we must choose Russia. Our
consciences are clear ; the choice is not of our seeking ; it is forced upon us, it is forced upon the South-
eastern nations, by the professed enemies of Russia.
It is those professed enemies of Russia who are doing
the work of Russia. It is they who are allowing
Russia to take on herself alone the office in which
England and all civilized nations ought to join with
her, that of the protector of the oppressed nations.
The policy of reason is to hinder any evil designs
which Russia may be thought to have—though I
know of no reason for always attributing evil designs
to Russia more than to any other power—by frank
and cordial alliance with her in designs which, at least
in profession, are good. The deliverance of the subject
nations ought to be, if possible, the work of all Europe.
Failing that, it should be the work of Russia and
England together. But if England holds back and
leaves Russia to do the work alone, the fault lies with
England and not with Russia. If the designs of
Russia are good, we lose the glory of sharing in
them ; if her designs are evil, we fail to employ the
best means of thwarting them. The policy with
which England entered into the Conference, the
resolve that, in no case whatever, was any thing to
be done, that in no case should the Turk be either
helped or coerced, was the very policy which Russia,
if she has any hidden designs, would wish England
to follow.

The disarmament of Russia at this moment would

be to take away from the subject nations their last hope, that which the policy of Lord Derby has made their last hope. It would be to leave those nations helpless in the clutches of their tyrants. Intervention must come sooner or later. As long as the Turk rules, the present state of things will go on. As long as the Turk rules, there will always be revolts, there will always be massacres. Europe cannot endure this state of things for ever. One European nation at least stands ready to step in and put an end to it. We wish that that nation did not stand alone; but if, by the fault of other nations, she does stand alone, we cannot blame her, we cannot thwart her. Lord Beaconsfield and Lord Derby have brought things to such a pass that there is no hope but in Russia. It is something that, even in their hands, the Protocol is not so drawn up as not to cut off that only hope.

Otherwise the Protocol, as a document, and the other documents which follow it, are simply talk of the usual kind. The Protocol talks about this and that circular and declaration of the Turk as if it meant something. It talks "of good intentions on the part of the Porte"—the "Porte" being the usual euphemism for the Ring that ordered the massacres. It talks of their "honour"—the honour of the men whose falsehoods Lord Salisbury and General Ignatieff rebuked to their faces. It talks of their "loyalty"— the loyalty of the men whose promises are, in the schoolboy proverb, like pie-crust. It talks about "reforms," as if the Turk would ever make reforms. It

"invites the Porte," in the queer, cumbrous, language
of diplomacy, "to consolidate the pacification by re-
placing its armies on a peace-footing, excepting the
number of troops indispensable for the maintenance
of order." What is "order"? By order the Turk
means one thing ; the Bulgarian or the Thessalian
means another thing. By order the Turk means a
state of things in which the Bulgarian and the Thessalian lie still, while the Turk deals with them as he
chooses. The number of troops indispensable for the
maintenance of order in this sense may be got at, if
we know how many unarmed Christians can be kept
in bondage by one armed Mussulman. In the eyes
of the Bulgarian and the Thessalian, order means a
state of things for which it is in the first place indispensable that there should be no armed Turks in
his country at all. Where the armed Turk is, there
can be no order ; for the presence of the armed Turk
means the commission of every form of outrage without fear of punishment. Turkish troops can never be
put on a peace-footing ; because, where Turkish troops
are there can be no peace, except in that old sense
in which men call it peace when they have made a
wilderness.

And, to do all these wonderful measures of reform,
the Turk is to "take advantage of the present lull."
Where is the "lull"? Certainly nowhere in the lands
east of the Hadriatic. There is no lull in Bulgaria,
where the Turk goes on with his usual work of blood
and outrage day by day. There is no lull in Free

Bosnia, where the victorious patriots have driven out the Turk, and where they stand with their arms in their hands lest he should come in again. There is no lull on the Black Mountain, where the triumphant champions of freedom, the men to whom the back of a Turk is the most familiar of all sights, stand ready to march, ready to extend their own freedom to their suffering brethren. While all this is going on, diplomatists see a lull. They meet and talk, and say that, "if" the things happen which are happening every day, then they will meet again and have another talk.

The sayings and doings of Lord Derby have long since passed out of the range of practical politics. He seems to have lost even that amount of practical vigour which is involved in forbidding an act of humanity or in exhorting the Turk to suppress an insurrection. Of all things absolutely helpless the most helpless surely is the conditional signature of the Protocol. Yet, if anything, the long letter which accompanies the Protocol is more helpless still. This part of the document is really worth preserving.

" Under these circumstances it appears to the Russian Government that the most practical solution, and the one best fitted to secure the maintenance of general peace, would be the signature by the Powers of a Protocol which should, so to speak, terminate the incident.

" This Protocol might be signed in London by the representatives of the Great Powers, and under the direct inspiration of the Cabinet of St. James.

" The Protocol would contain no more than the principles upon which the several Governments would have based their reply to the Russian Circular. It would be desirable that it should affirm that the present state of affairs was one which concerned the whole of Europe, and should place on record that the improvement of the condition of the Christian population of Turkey will continue to be an object of interest to all the Powers.

" The Porte having repeatedly declared that it engaged to introduce reforms, it would be desirable to enumerate them on the basis of Safvet Pacha's Circular. In this way there could be no subsequent misunderstanding as to the promises made by Turkey.

" As a period of some months would not be sufficient to accomplish these reforms, it would be preferable not to fix any precise limit of time. It would rest with all the powers to determine by general agreement whether Turkey was progressing in a satisfactory manner in her work of regeneration.

" The Protocol should mention that Europe will continue to watch the progressive execution of the reforms by means of their diplomatic representatives.

" If the hopes of the Powers should once more be disappointed, and the condition of the Christian subjects of the Sultan should not be improved, the Powers would reserve to themselves to consider in common the action which they would deem indispensable to secure the well-being of the Christian population of Turkey and the interests of the general peace.

" Count Schouvaloff hoped that I should appreciate the moderate and conciliatory spirit which actuated his Government in this expression or their views. They seemed to him to contain nothing incompatible with the principles on which the policy of England was based, and their application would secure the maintenance of general peace."

It appears then that, on March 31, 1877, Lord Derby still believed that the Turk was going to reform ; he still believed that, in watching his doings, there would be something else to watch than the kind of doings which the Turk has always done for the last five hundred years. Such an example of the charity which believeth all things can be surpassed only by the charity of Origen and Tillotson, both of whom, according to Lord Macaulay, did not despair of the reformation of a yet older offender. But, in the practical, everyday, world in

which we live, these illusions of a charitable sentimentalism cannot be taken into account. The
months during which Lord Derby is willing to look
on, hoping for the regeneration of Turkey, may be
profitably spent in accomplishing the regeneration
of Turkey by the only means by which it can be
regenerated, by putting an end to the rule of the Turk.
If Lord Derby expects the regeneration of Turkey
to be brought about by any other means, he will
no more see that done in 1877 than he or anybody
else has seen it done in any other year since 1356.

On the whole then, "the inspiration of the Cabinet
of St. James" does not seem likely to do much towards "terminating the incident," if, by "terminating
the incident" is meant putting an end to the "eternal
Eastern Question" and its causes. The phrase is not
a bad one. The presence of the Turk, and the
"eternal Eastern Question" which his presence causes,
is really only an "incident," though it is an incident
which has gone on for five hundred years. The Turk's
presence in Europe is incidental. It is something
strange, abnormal, contrary to the general system of
Europe, something which keeps that system always
out of gear, something which supplies a never-failing
stock of difficulties and complications. The Turk in
Europe, in short, answers to Lord Palmerston's definition of dirt. He is "matter in the wrong place."
The sooner the "incident" of his presence is
"terminated," by the help of whatever "inspiration,"
the better. An inspiration likely to terminate that

incident might have come from the Cabinet of St. James in the days of Canning. It is not likely to come from one who proposes to fold his hands for some months to see what the Turk will do. Those who have their eyes open, and who do not talk about "terminating incidents," know perfectly well that the Turk will, during those months, go on doing as he has done in so many earlier months. He will go on making things look smooth at Constantinople, while he does his usual work in Bulgaria and Crete.

But there is yet another danger. If everything rested with Lord Derby, with a man who is steadfastly purposed to employ himself with a vigorous doing of nothing, we should at least have one kind of safety. In the hands of Lord Derby, if we do no good, we shall do no harm, except so far as the doing of nothing is really the worst form of the doing of harm. From him, if we hope for no active good, we need fear no active mischief. But there is another power against which England and Europe ought to be yet more carefully on their guard. It is no use mincing matters. The time has come to speak out plainly. No well disposed person would reproach another either with his nationality or his religion, unless that nationality or that religion leads to some direct mischief. No one wishes to place the Jew, whether Jew by birth or by religion, under any dis-ability as compared with the European Christian. But it will not do to have the policy of England, the welfare of Europe, sacrificed to Hebrew sentiment.

The danger is no imaginary one. Every one must have marked that the one subject on which Lord Beaconsfield, through his whole career, has been in earnest has been whatever has touched his own people. A mocker about everything else, he has been thoroughly serious about this. His national sympathies led him to the most honourable action of his life, when he forsook his party for the sake of his nation, and drew forth the next day from the Standard newspaper the remark that "no Jew could be a gentleman." On that day the Jew was a gentleman in the highest sense. He acted as one who could brave much and risk much for a real conviction. His zeal for his own people is really the best feature in Lord Beaconsfield's career. But we cannot sacrifice our people, the people of Aryan and Christian Europe, to the most genuine belief in an Asian mystery. We cannot have England or Europe governed by a Hebrew policy. While Lord Derby simply wishes to do nothing one way or another, Lord Beaconsfield is the active friend of the Turk. The alliance runs through all Europe. Throughout the East, the Turk and the Jew are leagued against the Christian. In theory the Jew under Mahometan rule is condemned to equal degradation with the Christian. In practice the yoke presses much more lightly upon the Jew. As he is never a cultivator of the soil, as he commonly lives in the large towns, the worst forms of Turkish oppression do not touch him. He has also endless ways of making himself useful to the Turk, and oppressive to the Christian. The Jew is the tool of the Turk, and is therefore yet more hated than the Turk. This is the key to the supposed intolerance of Servia with regard to the Jews. I can speak for Servia; I have no information as to Roumania. The Servian legislation is not aimed at Jews as Jews, for Jews are eligible to the highest offices in Servia; it is aimed at certain corrupting callings which in point of fact are practised only by Jews. Strike out the word "Jew," and instead name certain callings which none but Jews practise, and the law of Servia might perhaps still be open to criticism on the ground of political economy; it could be open to none on the ground of religious toleration. The union of the Jew and the Turk against the Christian came out in its strongest form when Sultan Mahmoud gave the body of the martyred Patriarch to be dragged by the Jews through the streets of Constantinople. We cannot have the policy of Europe dealt with in the like sort. There is all the difference in the world between the degraded Jews of the East and the cultivated and honourable Jews of the West. But blood is stronger than water, and Hebrew rule is sure to lead to a Hebrew policy. Throughout Europe, the most fiercely Turkish part of the press is largely in Jewish hands. It may be assumed everywhere, with the smallest class of exceptions, that the Jew is the friend of the Turk and the enemy of the Christian. The outspoken voice of the English people saved us last autumn from a war with Russia on behalf of the Turk. The brags of the Mansion-House were answered by the protest of Saint James's Hall. But we must be on our guard. If Russia once goes to war with the Turk, a thousand opportunities may be found for picking a quarrel. Every step must be watched. As we cannot have the action of Canning, we must at least make sure that the inaction of Lord Derby shall be the worst thing that we have.

As I have for many years read, thought and written, much about the present subject and other subjects closely connected with it—as they have, I may say, been through life my chief secondary object of study, I have thought it worth while to give a list of the chief articles which I have written on such matters during the last three and twenty years. I forbear to mention mere letters in newspapers, which are endless. I think the dates will shew that my attention to these matters is at least not anything new.

The Byzantine Empire. North British Review. February, 1855.

Mahometanism in the East and West. North British Review. August, 1855.

The Greek People and the Greek Kingdom. Edinburgh Review. April, 1856.

The Eastern Church. Edinburgh Review. April, 1858.

Mediæval and Modern Greece. National Review. January, 1864.

Mahomet. British Quarterly Review. January, 1872.

Public and Private Morality. Fortnightly Review. April, 1873.

The True Eastern Question. Fortnightly Review. December, 1875.

Montenegro. Macmillan's Magazine. January, 1876.

The Illyrian Emperors and their Land. British Quarterly Review. July, 1876.

The Turks in Europe. British Quarterly Review. October, 1876.

Present Aspects of the Eastern Question. Fortnightly Review. October, 1876.

The Geographical Aspect of the Eastern Question. Fortnightly Review. January, 1877.

The English People in relation to the Eastern Question. Contemporary Review. February, 1877.

Race and Language. Contemporary Review. March, 1877.

I may add that the present volume is in some sort an expansion of the argument of a small tract called the " Turks in Europe," which I lately wrote as the first number of the series called " Politics for the People."

SOMERLEAZE, WELLS, SOMERSET,
April 9th, 1877.

CONTENTS.

OTTOMAN POWER IN EUROPE;

ITS NATURE, ITS GROWTH, AND ITS DECLINE.

CHAPTER I.

EASTERN AND WESTERN EUROPE.

THE rule of the Ottoman Turks in Europe is in itself a phænomenon without a parallel in history. For a length of time ranging in different parts from two to five hundred years, a large part of the fairest and most historic regions of the earth, a large part of the most renowned cities, the ancient seats of empire and civilization, have groaned under the yoke of foreign rulers, rulers whose rule is in no way changed by lapse of time, but who remain at the end of five hundred years as much strangers as they were at the beginning. In the lands where European civilization first had its birth, the European has been ruled by the Asiatic, the civilized man by the barbarian. There have been other phænomena in European history which have approached to this ; but there is none that supplies an exact parallel. A race which stands apart

B

from all the other races of Europe in all which makes
those races European, in all which distinguishes European man from Asiatic or African man, has held an
abiding dominion over those parts of Europe which
are in their history preeminently European, over
those parts of Europe from which the rest have learned
wellnigh all that has made Europe what it is. Alike
in Europe and in Asia, the ancient seats of European
dominion, the cities whence European man once ruled
over Asia, are now in the hands of the Asiatic who rules
in Europe. The earliest homes of European culture
and European history have fallen under the rule of a
race to whom European culture and European history
are strange. The spots whence Christian teaching
first went forth to win the nations of Europe within
the Christian fold have passed into the hands of
votaries of the faith which is the most direct enemy
and rival of Christianity. Looked at as historical
events, these changes might pass as being merely
among the strangest among the strange revolutions
of history. But the phænomena of Turkish rule go
deeper than this. Changes of this kind have happened
in all parts of the world. They have happened with
special frequency in the Eastern world. It is not
merely that one dynasty or one race has overthrown
another. It is not merely that a people of conquerors have held a people of subjects in bondage.
If this were all, there would be parallels enough.
The great and strange phænomenon is that, while
Europe believes itself to be the quarter of the world
which takes the lead of all others, there is still a large
part of Europe, and that the part of Europe which has,
so to speak, made the rest of Europe European, which
abides under the dominion of rulers who have nothing

to do with Europe beyond the fact that they live and bear rule within its borders.

The phænomena of Turkish rule in Europe are so strange that their very strangeness sometimes in a manner hides itself. Our usual modes of speaking are at fault. It is hard to describe the actual state of things, except by the use of words which belong to another state of things, and which, when applied to the state of things which exists in South-eastern Europe, have no meaning. If we use such words as *nation*, *people*, *government*, *law*, *sovereign*, *subject*, we must give them all special and new definitions. If we fancy that South-eastern Europe contains anything which answers to the meaning of those words in Western Europe, we are altogether deceived. We have a political and social nomenclature which suits the nations of Western Europe, as forming one political and social world. We have no special nomenclature to describe an opposite state of things at the other end of Europe ; and, if we transport our Western nomenclature there, we find ourselves using words which have nothing to answer to them. In fact the gap which divides the Turk from the nations of Europe is so wide and impassable that ordinary language fails to express it. It is so wide and impassable that we are sometimes tempted to forget how wide and impassable it is. The nations of civilized Europe have so much in common with one another that their differences strike us all the more because they have so much in common. We are therefore apt to forget how much they really have in common, how they stand together as members of one body, bound together by many ties, how they are kinsfolk whose points of unlikeness are after all trifling compared with their points of likeness. As opposed to the Turk, they are one body. They have a crowd of things in common in which the Turk has no share. To understand then what the Turk really is, how strange an anomaly his presence in Europe is, it will be well to run through the chief points of likeness between the nations of civilized Europe, to point out the chief things which they all share as common possessions. When we clearly understand how much all European nations, in spite of political and religious differences, really have in common, we shall better understand how utterly the Turk is a stranger to all of them alike.

Fully to understand the nature of this common store which belongs to the nations of civilized Europe, but in which the Turks have no share, we must go back to the very beginning of things. All the chief nations of Europe belong to one branch of the human family ; they all speak tongues which can be shown to have been at first the same tongue. There was a time when the forefathers of all the nations of Europe, Greek, Latin, Teutonic, Slavonic, and Lithuanian, were all one people, when they marched in one common company from the common home far away. Setting aside a few remnants of earlier races which our forefathers found in Europe, setting aside a few settlements which have in historic times been made in Europe by men of other races, all the nations of Europe belong to the one common Aryan stock. And those which do not, the earlier remnants, the later settlers, have all, with one exception, been brought more or less thoroughly within the range of Aryan influences. If not European by birth, they have become European by adoption. Here then is one great common possession, namely, real original unity of race and speech. (¹) And it surely cannot be doubted that this original unity of race and speech had a most powerful, though an unconscious, influence, in bringing the European nations together as members of one great commonwealth, in distinction from those who have no share in this ancestral possession. The original unity worked for ages before men knew anything of its being; it bound men together who had no thought whatever of the tie which bound them. The Gaul, the Roman, the Goth, had no knowledge of their original kindred. But that original kindred did its work all the same. It enabled Gaul, Roman and Goth, to be all fused together into one society, a society in which the Hun and the Saracen had no share. First and foremost then among the common possessions of civilized Europe, we must place the common possession of Aryan blood and speech. Throughout Europe that which is Aryan is the rule ; that which is not Aryan is the exception. And for the most part that which is not Aryan has more or less thoroughly put on an Aryan guise. Here then is the first common possession which marks off Aryan Europe from those who have no share in the common heritage.

But original community of descent and language are not all. By themselves they might not have been enough to form the nations of Europe into one great society. We have far-off kinsfolk, sprung from the same ancestral stock, speaking dialects of the same ancestral language, who have been parted off so long and so utterly that the original kindred has now become mere matter of curious interest, with little or no working upon practical affairs. If Latin, Teuton and Slave are all kinsmen to one another, the Persian

and the Hindoo are kinsmen no less. And yet the
Persian and the Hindoo are not, like the Latin, the
Teuton, and the Slave, members of one great commonwealth of nations. The geographical separation
between the Eastern and the Western Aryans has
caused the Western Aryans to form a distinct
commonwealth of nations, quite apart from their
Eastern kinsfolk. The Western Aryans have settled
in lands which are geographically continuous, and
that geographical continuity has enabled them to add
to original tie of race and speech, the further tie of
partnership in a common history. They all form
part of one historic world, the world of Rome. They
all share, more or less fully, in the memories which are
common to all who have been brought within the
magic influence of either of the two seats of Roman
dominion. The modern nations of Europe were
either once subjects of the Roman Empire, or else
they are settlers within that Empire, in the character
half of conquerors, half of disciples. Or even if they lie
beyond the bounds of the older Empire, even if they
never submitted to its political authority, they have
still bowed beneath its moral influence. All Europe,
Eastern and Western, has a common right in Rome
and in all that springs from Rome, in the laws, the
arts, the languages, the general culture, which Rome
taught them. Of that Roman influence there have
been two centres; Western Europe sat at the feet of
the Old Rome by the Tiber ; Eastern Europe sat at
the feet of the New Rome by the Bosporos. From
Rome, Old and New, from the city of Romulus and
from the city of Constantine, has come the civilization
which distinguishes Europe from Africa and Asia.
In that heritage all Europe has a share. From that

source all Europe has learned a crowd of ideas and memories and sympathies, in which those nations which stood outside the Roman world never had a share. All Europe alike has its right in those two languages of the Roman world which have ever been, in one shape or another, the groundwork of European culture. The Greek and the Latin tongues, the tongue of poetry and science, the tongue of law and rule, the undying literature of those two tongues, the endless train of thoughts and feelings which have their root in that literature, all these are a common and an exclusive possession of civilized Europe. They are a common heritage which parts off Roman Europe from those nations which never came under the abiding spell of Roman influence.

But besides their common origin and common history, there is another common possession of the nations of Europe, a possession which is the greatest result of their common history, the greatest gift which Rome gave alike to her children, her subjects, her conquerors, and her far-off disciples. Besides a common origin and a common history, the nations of Europe have a common religion. Besides being Aryan and Roman, Europe is also Christian. In its historic aspect, Christianity is the religion of the Roman Empire, the religion of all those lands which either formed part of the Roman Empire or which received their culture from Rome, Old or New. It is the religion of Europe; if it is no longer the religion of the lands out of Europe which once were Roman, it is because in those lands it has undergone more or less of physical uprooting. In its origin Semitic and Asiatic, Christianity became in its history preeminently European and Aryan. Born in a remote province of the Empire, it became the religion of the Empire; it became the religion of all the nations to which the Empire gave its creed as well as its law and its culture. But beyond those limits it hardly spread. It is the creed of civilized Europe and America, because civilized Europe and America share in the common heritage of Rome. It is not the creed of Asia and Africa; because over the greater part of Asia and Africa the influence of Rome never spread, and where it did spread it has been rooted out by the events of later history. Nor does it really affect this common possession that the nations of Europe have accepted Christianity in various forms, that each great division of nations has moulded the common possession into a shape of its own, according to its own national character and national feelings. To go no deeper into the divisions of Christendom, there is on the face of things a Greek, a Latin, and a Teutonic Christianity, each of which has features which are special to itself, in ceremony, in discipline, and even in doctrine. And these differences have led to divisions, hatreds, persecutions, wars. And yet, among all this division, there is real unity. Christianity is, after all, a common possession, a common tie, even among nations who are almost ready to refuse to one another the name of Christians. They may carry on their disputes even in the face of men of another faith, and yet, as compared with men of another faith, their union is stronger than their diversity. Between the professors of any two forms of Christianity the points of likeness are, after all, more and stronger than the points of unlikeness. In most cases this is true even of mere dogma. In all cases it is true of those indirect results of Christian teaching which are the truest common possession of

Christian nations. What those results are we will go on to examine further ; but we have already found a third note, a third possession, which the nations of civilized Europe—reckoning also of course their colonies in other lands—have in common and have almost exclusively. Civilized Europe, besides being Aryan and Roman, is also Christian.

We now go a step further. The common origin of the European nations, combined with their geographical position, allowed them to have a common history. That common history gave them a common creed. And that common history and common creed working together have given them a common civilization, a common morality, a common possession of political, social, and intellectual life. Community of origin and community of history gave the European nations a common possession of political and intellectual instincts, and their common faith, to say the least, did not stand in the way of the developement of those common political and intellectual instincts. This last assertion needs, if not some qualification, at least some explanation. Men who have given themselves out as representatives of the Christian religion, men who have borne the names of Christian teachers and Christian rulers, have often stood in the way of those instincts. Political freedom and intellectual life have often been suppressed and proscribed in the name of the Christian religion. Persecutions and wars against men professing other creeds, against men professing other forms of Christianity, have often been decreed in the name of Christianity. But Christianity itself has done none of those things. Those who have done them have not obeyed but disobeyed the genuine teaching of Christianity. That

this is so will appear more plainly when we come to
speak of the practical working of another religion.
The historical work of Christianity has been this.
The common creed of Europe, working together with
the common origin and common history of Europe,
has produced the common civilization of Europe.
The common creed has strengthened whatever was
good, it has weakened whatever was evil, in the state
of European society when that common creed was
first adopted. It has been enabled to do so mainly
through the negative side of its teaching. Christianity
lays down no political or civil precepts. It prescribes
no form of government ; it forbids no form of government. Its precepts are purely moral. It lays down
no code of laws. It simply lays down moral precepts,
according to which its individual professors are bound
to shape their private actions, and therefore according
to which communities made up of those professors
are bound to shape their public actions. It prescribes
justice and mercy. It prescribes good will and good
deeds to brethren in the faith in the first instance, but
to men of other creeds as well. To do good unto all
men, specially unto such as are of the household of
faith, is the sum of its teaching.

In short, Christianity is so far from laying down
any political or civil code that it does not even lay
down a moral code. The practical application of its
moral precepts to political and social questions is left
to its disciples to work out for themselves. Take for
instance the two great features which distinguish
Eastern from Western society, features which are
closely connected with one another, and of which it
may be safely said that one at least implies the
other. Eastern society not only allows slavery and

polygamy, but it is grounded upon them. An Eastern nation from which slavery and polygamy were wholly swept away would cease to be an Eastern nation. It would, whatever its geographical position, have, in the most important social respects, become Western. To say that Eastern society is grounded on slavery and polygamy of course does not imply that each particular man in an Eastern nation is necessarily either a slave-owner or a master of many wives. Slavery and polygamy on any great scale must always be in their own nature the privileges of the few. But Eastern society is founded on those institutions in the same sense in which it might be said that some forms of Western society have been founded on those ideas which, for want of better words, may be called by the inaccurate, but not wholly meaningless, names of feudal and chivalrous. The possibility of slavery and polygamy in all cases, their presence in many cases, give Eastern society its distinctive character. The characteristics of Western society, on the other hand, are that polygamy has never existed, and that slavery has everywhere died out. We may say that polygamy has never existed; for the few cases to the contrary are so purely exceptional as to have no practical bearing on the matter.([2]) And we may say that slavery has everywhere died out, when it has vanished from every part of Christian Europe and even from the great mass of European colonies. This character of Western society is the fruit of Christianity working on the earlier institutions of the European nations. With regard to polygamy there was hardly any need to legislate. Christianity was first preached to societies where monogamy was the law ; amid great licentiousness of manners and a

lax law of divorce, no subject of the Roman Empire
could have more than one lawful wife at a time. And
what was the law of the Roman Empire was in this
respect the general law of the Teutonic nations also.
Here then the business of Christianity was, not to
lay down any new principle, but to work a general
purification of morals and to abridge the licence of
divorce. It is on this last head that rules are laid
down in the Gospel which come nearer to the nature
of civil precepts than any other. But it would be
hard to find any direct prohibition of polygamy in
the Christian Scriptures. The institution was allowed
by the Old Law, and it is not in so many words
taken away by the New. But every moral precept
of Christianity tells against it. And this tendency,
working together with the teaching both of Roman
and of Teutonic law, has caused all Christian
nations to take monogamy for granted as something
absolutely essential to a Christian society. With
slavery on the other hand Christianity has had to
fight a much harder battle. In the case of polygamy,
Christian teaching could go hand in hand with Roman
and Teutonic law. In the case of slavery, Christian
teaching found both Roman and Teutonic law
arranged against it. The New Testament contains
no precept which directly forbids slavery; indeed
it assumes it as one of the ordinary conditions of
that Roman society to which Christianity was first
preached. But the moral precepts of Christianity are
distinctly inconsistent with slavery, and they have in
the end, slowly but surely, done their work. Men first
learned that it was a sin against Christian fellowship
to hold a fellow Christian in bondage. Thus, first
actual slavery, and then the milder forms of serfdom

and villainage, have gradually died out or have been abolished in all European nations. The rule which men thus learned to apply to men of their own creed and their own colour they learned more slowly to apply to men of other creeds and other colours. The abolition of the slavery of the black man in European colonies has followed the abolition of the slavery of the white man in Europe itself. Personal slavery has so long died out in Western Europe, even villainage has so long died out in England, that we are apt to forget that slavery remained a common institution in all Western Europe, and not least in our own island, for ages after the establishment of Christianity. Good men in the eleventh and twelfth centuries preached against the bondage and sale of fellow Christians, as good men in the eighteenth and nineteenth centuries have preached against the bondage and sale of fellow men. But in the end the implied teaching of the Gospel has triumphed. As Christianity, working along with Roman law, effectually shut out polygamy, so in the end Christianity, even in the teeth of Roman law, has effectually driven out slavery.

We may fairly say that, if there were no other differences, these two points alone would be enough to distinguish Eastern and Western society. The difference between a polygamous community and one in which polygamy is forbidden or unknown is an essential difference, a difference which runs through everything, a difference of another kind from ordinary differences in religion, manners, or forms of government. It is a difference which directly affects the condition of half the human species, and which indirectly affects the condition of the other half. The whole social state of a polygamous and a monogamous people is wholly different. It is a difference which does not admit of degrees, a difference in which the first step is everything. And it should further be noticed that polygamy practically implies slavery, and that it is the greatest encouragement of slavery. The difference of slavery or no slavery by itself does not make so wide a gap, and it does admit of degrees. We might say that the prohibition of polygamy is implied in the earliest conception of Western society; the prohibition of slavery belongs only to its fullest developement. But both prohibitions alike are characteristic of Western society as we now conceive it; they form an irreconcileable difference between that society and any society which allows either of the two great evils, one of which we never knew, while from the other we have set ourselves free.

Now as the European nations have all these common possessions, historical, religious, and social, it has naturally followed that they have all tended more or less strongly to a common type of government and polity. It has often been shown that the various governments of Europe, notwithstanding all their points of unlikeness, and notwithstanding the widely different courses which they have run, have all sprung out of certain common elements, and that they have all along kept certain great ideas in common. And, for a good while past, all of them seem to be, as it were, converging towards one model. The worst European governments in the worst times have kept up a certain show of right, a certain profession of regard for law, even where the laws were worst in themselves and were worst administered. And in later times most European governments, even those which have been in some things unjust and oppressive, have tended more and more towards a system which does tolerably fair justice between man and man, at all events in matters where the interest of the government is not concerned. Where European governments have become most nearly despotic, it has always been by the overthrow or dying out of earlier and freer institutions. And in every European country but one, despotism has in its turn died out or been overthrown. Russia is now the only European country which has not some kind of political constitution, some measure of political freedom, greater or less. In making this exception, we must remember, on the one hand, that Russia is, both through its geographical position and through its former bondage to Asiatic rulers, the least European of European countries. And we must remember also that, though Russia has as yet no political constitution, yet even in Russia there are many tendencies at work in the direction of freedom, and that public opinion is beginning to have a power there which would have seemed impossible only a short time back. But of the countries of Western Europe, all at this moment have constitutions of some kind. We may say, at all events by comparison with other times and places, that all the governments of Western Europe, though doubtless some are better than others, all fairly discharge the first duties of government. It is only in a very few parts of Western Europe, that any great crime of one man against another is likely to go unpunished. And, even where it is so, the fault can hardly be said to rest either with the law or with the government, but rather with some local cause which makes it hard to put the law in force. One Western government is doubtless better than another, whether in the law itself or in the administration of the law. But all of them fairly discharge the great duty of defending their subjects from wrong to their persons or properties. In all of them the voice of the nation has some way, more or less perfect, of making itself known. In all of them the ruler has a right to allegiance from the subject, because the subject receives protection from the ruler. In short, in Western Europe, and above all in England, we are so used to the rule of law that we can hardly understand the absence of law. We can understand the temporary suspension of law through a state of war or revolution ; we cannot understand its abiding absence. In one sense indeed the utter absence of law is impossible. In every society, even the rudest, there is some check, either of religion or of traditional custom, upon the personal will of the ruler. But the regular legal order of things to which Western Europe is used, and to which England has very long been used, is by no means a thing which has existed in all times and places. The notion of an appeal to the law in the case of any wrong is so familiar to our minds that we find it hard to conceive a state of things where no such appeal is to be had. But it is specially important to remember that the good administration of justice, an administration which has been getting better and better for nearly two hundred years, and to which we are so thoroughly accustomed that we are apt to take it for granted, is a thing which has been rare in the history of the world, and which in its perfect form is not very old among ourselves.

Speaking roughly then, and by comparison with other times and places, we may say that in all the countries of Western Europe the main ends of government are well carried out. This or that government may be bad in some particular points; but on the whole it is an instrument of good. To say the very least, it does more good than it does harm. And more than this, as a rule, the governments of Western Europe are national governments. There are particular parts in several of the countries of Western Europe in which men complain, with greater or less reason, that they are not under national governments, that they are under governments which are not of their own choosing and which they would willingly throw off. But the parts where complaints of this kind are made make up but a very small part of Western Europe. They are mere exceptions to a general rule. And, even where people complain of a foreign dominion, that foreign dominion does not, as compared with other times and places, carry with it any monstrous oppression. In no part of Western Europe is there such a sight to be seen as that of a large country where the people of the land are in bondage to foreign rulers, where they are shut out from any real share in the government of their own land, and where they cannot get any redress from their foreign rulers, even for their greatest wrongs. Even the exceptional cases which have just been spoken of are something very different from this. And, setting those exceptional cases aside, the whole of Western Europe may be fairly said to be under governments which are really national governments, governments which the people of the land may wish to improve in this or that point, but which they do not wish to throw off altogether. The nation and the Government have common interests, common feelings. The Government may fail rightly to understand the

C

interests, feelings, and wishes of the nation ; but it has not, openly and avowedly, interests, feelings, and wishes opposed to those of the nation.   The King or other chief of the Government is the acknowledged head of the nation.   Even if in any case he chances to be of foreign birth, he throws off as far as he can the character of a stranger, and puts on as far as he can the cha- racter of a native ruler.   If not a countryman by birth, he becomes a countryman by adoption.   His govern- ment may be better or worse ; his personal character may make him more or less popular ; but in any case the nation accepts him as its leader at home and its representative abroad.   The land, the nation, and the chief of the nation are all bound together.   The interests of England and the interests of the English, the interests of France and the interests of the French, are phrases of exactly the same meaning. Nor does it come into any man's head that the Queen of Great Britain or the President of the French Republic has, in any public matter at home or abroad, any personal interests opposite to or separate from the interests of the lands and nations over which they severally rule.

Now it should here be noticed that, though nearly the whole of Western Europe is now under national governments, it is far from being true that all those governments were national governments from the beginning.   Most of them had their beginning in conquest; most of them began in the forcible settle- ment of one people in a land occupied by another people.   But in most cases it has gradually come to be forgotten that the government had its begin- ning in conquest.   The conquerors and conquered have, sooner or later, learned to feel as one people, and to acknowledge a common head in the ruler of their common land. Sometimes the conquerors have learned the language and manners of the conquered ; sometimes the conquered have learned the language and manners of the conquerors. Sometimes the conquerors have taken the name of the conquered ; sometimes the conquered have taken the name of the conquerors. In either case, conquered and conquerors have, sooner or later, become one people ; and, in some cases, even where they have not so thoroughly become one people as this, even where the languages of the conquerors and the conquered have gone on side by side, it has been found that old wrongs can be thoroughly forgotten, and that the two nations have practically become one in face of all other nations. Thus, in the old days of the Roman dominion, when the Roman Empire was spread over all the lands around the Mediterranean sea, the conquered nations were, step by step, admitted to the rights of Romans. They adopted the language and manners of Rome ; they forgot their old national names and feelings, and spoke of themselves only as Romans. So in later times, when the German people of the Franks settled in a large part of Gaul and gradually spread their power over the rest, the conquerors and the conquered gradually became one people. The conquerors learned the language of the conquered, and the conquered came, step by step, to call themselves by the name of the conquerors. It matters to no man in France now, whether his forefathers long ago were of Iberian, Celtic, Roman, Gothic, Burgundian, or Frankish blood. All are now thoroughly mingled together in the one French nation. So in our own island, where English, Scots,

and Welsh have been brought together, partly by
conquest, partly by treaties, though old national
feelings are not forgotten, though even distinct
languages are still to some extent in use, yet all
form politically one nation. No man in Great
Britain wishes to throw off the common government
of Great Britain, or to cut off his own part of Great
Britain from the rest. So again, when England
was conquered by the Normans, and a foreign
king and a foreign nobility bore rule over the land,
still the conquerors and the conquered drew near
together in a wonderfully short time. The conquerors
gradually learned to speak the tongues of the conquered, to share their feelings, and to call themselves
by their name. It matters nothing to any Englishman now whether his forefathers ages back were
of Old-English or of Norman birth. It mattered but
little even so soon after the Conquest as the reign of
Henry the Second. In all these cases, governments
which began in conquest have, sooner or later, sometimes very soon indeed, become national governments.
And we may remark that the tendency of conquerors
and conquered to be in this way fused together is
especially characteristic of Western Europe, and
above all, of those parts of Western Europe which
formed parts of the Roman Empire. For the influence of Rome on men's minds was such that,
within the provinces which had become thoroughly
Roman, all conquerors, at least all Aryan conquerors,
came so far under its power as at least to learn to
speak some form of the Roman language. In Italy
above all, though the land has been conquered over
and over again, though till lately it was divided
among many separate governments, yet all the

successive conquerors had learned the speech of
the land, and had become one with the people of
the land where they settled. One can have no doubt
that, in all these cases, the common origin of the
European nations, even though they knew nothing
about it, had a real effect in making it easier for
different nations to join into one. And in the lands
which had become thoroughly Roman the process
of union was easier still.

We have thus seen how many things all the nations
of Europe, among all their differences, really have
in common. They have a common origin, a common
history, a common religion, a common civilization,
common social, moral, and political ideas. And
the result of all this is that they, for the most part,
live under national governments, under fairly good
governments—that, even where the government began
in conquest the conquerors and the conquered have
commonly been able to come together as one people—
that there is no large part of Western Europe where
the people of the land can even pretend that they
are under foreign rulers—that in the few parts where
there is foreign rule, that foreign rule does not carry
with it any very gross oppression. We have seen
that in the countries of Western Europe there is
no separation of interest or feeling between the
land, the people, and the government. The nation
is a body of which the King or other ruler is the head.
When we have well taken in all these things, we shall
be really able to understand the peculiar position of
the Turks in South-eastern Europe, and how utterly
it differs from anything to which we are used in
Western Europe.

Thus the Turks have given their name to the land

which they conquered, exactly as the Franks have given their name to the land which they conquered. The one land is called Turkey, as the other is called France. But the history of the Turks in Greece, Bulgaria, Servia, and the other lands which they conquered has been quite different from the history of the Franks in Gaul. The Franks in Gaul have been altogether lost in the general mass of the people of the land. But the Turks in Turkey are just as distinct now from the mass of the people of the land as they were when they first came into it. It is not a question whether a man's remote forefathers were Turks or not; the question is a much more immediate and practical one, whether a man is himself a Turk or not. The Turks, though they have been in some parts of Turkey for five hundred years, have still never become the people of the land, nor have they in any way become one with the people of the land. They still remain as they were when they first came in, a people of strangers bearing rule over the people of the land, but in every way distinct from them. They have not adopted the language and manners of the people of the land, nor have the people of the land adopted their language and manners. After dwelling in the same land for so many ages, they have never become the country-men of the people of the land; they still remain foreigners and oppressors. The process of conquest, which in all western conquests came to an end sooner or later, still goes on in the lands conquered by the Turk. So far as there is any law and government at all, it is carried on for the interests of the conquering strangers, and not for the interest of the people of the land. The so-called sovereign is in no sense the head of the people of the land, but is simply the head of the conquering strangers.

Now when we have thoroughly taken in the real nature of such a state of things as this, we at once ask how it came about. We ask why it is that there is in South-eastern Europe a state of things so different from anything to which we are used in Western Europe? Why is it that, while in the West the differences between conquerors and conquered have been everywhere gradually forgotten, in the East the difference remains as strong at the end of five hundred years as it was at the beginning? Why has the Turk failed to assimilate the people of the land, and why have the people of the land failed no less to assimilate the Turk? Why has the Turk not been able to do as the Roman did of old, to win the people of the land to his own speech and manners, to make them in short Turks, as the people of Gaul and Spain became Romans? Or why, on the other hand, could not the Turk lose himself among the people of the land whom he conquered, as the Frank lost himself in Gaul, as the Lombard did in Italy, as the Norman did in England? Why is it that the people of the land and their conquerors have never in all these years been fused into one people, in the same way which happened in all the other cases which we have mentioned? Why is it that, while, in all these other cases, a government which began in conquest has gradually become a national government, discharging the duties of government, while it has often become a thoroughly free government, the Turk has in all these ages never given so much as common protection for life, property, and personal rights to the nations under his rule? The causes are many; some of them are to be found in the earlier history of the lands which the Turk invaded; some are to be found in the peculiar position of the Turk himself. We may say that the first set of causes made it harder for any conquering people in those lands to become naturalized as they did in the West, and that the peculiar position and character of the Turk made what in any case would have been hard altogether impossible.

We have thus traced out the chief points in which the nations of Western Europe agree with one another, and we have shewn in a general way how their state differs from the state of the South-eastern lands which are under the rule of the Turks. We must now go on to trace out more in detail what the rule of the Turks is, and the causes which made it what it is. But before we go into these points, it will be well to set forth rather more at length some of the points which, even were the Turks away, would still distinguish Western and Eastern Europe. These differences ought to be well understood, because they certainly helped the advance of the Turks when they invaded these lands, and because they have a direct bearing on the relation of the Turks to the subject nations and of the subject nations to one another. These points of difference between Eastern and Western Europe, which were points of difference before the Turks came, and which will remain points of difference even if the Turks are taken away, will fittingly form the subject of a separate chapter.

NOTES.

(1, p. 5.) In speaking thus I am fully aware that, in a strictly scientific sense, speech is no sure index of race. What Mr. Sayce says at the beginning of the fifth chapter of his Principles of Comparative Philology is perfectly true from a purely scientific view. That is to say, no nation is of absolutely pure descent. No nation can make out such a pedigree as would satisfy a lawyer in the case of a man claiming an estate or a peerage. But for practical and historical purposes, speech is, not indeed a sure index, but a presumption of race. We assume speech as the index of race, except when we know historically that a nation has changed its speech; and for historical and practical purposes we do not need that absolute purity of race which is demanded by the scientific inquirer. We may compare a nation to a Roman *gens*, which started as a family, but which in course of time admitted many members who were not naturally descended from the original forefather. We apply in short the Roman law of adoption to nations as well as to families. For historical purposes, we assume Teutons, Slaves, or any other people marked out by distinction of speech, to be for historical purposes a race, even though there will always be some admixture of blood, and in some cases a great deal. It is possible for instance that the Gaulish or the Greek nations, at the first time when we hear of them, were largely made up of people who were not Greeks or Gauls by blood, but had simply adopted the Gaulish or the Greek tongue. About this history can say nothing. But history can say for certain that in after ages the Gauls exchanged their own tongue for Latin, while the Greeks kept their own tongue. I therefore do not scruple to speak of race and speech in a manner which is perfectly true for my present purpose, though it may not be quite scientifically accurate. For instance I should say that among the Slavonic nations there is unity of race and speech. The Slaves may in præ-historic times have assimilated other nations, as we know that they assimilated the original Bulgarians. But for all practical purposes they form one race, marked out by the use of a kindred speech. To speak of the Slavonic race is historically true, though it may not be scientifically accurate. But to speak of the "Latin race" is neither scientifically accurate nor historically true. For the so-called Latin race is simply made up of nations which at different times adopted the Latin language, but which we know had no further connexion with the original Latin than coming of the same common Aryan stock, while some of them, namely, whatever is of Iberian descent, are not Aryan at all. The reader will thus understand in what sense I use the word race in these chapters. The people of Hydra are Greek by speech, Albanian by race. The people of Psara are Greek both by speech and race, even though they may in præ-historic times have had Karian or Phœnician forefathers. I have worked this matter out at greater length in the *Contemporary Review* for March, 1877.

(2, p. 11.) Polygamy was utterly unknown both to Greek and to Roman law. The story of Anaxandridês King of Sparta (Herodotus, v. 40), who was specially allowed for a special reason to have two wives at once, only brings the general rule into greater prominence. So something like polygamy seems to have been practised by one or two of the later Macedonian kings, besides the well-known case of Alexander himself. But this only shows that they had partially adopted Eastern manners, and the practice never became usual even among kings, much less among other men. Among the Germans, Tacitus (Germania, 18), speaks of polygamy as practised only by a few for special reasons— " Prope soli barbarorum singulis uxoribus contenti sunt, exceptis admo- dum paucis, qui non libidine, sed ob nobilitatem, plurimis nuptiis ambiuntur." So even in Christian times the Merwing Dagobert (Fredegar, c. 50) had three acknowledged queens at once. " Tres habebat ad instar Salomonis reginas, maxime et plurimas concubinas." But all such cases are exceptional. It was not legal polygamy, but a lax law of divorce, with which Christianity had to struggle, alike among Greeks, Romans, and Teutons.

CHAPTER II.

THE object of the present chapter is to point out those features in the history and condition of South-eastern Europe which would, even if the Turk were away, make it different in many things from Western Europe. These points of difference may be shortly summed up in one, that distinctions of race and creed are far more lasting in Eastern Europe than they are in Western. The great case, the case where there is the widest difference of all, is of course the difference between the Turk and his Christian subjects. But the wide gap between race and race, between creed and creed, though it takes its strongest and most repulsive form in the case of the Turk, is not altogether peculiar to his case. If we go back to the times before the Turk came, we should still find in South-eastern Europe a state of things quite different to that to which we are used in Western Europe. The difference will of course not be so great, nor will it be at all of the same kind, as the difference which has been made by the coming of the Turk. Still there is a widely marked difference, and a difference the causes of which it is well worth our while to search out.

A very small amount of thought will shew that all differences of race and speech are much more marked and much more lasting in the East of Europe than they are in the West. It will also shew that differences in religion have greater importance in the East than they have in the West, and that they put on more of the character of national differences. In the West, as we have seen, the different races which have settled in each of the great countries of Western Europe have come together to form one distinct nation in each. In each land, say England, France, Germany, one type of man, marked by the use of one language, is the rule. Everything which departs from that rule, everything which uses any other language, is exceptional. And anything that departs from the general rule takes for the most part the form of mere fragments or survivals, objects of curious historical and linguistic interest, but having no bearing on practical politics. The political unity of France is not threatened because Flemish, Walloon, Breton, Basque, and Provençal are all spoken within the French border. The political unity of Great Britain is not threatened because Welsh and Gaelic are spoken within its coasts. The recent conquests of Germany stand on a different ground, because they are recent conquests, and because each of the disaffected districts lies in close neighbourhood to a larger population of its own speech. If the Breton-speaking districts of France joined on to a large independent Breton-speaking state, the Breton element in France would not be so politically unimportant as it now is. Ireland stands on a different ground, partly because two great islands never can be so thoroughly united as a continuous territory, partly because for some centuries a variety of causes made the state of things in Ireland rather Eastern than Western.([1])   With these exceptions, the rule holds good.   In Western Europe each land has a dominant type, Roman or Teutonic; whatever departs from both those types is everywhere exceptional and politically unimportant.   And the exceptional districts, where there are any, mark their character as survivals by their geographical position.   The old tongues, those which are older than both Roman and Teutonic, live on only in corners by themselves.   In no part of Western Europe do we find districts inhabited by men differing in speech and national feeling, lying in distinct patches here and there over a large country. A district like one of our larger counties in which one parish, perhaps one hundred, spoke Welsh, another Latin, another English, another Danish, another Old-French, another the tongue of more modern settlers, Flemings, Huguenots or Palatines, is something which we find hard to conceive, and which, as applied to our own land or to any other Western land, sounds absurd on the face of it.

When we pass into South-eastern Europe, this state of things, the very idea of which seems absurd in the West, is found to be perfectly real. All the races which we find dwelling there at the beginning of recorded history, together with several races which have come in since, all remain, not as mere fragments or survivals, but as nations, each with its national language and national feelings, and each having its greater or less share of practical importance in the politics of the present moment.   Setting aside races which have simply passed through the country without occupying it, we may say that all the races

which have ever settled in the country are there still as
distinct races. And, though each race has its own particular region where it forms the whole people or the
great majority of the people, still there are large districts where different races really live side by side in the
very way which seems so absurd when we try to conceive it in any Western country. We cannot conceive
a Welsh, an English, and a Norman village side by
side ; but a Greek, a Bulgarian, and a Turkish village
side by side is a thing which may be seen in many
parts of Thrace. The oldest races in those lands, those
which answer to Basques and Bretons in Western
Europe, hold quite another position from that of
Basques and Bretons in Western Europe. They form
three living and vigorous nations, Greek, Albanian,
and Rouman. They stand as nations alongside of
the Slaves who came in later, and who answer roughly
to the Teutons in the West, while all alike are under
the rule of the Turk, who has nothing answering to
him in the West. But it must be further remembered
that this abiding life of races and languages is
not confined to the lands which are under the Turk.
It comes out in its strongest form in these lands ; but
it comes out also in a form nearly as strong in the lands
which form the Austro-Hungarian monarchy. It is in
short a characteristic of Eastern Europe generally as
distinguished from Western. And the causes of this
difference will be easily seen, if we look carefully into
the history of Eastern Europe as distinguished from
Western.

The main causes of this difference between Eastern
and Western Europe are twofold. The first cause
is the different position which the Roman Empire
held in the West of Europe and in the East. The

second cause is the presence in the East of certain elements which have nothing answering to them in the West. East and West have three elements in common, while the East has a fourth element which it has all to itself. First, there are, both in East and West, the nations which were there before the Roman power began. Secondly, there is the Roman power itself, still existing in its effects. Thirdly, there are the Aryan nations which came in since the establishment of the Roman power. All these are common to West and East; only their proportions and relations to one another are not the same in the East as they are in the West, a difference which is caused by the different positions which the Roman power held in the two cases. But, fourthly, the East has a fourth element which is not to be found in the West, namely the non-Aryan races which have come in since the establishment of the Roman power. Among these the Turks are the most important; but they are not the only non-Aryan settlers, and the difference between the settlement of the Turks and the settlements of the other non-Aryan races forms one of the most instructive parts of our whole subject.

In examining these two causes of those differences between Eastern and Western Europe which lie on the surface, we shall find that the condition of the earlier nations which were there before the Romans came, and over whom they extended their power, was altogether different in the East from what it was in the West. In the West, in Gaul and Spain, the Romans found nations much less civilized than themselves, nations which were ready to look up to their conquerors as masters and to adopt the language, the manners, and the name of Romans. In the West therefore the first element, the element older than the Roman dominion, has lingered on only in the shape of fragments and survivals. The great mass of the people of those lands became practically Roman. In the West the second element in our list, the Roman element, swallowed up nearly the whole of the first. But in Eastern Europe the Romans found a nation more civilized than themselves, a nation which they conquered politically, but to which in everything else they were as ready to look up, as the nations of the West were ready to look up to them. This was the Greek nation. When the Romans conquered the South-eastern lands, they found there three great races, the Greek, the Illyrian, and the Thracian. Those three races are all there still. The Greeks speak for themselves. The Illyrians are represented by the modern Albanians. The Thracians are represented, there seems every reason to believe, by the modern Roumans.([2]) Now had the whole of the South-eastern lands been inhabited by Illyrians and Thracians, those lands would doubtless have become as thoroughly Roman as the Western lands became. There would be in the East Romance and Slavonic nations, as there are in the West Romance and Teutonic nations, with perhaps some fragments and survivals of Illyrian and Thracian lingering on, as Basque and Breton have lingered on in the West. But the position of the Greek nation, its long history and its high civilization, hindered this. The Greeks could not become Romans in any but the most purely political sense. Like other subjects of the Roman Empire, they gradually took the Roman name; but they kept their own language, literature, and civilization. In short we may say that the Roman Empire in the East became Greek, and that the Greek nation became Roman. The Eastern Empire and the Greek-speaking lands became nearly coextensive. Greek became the one language of the Eastern Roman Empire, while those that spoke it still called themselves Romans.([3]) Till quite lately, that is till the modern ideas of nationality began to spread, the Greek-speaking subjects of the Turk called themselves by no name but that of Romans. This people, who might be called either Greek or Roman, but who have now again taken up the Greek name, has lived on as a distinct nation to our own time. It is a nation which has largely assimilated its neighbours, but which has not been assimilated by them.

While the Greeks thus took the Roman name without adopting the Latin language, another people in the Eastern peninsula adopted both name and language, exactly as the nations of the West did. If, as there is good reason to believe, the modern Roumans represent the old Thracians, that nation came under the general law, exactly like the Western nations. The Thracians became thoroughly Roman in speech, as they have ever since kept the Roman name. They form in fact one of the Romance nations, just as much as the people of Gaul or Spain. They are a Romance nation on the Eastern side of the Hadriatic instead of on the Western. The third nation, that of the Illyrians, Skipetar, or Albanians, have been largely assimilated by the Greeks. Though they may be truly said to exist as a nation, still their existence as a nation has been mainly owing to their being a wild people living in a wild country. They hold a position between that

D

of a nation like the Greeks and that of a mere survival of a nation like the Basques. The Roumans too, though they learned the Roman language and have kept the Roman name, can never have so fully adopted the Roman civilization as the Gauls and Spaniards did. In short, the existence of a highly civilized people like the Greeks hindered in every way the influence of Rome from being so thorough in the East as it was in the West. The Greek nation lived on, and alongside of itself, it preserved the other two ancient nations of the peninsula. Thus all three have lived on to the present as distinct nations. Two of them, the Greeks and the Illyrians, still keep their own languages, while the third, the old Thracians, speak a Romance language and call themselves Roumans.

Thus the existence of the Greek nation with its higher civilization has influenced the relations of the Roman power to the old nations of the peninsula, and it has kept them alive as nations. It also affected the relations of the Roman power to the Aryan nations which came in afterwards. These are, to sum it up in a word, the Slaves. The Slavonic nations hold in the East a place answering to˙that which is held by the Teutonic nations in the West. They were the later Aryan settlers, the settlers who came into the Empire after the establishment of the Roman power. The Teutonic nations themselves founded no lasting settlements within the Eastern Empire.[4] The Goths used the Eastern Empire as a highway to the West; they marched through it at pleasure, but it was not till they had reached the West that they founded lasting Gothic kingdoms.[5] On the northern frontier of the Eastern Empire Teutonic kingdoms were founded by the Gepidæ and the Lombards.

But even these were not lasting. The Gepidæ were cut off altogether, and the Lombards passed into Italy, to find their real place in history there. The place in history which in the West belongs to the Teutonic nations which founded kingdoms in Gaul, Spain, and Italy, is filled in the East by the Slavonic nations who made their way into the Empire, and were the forefathers of the present inhabitants of Croatia and Dalmatia, of enslaved Bosnia and Bulgaria, of liberated Servia and of unconquered Montenegro. Just like the Teutons in the West, the Slaves in the East came into the Empire in all manner of characters, as captives, as mercenaries, as allies, at last as conquerors. In the sixth century they carried havoc through all the provinces between the Hadriatic and the Euxine; in the seventh century the Emperors found it wise to allow them to make permanent settlements in those provinces which in time grew into regular kingdoms. From this time we must count the Slavonic people and the Slavonic languages as one great element, in number perhaps the greatest element, in the lands which form the great eastern peninsula of Europe.

But though the Slaves in the East thus answer in many ways to the Teutons in the West, their position with regard to the Eastern Empire was not quite the same as that of the Teutons towards the Western Empire. The Western Empire was purely Roman. The Eastern Empire was from one side Roman, and from another side Greek. Its capital was the old Greek city of Byzantium, refounded and enlarged to become the New Rome or Constantinople. Its capital then was at once Greek and Roman, and so was the dominion of which it was the head. It was politically Roman, but intellectually Greek. Its political traditions, its laws, the succession and titles of its Emperors, were all Roman, and, down to its final conquest by the Turks, it never knew any name but the Roman Empire. Latin remained for some ages the language of government and warfare. Byzantine Greek is full of Latin technical terms, very much as English is, through the effects of the Norman Conquest, full of French technical terms. But Greek was the language of literature and religion, and in the end it drove Latin out for all purposes. Thus, while the nations which pressed into the Western Empire came within the reach of an undivided Roman influence, those which pressed into the East came within the reach of a divided influence, partly Greek, partly Latin. Such a divided influence was in itself less strong than the purely Latin influence in the West. Add to this that the Roman power in the East was centred in a single city in a way in which it was not in the West. The moral power of the Old Rome has been far greater than that of the New. But the physical power of the New Rome as a city has been far greater than that of the Old. The Roman Empire grew out of the Old Rome : but, when the Roman power was at its height, the local Rome itself had ceased to be the ruling city. All Western Europe had, so to speak, become Rome, and the local Rome itself was not more Roman than other parts. Its geographical position, which had made it the head of Italy, hindered it from remaining the political head of Western Europe. The city of Rome was taken over and over again by Teutonic conquerors ; but by that very means its conquerors came more and more under Roman influences. Thus in the West the political succession of the Old Rome passed

away to Teutonic kings, while Rome herself, through
the absence of the Emperors, became the seat of a
new kind of dominion under her bishops.   The New
Rome, on the other hand, was a great city, a great
fortress, which, as a city and fortress, commanded the
whole Eastern Empire, and which for nine hundred
years no foreign invader could ever take.   Hence,
in the West, as the Roman power died out politically,
its moral influence was strengthened.   In the East it
lived on as a political power, a power centred in one
great city, a city which the nations which pressed
into the Empire were always trying to take but never
could.   The Slaves who pressed into the Eastern
Empire admired and reverenced and looked up to the
New Rome.   They learned its religion, and much of
its civilization.   Still it remained a separate political
power, with which they were often at war.   It followed
from all this that the Slaves in the Eastern Empire
remained distinct, in a way in which Goths, Franks,
and Burgundians in the Western Empire did not.
They learned much from the half Roman, half Greek,
power with which they had to do ; but they did not
themselves become either Greek or Roman, in the way
in which the Teutonic conquerors in the Western
Empire became Roman.   Thus, as the existence of
the Greek nation and Greek civilization preserved the
older nations as distinct nations, so the half Greek,
half Roman, character of the Eastern Empire, combined with the centring of its whole power in a
single city, kept the new comers, that is chiefly the
Slaves, also apart as distinct nations.   Thus, while in
the West everything except a few survivals of earlier
nations, is either Roman or Teutonic, in the East,
Greeks, Illyrians, Thracians or Roumans, and Slaves,

all stood side by side as distinct nations when the next set of invaders came, and they remain as distinct nations still.

We thus see that, even with regard to the three elements which Eastern and Western Europe may be said to have in common, there are some marked differences between the two. In both there were the nations who were there before the Roman times, there was the Roman power itself, and there were the Aryan nations which had come in since the establishment of the Roman power. But we have seen that the relations between these three elements were not quite the same in the East and in the West. In the East the distinctions of race and language were broader and more lasting than they were in the West. Still, with all their differences and rivalries, these nations had much in common; they all had their share in those things which are the common heritage of Christian Europe. They were all Aryan; they were all Christian; they had all come more or less fully under Greek and Roman influences. Still various causes had made it hard for them to unite, and they remained distinct and often hostile nations. These points become of importance when we come to the fourth element in Eastern Europe, the settlement in it of nations wholly foreign alike to Greeks, Albanians, Thracians, and Slaves—nations, in a word, which were neither Aryan nor Christian. The last and greatest of these were the Ottoman Turks. But before we come to the history of the Ottoman Turks, it will be well to compare their settlement with the earlier settlements of other nations more or less akin to them,[6] as this comparison will be found to be one of the most instructive parts of our subject.

The relations of Eastern and of Western Europe to those nations which were neither Aryan nor Christian have been widely different. One might have expected that the Semitic nations, the nations of South-western Asia, the Phœnicians, Hebrews, and Arabs, would have played a greater part in the history of Eastern Europe than they played in the history of Western Europe. Yet the contrary has been the case both in earlier and in later times. Whatever influence the Phœnicians may have had on the Greeks in the earliest times, the Phœnician settlements in Europe in historical times were all in the West, in Spain, in Sicily, in the other islands of the Western Mediterranean. So it was ages after with the Arabs or Saracens. They robbed the Eastern Empire of Syria, Egypt, and Africa; they ravaged Asia Minor; they twice besieged Constantinople itself; but they formed no lasting settlement within the bounds of Eastern Europe. But in the West they conquered nearly the whole of Spain, and they kept part of that conquest for nearly eight hundred years. They held Sicily for a shorter, but a considerable time; and the only European province of the Eastern Empire which they ever won, the island of Crete, was won by a band of adventurers from Spain. Thus the strictly Semitic power, the power of the Saracen as distinguished from that of the Turk, has really been stronger in Western than in Eastern Europe. Yet we cannot reckon the Semitic power as one of the elements in Western Europe. It was only in Spain that the Saracen power was really abiding, and even from Spain it has utterly passed away. It could pass utterly away, because, though it lasted so long, it was always an alien power in Europe, and

never really took root. We need not count the
Semitic power as an element either in Eastern or
Western Europe; for in Eastern Europe the Semitic
nations never settled, and from Western Europe they
are quite gone. The case is quite different with
regard to that class of nations which form an important element in Eastern Europe, but which have
nothing answering to them in the West. This is the
group of nations to which the Turks belong, and of
which in Europe the Ottoman Turks are the most
prominent members.

Taking then the Turk as the greatest and the most
prominent specimen of those nations in Eastern
Europe which did not originally belong to the
European community of nations, and leaving out of
sight for a moment, the fact that he is only
one member of that class, let us ask how the
Turk looks as compared with the other nations of
the Eastern peninsula, Greek, Albanian, Rouman,
and Slave. We have seen that two chief causes had
combined to keep those nations distinct, and to make
any union among them very hard. At last there
came among them, in the form of the Ottoman Turk,
a people with whom union was not only hard but
impossible, a people who were kept distinct, not by
special circumstances, but by the inherent nature of
the case. Had the Turk been other than what he
really was, he might simply have become a new
nation alongside of the other South-eastern nations.
Being what he was, the Turk could not do this. He
could not sit down alongside of the other nations.
He could not assimilate the other nations or be assimilated by them. He could not sit down among the
other nations as a constant neighbour and occasional

enemy. If he came among them at all, he could come only as a ruler, and, if as a ruler, then as an oppressor. We must now trace out what are the causes which, even in Eastern Europe where the lasting distinction of races is a characteristic of the history of the country, have given the Turk a position wholly unlike the position of any of the other races.

Why then has the conquest made by the Turks been of a nature so different, not only from other conquests made in Western Europe, but even from other conquests made in Eastern Europe? Why is the position of the Turks as a distinct people something quite unlike the position of any other people, even in lands where nations have a tendency to remain specially distinct? The reason is because the Turk has no share in any of those things which, among all differences, are shared in common by the European nations. The Turk belongs to another branch of the human family from the nations of Europe. He has no share in the common history of these nations, in their common memories, their common feelings, their common civilization. Lastly, what is more important than all the rest, he does not profess any of the forms of the Christian religion, but follows the religion of Mahomet.

First then, the Turk has no share in that original kindred of race and language which binds together all the European nations. The original Turks did not belong to the Aryan branch of mankind, and their original speech is not an Aryan speech. The Turks and their speech belong to altogether another class of nations and languages. They were wholly distinct alike from the Aryan inhabitants of Europe

and from the inhabitants of Western Asia, who,
wherever they were not Aryan, mainly belonged to
the Semitic family. The Semitic nations must, in all
those points which distinguish Eastern from Western
life, be set down as belonging to the Eastern division. Yet in some points of language they come
nearer to the Aryans than the other non-Aryan
nations, and some of them have reached a higher stage
of civilization and civil polity than any of the nations
which lie beyond both the Aryan and the Semitic
range. It is not needful for our purpose to go deep
into any scientific enquiry, as to the exact relations of
those nations and languages of Asia and Northern
Europe which are neither Aryan nor Semitic. For our
purpose, it will be enough to class all those of them
with which our subject has anything to do under a
name which is sometimes given to them, that of
Turanian. The old Persians, who spoke an Aryan
tongue, called their own land *Iran*, and the barbarous
land to the north of it they called *Turan.* In their
eyes Iran was the land of light, and Turan was the
land of darkness. From this Turan, the land of
Central Asia, came the many Turkish settlements
which made their way, first into Western Asia and
then into Europe. The Turks are thus far more distant from any of the Aryan, or even from any of the
Semitic nations, of Europe and Asia than any one of
those nations can be from any other. From us Europeans they are more distant than the Persians and
Hindoos, who are Aryan kinsfolk, though we and they
have been so long parted. They are more distant—
a fact which it is very important to notice—even than
their Semitic forerunners and teachers in the Mahometan religion, the Arabs or Saracens. It is true

that the original Turkish blood must have been
greatly modified, as their language has been greatly
modified, by their passage through Persia and Asia
Minor. It must also have been greatly modified by
their being joined by many European renegades, and
by their custom of forcing the youth of the nations
whom they conquered to serve in their armies and to
embrace their religion. In this way we might say
that the Turks in Europe are an artificial nation, and
it is certain that many of them must be, in actual
descent, of European blood. But the original stock
was something altogether foreign to Europe, and, in
a case like this, it is the original stock which gives the
character to the whole. The Turks in Europe have
neither assimilated the nations which they have conquered, nor have they been assimilated by them.
They have simply adopted a great many renegades,
one by one. And those renegades have of course
been assimilated by the body which they have joined.
They have practically become Turks.

Now we cannot reasonably doubt that this original
difference in blood and language has made it harder
than it would otherwise have been for the Turks
to become partakers of the common possessions of
the European nations, in short for them to become
an European nation. It would in any case have
made it harder for them, either, like conquerors in
Western Europe, to become one people with the conquered, or, like conquerors in Eastern Europe, to sit
down as a distinct nation alongside of other nations.
But there is no reason to believe that, had other
circumstances been favourable, the original difference
of race would of itself have made it impossible for
them to do so. Experience teaches us the contrary.

For other Turanian nations beside the Ottoman
Turks have also made their way into Europe, and
the history of some of those nations has been quite
unlike the history of the Ottoman Turks. These
other Turanian nations came into Europe much earlier
than the Turks, and they came by a different road.
In chronological strictness then they should have
been mentioned before the Turks; but, in order to
make the difference between their history and that
of the Ottoman Turks more clear, it seemed well first
of all to draw a general picture of the position of
the Ottoman Turks. The chief point to be shown is
that, while in any case it was harder for a Turanian
than for an Aryan people to enter into the European
fellowship, yet, in the case of other Turanian nations,
though hard, it was not impossible. In the case of
the Ottoman Turks certain special circumstances
made it altogether impossible.

Setting aside any curious questions as to the remains of Turanian nations in Europe earlier than
the coming of the Aryans, the historical incursions of
the Turanian nations, their attacks upon the Aryan
nations of Europe, began more than a thousand
years before the coming of the Ottoman Turks, in
the fourth century of our æra. Thus the Huns began
to make themselves terrible to Romans, Teutons and
Slaves. But in Western Europe neither the Huns
nor any other Turanian people ever made any lasting
settlements.[7] When Attila and his Huns invaded
Gaul in the fifth century, Romans, Goths, and Franks
all joined together. They smote the barbarians on
the Catalaunian fields, and saved Western Europe
from a Turanian occupation. In the East things
took a different course. There Turanian settlers,

ages before the coming of the Ottoman Turks, grew up into great kingdoms. Passing by a crowd of nations which play an important part in Byzantine history but which have left no modern traces behind them, we must mark that the Avars founded a great kingdom on the northern borders of the Eastern Empire and often carried havoc through the lands of the Empire itself. The Avars passed away beneath the sword of Charles the Great; but two other Turanian settlements must be specially noticed, because they throw much light on the present question. Long before the Turks came into Europe, the Magyars or Hungarians had come; and, before the Magyars came, the Bulgarians had come. Both the Magyars and the Bulgarians were in their origin Turanian nations, nations as foreign to the Aryan people of Europe as the Ottoman Turks themselves. But their history shows that a Turanian nation settling in Europe may either be assimilated with an existing European nation or may sit down as an European nation alongside of others. The Bulgarians have done one of these things; the Magyars have done the other; the Ottoman Turks have done neither.

So much has been heard lately of the Bulgarians as being in our times the special victims of the Turk that some people may find it strange to hear who the original Bulgarians were. They were a people more or less nearly akin to the Turks, and they came into Europe as barbarian conquerors who were as much dreaded by the nations of South-eastern Europe as the Turks themselves were afterwards. The old Bulgarians were a Turanian people, who settled in a large part of the South-eastern peninsula, in lands which had been already occupied by Slaves. They came in as barbarian conquerors; but, exactly as happened to so many conquerors in Western Europe, they were presently assimilated by their Slavonic subjects and neighbours. They learned the Slavonic speech; they gradually lost all traces of their foreign origin. Those whom we now call Bulgarians are a Slavonic people speaking a Slavonic tongue, and they have nothing Turanian about them except the name which they borrowed from their Turanian masters. Their case has been not unlike that of the settlements of the Franks in Gaul or of the Normans in England. When we call their land Bulgaria and its people Bulgarians, it is almost as if our own land were called Normandy and ourselves Normans. It is in some points as when the land and people of Gaul came to be called France and French from their Frankish conquerors. The Bulgarians entered the Empire in the seventh century, and embraced Christianity in the ninth. They rose to great power in the South-eastern lands, and played a great part in their history. But all their later history, from a comparatively short time after the first Bulgarian conquest, has been that of a Slavonic and not that of a Turanian people. The history of the Bulgarians therefore shows that it is quite possible, if circumstances are favourable, for a Turanian people to settle among the Aryans of Europe and to be thoroughly assimilated by the Aryan nation among whom they settled.

The other case of earlier Turanian settlement, that of the Magyars or Hungarians, shows that Turanian settlers can, even when they are not assimilated, sit down in Europe and become an European nation. The Magyars, who two hundred years ago were among the subjects and victims of the Turks, have lately taken to profess great friendship for the Turks on the ground of common origin. This is certainly carrying the doctrine of race very far indeed. But there is just this much of truth in it, that the Turanian Magyars came into Europe, like the Bulgarians, as a race of Turanian conquerors. They came in the last years of the ninth century. For a while they were the terror of East and West. But in the West they simply ravaged ; in the East they sat down as a distinct nation. And to this day they still keep marked traces of their foreign origin, while the original Bulgarians lost all traces of theirs in about two hundred years. The Magyars still remain a distinct nation, speaking their own Turanian tongue. In the kingdom of Hungary to which they have given their name, they still abide as in some sort a ruling race among its Slavonic inhabitants, though they certainly do not hold them in the same kind of bondage in which the Turks hold their subject nations. We therefore cannot say that the Magyars have been assimilated, like the old Bulgarians ; but we may fairly say that they have been incorporated among the nations of Europe. For, not very long after their settlement, they adopted the religion and the general civilization of Europe, and they have ever since been reckoned as an European nation. It has been a point of great importance in the history of Eastern Europe that the Magyars, though geographically they belong rather to Eastern than to Western Europe, got their Christianity and civilization from the West, and not from the East. But our present point is that, though they kept

their own tongue and remained a distinct nation,
they did adopt the religion and civilization of Europe
in some shape. Thus, though their history has not
been the same as the history of the Bulgarians, it has
been very different from the history of the Turks.
And it should always be remembered that both
Bulgarians and Magyars have been among the
nations whom the Turks have overcome and borne
rule over. Their original kindred with the Turks
has not enabled them, any more than any of the
other nations whom the Turks overcame, either to
assimilate the Turks to themselves, or to be assimilated by them.

It is therefore most important constantly to bear in
mind the history of the Bulgarians and Magyars, and
the difference between their case and that of the
Turks. Two of the Turanian nations which settled
in Europe have become more or less thoroughly
European. The third has not become European
at all. This shows that even difference of origin,
though very important, is not of itself enough to
account for the fact that the Turks, though they have
been so long settled in Europe, have never become
European. The cause of that fact must be sought
in difference of origin, combined with certain other
circumstances which have affected the settlement of
the Turks, but which did not affect the settlements of
the Bulgarians or the Magyars.

We have thus traced out the special characteristics
of the nations of South-eastern Europe, as compared
with the nations of the West. We have seen how the
earlier nations which were there before the Roman
conquest still abide as nations. We have seen how
one of them did in a manner make the Roman Empire

its own, how in those lands the names Roman and Greek came to have much the same meaning. We have seen how, after the establishment of the Roman power, the Slavonic nations settled in the Eastern Empire, much in the same way in which the Teutonic nations settled in the Western Empire, but with some important differences, differences which arose out of the earlier history of those lands and which have affected their later history. We have seen further how in the East there was a fourth element which has nothing answering to it in the West, namely the settlement of nations which were not European or Aryan at all. We have seen that some of these non-Aryan settlers could be assimilated by their Aryan neighbours, while others could sit down alongside of them as one nation among others. That is, in different ways, they could both become more or less thoroughly European. Lastly we have seen that another race of non-Aryan settlers has been able to do none of these things, but has always remained distinct. It has conquered a large part of Europe and held several European nations in bondage, but it has never itself in any sort become European. We must now go on to ask what were the special reasons which hindered the Ottoman Turks from doing as the Bulgarians did, or even as the Magyars did, what in short has hindered them from ever becoming an European nation.

E

NOTES.

(1, p. 29.) The truth is that during the last century the state of things in Ireland was the nearest parallel in Western Europe to the state of things in South-eastern Europe. The rule of the English in Ireland was, we may hope, never quite so bad as the rule of the Turk in South-eastern Europe, but it was a rule of essentially the same kind. It was a rule of race over race, of creed over creed, exactly like the rule of the Turk; and, just as in the East, nationality and religion went together. The subject class, the great Roman Catholic majority of the island, consisted of the native Irish and of those of the earlier English and Norman settlers who had practically become Irish, "Hibernis ipsis Hiberniores," as the phrase ran. The ruling Protestant body consisted of those settlers, mainly later settlers, from Great Britain who kept their own nationality, and were Protestant in religion. Practically the state of things in Ireland was of the same kind as the state of things in Turkey; but the historical origin of the two cases was different. In the case of the Turk and his subjects, the distinction was both national and religious from the beginning. In the case of Ireland a distinction which was originally national afterwards became religious. That is to say, in the sixteenth century the native Irish, and those of the settlers who had become Irish, clave to the Roman Catholic religion, while the ruling English caste became Protestant. Thus the distinction became more marked, as it is easier to tell what religion a man professes than to tell from what blood he springs. Thus, while the earlier laws are against the Irish as Irish, the later laws are against Roman Catholics as Roman Catholics. The state of the Roman Catholic in Ireland while the penal laws lasted was closely akin to the state of the Christians in Turkey. It was a state of disability and degradation, but not of religious persecution strictly so called. But the main difference between the two cases is that in Ireland wrongs have been redressed, while in Turkey they have not. On this head I shall have something to say in a later chapter.

(2, p. 32.) I do not put forth this theory of the Thracian origin of the Roumans with perfect confidence, but it seems to me more likely than any other. It is commonly taken for granted that the Roumans are the descendants of Roman colonists in Dacia, and of Dacians who adopted the Latin language. The phænomena of Dacia would thus be the same as the phænomena of Gaul and Spain. But then it should be remembered that Dacia was, of all the provinces of the older Roman Empire, the last won, and the first lost. Conquered by Trajan, given up by Aurelian, it was Roman only for about one hundred and seventy years. The land was from that time onwards the highway of every nation which pressed into Europe from the lands north of the Euxine; and it is most strange if Latin should have lived on there when it died out in the neighbouring lands, or never made its way into them. But in truth the Roumans or Vlachs are even now by no means confined to Dacia. They are still found in many other parts of the peninsula, and their settlement in the present Roumania was most likely owing to a later migration. The Rouman power in those lands seems to have begun only in the thirteenth century. (See Jirecek, Geschichte der Bulgaren, p. 265.) It is much easier to suppose that these Latin-speaking people in the Eastern peninsula represent, not specially Dacians or Roman colonists in Dacia, but the great Thracian race generally, of which the Dacians were only a part. The Thracian coast was early studded with a fringe of Greek colonies, as it remains still; but the mass of the Thracian land was never Hellenized. It was thus ready at the time of the Roman Conquest to be Romanized, just as Gaul and Spain were. It adopted the Latin language, while Greece and the Hellenized lands clave to Greek. The Roumans would thus represent those of the Roman provincials of Thrace and Mœsia who kept on their adopted Roman nationality in the teeth of Slavonic conquests. The Vlachs or *Rumunje* and the Greeks or Ῥωμαῖοι both keep the Roman name, though in different forms. (See more in Jirecek, pp. 66, 74.)

(3, p. 33.) Ἕλλην, it must be remembered, from the New Testament onwards, meant *pagan*.

(4, p. 34.) The Tetraxite Goths in the land of Crim, if they are to be called subjects of the Empire, did not become so by settling within its bounds, but by entering into relations with it from outside.

(5, p. 34.) This is a point of special contrast between the Teutons and the Slaves in the East. The Teutons only marched through; the Slaves settled.

(6, p. 38.) I do not take on me to rule whether there is any real kindred, strictly so-called, between the Bulgarians, the Magyars, and the Ottoman Turks. They have for our purpose a kind of negative kindred. The speech of all these belongs to a class quite distinct from either the Aryan or Semitic.

(7, p. 44.) If there is any exception, it is the settlement of the Alans in Spain. But the Alans, if they were Turanian to start with, would seem to have been early brought under Teutonic influences, and they have left no traces behind them in modern times.

CHAPTER III.

WE must now go back to the points which we drew out in the first Chapter, the points in which European nations agree together, but in which the Turk differs from all of them, the things which they all have in common, but in which the Turk has no share. First among these we placed general kindred of race and speech, inasmuch as all the European nations, with the smallest exceptions, belong to Aryan stock, while the Turks belong to the Turanian stock. But we have further seen in the last chapter, that this original difference, had it stood by itself, would not have been enough to hinder the Turks from becoming Europeans by adoption. It doubtless would in any case have made it harder for them to do so; but it would not of itself have made it impossible. For, as we have seen, other Turanian nations, the Bulgarians and Magyars, have become European by adoption. We have now to see what it was by virtue of which the change which was hard, but still possible, in the case of the Bulgarians and Magyars has been altogether impossible in the case of the Ottoman Turks.

To answer this, we must go through our other points of likeness and unlikeness in order. The second point which we saw that the European nations had in common, besides their original Aryan kindred, was that they have a common history. They all have certain historic memories in common, memories which are chiefly derived from the dominion and influence of Rome. From these memories comes a vast common stock of what we may call literary and intellectual possessions. In all this the Bulgarians and Magyars, so far as they became European, came to have their share, if not by inheritance at least by adoption. The Bulgarians came under Greek, the Magyars under Latin, influences. But in all those memories, and in all that comes of those memories, as the Turks have no share by inheritance, so neither have they ever won any share by adoption. They have no share in that stock of common ideas and feelings which belongs to the European nations in general. They have no share in the two languages which are the common possession of Europe, the Greek and the Latin. They have their own languages and literature, of which we for the most part know nothing, as they for the most part know nothing of ours. They have their own Turkish language, as we have our own tongues, Teutonic, Romance, or Slavonic. What Greek and Latin have been to us, Arabic and Persian have been to them, They have occupied one of the two great seats of Roman power, one of the great seats of Greek civilization, but they have not thereby become Roman or Greek, or European in any way. While the Teutons in the West, while the Slaves in the East, came into the Roman Empire, as half conquerors, half disciples, the Turks have come in wholly as conquerors, not at all as disciples. Settled in Europe, they have remained untouched by all that distinguishes Europe and the colonies of Europe from Asia and Africa. The throne of the New Rome is occupied by an Asiatic ruler surrounded by an Asiatic people. Nor is this any the less true, because, not the Turkish people in general, but the ruling class among them, have very lately put on a certain European varnish. The nature of the Turkish power is not changed because certain classes of Turks learn to speak an European language and to wear an European dress. Such a mere varnish has nothing in common with the deep moral influence which the Western Rome had on the Teuton and the Eastern Rome on the Slave. ·The Turk still remains foreign to the feelings and habits and historic memories of Europe. Of the other two Turanian settlements in Europe this is not true. The modern Bulgarian is whatever the other Slaves are ; the Magyar, though he keeps his Turanian language, has his share in the great heritage of Western Europe, in the tongue and the civilization of Rome.

This brings us to the third point of difference between the Turks and the European nations, the point which is really the key to all the other points of difference. We have seen that it is not impossible for Turanians settled in Europe to become more or less thoroughly European, to obtain a share in much of those things which distinguishes European nations from others. But while other Turanian nations have done this, the Turks have never done it. Why is this? Why could not the Turks do either as the Bulgarians did or as the Magyars did ? The reason is because the Bulgarians and the Magyars embraced the common religion of Europe, while the Turks have never embraced it. Here is the great difference of all. As soon as the Bulgarians and Magyars became Christians,

the great difference between them and the other
nations of Europe was at once taken away. The
Bulgarians indeed, after some questioning and dis-
puting, embraced Christianity in its Eastern form,
while the Magyars embraced it in its Western form.
And many troubles and divisions in Europe have come
of this difference. Still both did become Christians,
and thus both became sharers in all those ideas and
feelings which are common to Christians of every sect,
but which are not shared by Pagans or Mahometans.
The Turks, on the other hand, entered Europe as
Mahometans, and Mahometans they still remain.
Here then is the great point of difference of all, that
point which makes it altogether impossible for the
Turks really to become an European nation. They
cannot become an European nation, as long as they
remain Mahometans ; and there is no known case of
any Mahometan nation accepting any other religion.

The question will now fairly be asked, why could
not the Turks lay aside their old religion, as the Bulgarians and Magyars laid aside theirs, and embrace
the religion of Europe as the Bulgarians and Magyars
embraced it. The answer may be given in a very few
words. The Bulgarians and Magyars could embrace
Christianity, because they were heathens ; the Ottoman Turks could not embrace Christianity, because
they were Mahometans. Because the Bulgarians and
Magyars were further off from the religion and civilization of Europe than the Turks were, for that very
reason they were able to adopt the religion and
civilization of Europe, and the Turks were not. This
is a case in which we may reverse the familiar proverb,
and say that no bread is practically better than half a
loaf. That is to say, a half civilization stands as a

hindrance in accepting a more perfect civilization. A half truth in religion stands in the way of accepting more perfect truth. Experience proves this in all ages of European history. The rude nations of Western, Northern, and Eastern Europe easily adopted the religion and civilization of Rome. No Mahometan nation has ever been known to accept Christianity ; no nation that has reached the half civilization of the East has ever been known to accept the full civilization of the West. This fact, the fact of the wide distinction in these matters between the Ottoman Turks and the earlier Turanian settlers in Europe, is the very key of our whole subject. The Turks are what they are, and they remain what they are, because their religion is Mahometan. It by no means follows that every Mahometan government must be as bad as the Ottoman government is now. For many Mahometan governments have been much better. But no Mahometan government can ever give to its subjects of other religions what we in Western Europe are used to look on as really good government. No Mahometan nation can really become part of the same community of nations as the Christian nations of Europe. These positions make it needful to look a little further into the nature of the Mahometan religion, and into the relations which, under a Mahometan government, must always exist, between its Mahometan subjects and its subjects of other religions.

This question is in itself a perfectly general one, not a special question between Mahometanism and Christianity, but a question between Mahometanism and all other religions. It is not needful here to enquire what would be the position of a nation of some third religion, neither Christian nor Mahometan. We need not ask whether such a nation could be really admitted into the European community, or whether it could give really good government to any Christian or Mahometan subjects that it might have. A great deal might be said in answer to such a question, as a matter of curious speculation. But the question is of no practical importance for our present subject. The only practical choice in Europe lies between Christianity and Mahometanism. The practical point is that, whatever a nation of some third religion might do, a Mahometan nation cannot live on terms of real community with Christian nations; a Mahometan government cannot give real equality and good government to its Christian subjects. The question in modern Europe lies between Christian and Mahometan, because all the nations of Europe besides the Turks are Christian. But it must be borne in mind that the question of the relation between Mahometan and Christians is only part of a greater question, that is, of the relation between Mahometans and men of other religions generally. What is true of Mahometans and Christians in Europe, is, or has been, true of Mahometans and Pagans in Asia. It is true that the opposition between Mahometanism and Christianity in Europe has been sharper than the opposition between Mahometanism and other religions elsewhere. And this has come of two causes; first, because Christianity and Mahometanism are more distinctively rival religions than any other two religions that can be named; secondly, because Christians in Europe, have, for nearly four hundred years past, had little to do with any Mahometans except the Ottoman Turks, that is, with the fiercest and the most bigoted of all Mahometans. (¹) Still, the relation between Mahometans and Christians in South-eastern Europe is only part of the general relation between Mahometans and men of other religions everywhere. What is true in the case of South-eastern Europe will be found to be true in the main, though it will often need some qualification, in every land where Mahometans have borne rule over men of any other creed.

The fact simply is that no Mahometan government ever has given or can give real equality to its subjects of other religions. It would be most unjust to put all Mahometan governments on a level in this matter. There have been Mahometan rulers who have avoided all wanton oppression of their non-Mahometan subjects ; but, even under the best Mahometan rulers, the infidel, as he is deemed in Mahometan eyes, has never been really put on a level with the true believers. Wherever Mahometans have borne rule, the Mahometan part of the population has always been a ruling race, and the Christian or other non-Mahometan part has always been a subject race. The truth is that this always must be so ; it is an essential part of the Mahometan religion that it should be so. The Koran, the sacred book of the Mahometans, bids the true believers to fight against the infidels, till the infidels either embrace Islam or submit to pay tribute. By paying tribute, they purchase the right to their lives and their property, which are otherwise held to be forfeited, and to the exercise of their religion on certain conditions. Their fate therefore is not the worst of all possible fates ; they are not, like some conquered nations, either swept away from the face of the earth or condemned to actual personal slavery. Nor are they subject to anything which can in strictness be called religious persecution. That is to say, the Christian, or rather the non-Mussulman, subject of a Mahometan government is not, simply as a non-Mussulman, subject to death, bonds, or other legal punishment. That he should be free from penalties of this kind is implied in this very notion of the tributary relation. His payment of tribute exempts him from any penalities of the kind. So far the position of the Christian under a Mahometan ruler is better than that of the Christian heretic has been under many Christian rulers. His religion is tolerated; but it is simply tolerated, and the toleration is of a purely contemptuous kind. There is no real religious equality. The Christian may freely embrace Islam, and no Christian may hinder him from so doing. But for a Mahometan to embrace Christianity is a crime to be punished with death. Thus the non-Mussulman subjects of a Mussulman ruler sink to the condition of a subject people. In the case of a people conquered by Mussulman invaders, they sink into bondmen in their own land. They remain a distinct and inferior community, reminded in every act of their lives that the Mussulmans are masters and that they are servants. They so remain as long as they are faithful to their religion : by forsaking it, they may at any moment pass over to the ranks of their conquerors. Thus every Christian under a Mussulman government is in truth confessor for his religion, as he might gain greatly by forsaking it. Still it is plain that such a state of things as this, grievous and degrading as it is, does not in theory involve any act of personal oppression. That is to say, though the Christian is treated in every thing as inferior to the Mussulman, yet his life, his property, and the honour of his family might be safe. Under any Mahometan ruler who did his duty according to his own law, they would be safe, because the Christian by the payment of tribute purchases his right to all these things. But the great evil of a law which condemns any class of people to degradation is that the practice under such a law is sure to be worse than the law itself. The relation between Christian and Mussulman under Mussulman rule is fixed, not by a law like an Act of Parliament, which may at any time be changed, but by a supposed divine law which cannot be changed. The relations between the Christian and the Mussulman, that is, the abiding subjection and degradation of the Christian, are matters of religious principle. The law enjoins neither persecution nor personal oppression : it enjoins toleration, though merely a contemptuous toleration. But when the toleration which the law enjoins is purely contemptuous, when the subjection of all religions but the dominant one is consecrated by a supposed divine sanction, it is almost certain that the practice will be worse than the law ; it is almost certain that contemptuous toleration will pass into an ordinary state of personal oppression, varied by occasional outbursts of actual persecution. So history shows that it has been. Instances may indeed be found in which Christians or other non-Mussulmans have fared better under a Mussulman government, than the law of the Koran prescribes ; as a rule, they have fared worse. It could in truth hardly be otherwise. When the members of one religious body feel themselves to be, simply on account of their religion, the superiors and masters of their neighbours

of another religion, the position is one which opens
every temptation to the worst passions of the human
heart. A man must have amazing command of himself, if, when it is his religious duty to treat a certain
class of men as subject and degraded, he does not
deal with them in a way which carries with it something yet more than subjection and degradation. A
bad man, even an average man, will be tempted every
moment to add direct insult and oppression beyond
what the letter of his law ordains. And so it has
been in the history of all Mahometan governments
which have borne rule over subjects of other religions,
especially over Christians. The best have been
what in Western Europe we should call bad; and
their tendency has been, like most bad things, to
get worse. The Christian subjects of Mahometan
powers have often been much better off than Christian
subjects of the Turk are now. But in no case have
they been what in Western Europe we should call
really well off, and the tendency has always been for
their condition to get gradually worse and worse.

The truth is that the Mahometan religion is, above
all others, an aggressive religion. Every religion
which does not confine itself to one nation, but which
proclaims itself as the one truth for all nations, must
be aggressive in one sense. That is to say, it must be
anxious to bring men within its pale; in other words
it must be a missionary religion. Now Mahometanism is eminently a missionary religion;([2]) but it is
something more. It is aggressive in another sense
than that of merely persuading men to embrace its
doctrines. It lays down the principle that the faith is
to be propagated by the sword. Other religions,
Christianity among them, have been propagated by

the sword; but it is Mahometanism only which lays
it down as a matter of religious duty that it should
be so propagated. No ruler who forced Christianity
by the sword on unwilling nations could say that
any precept of the Gospel bade him do so. And,
as the precepts of the Gospel have come to be better
understood, most Christians have agreed that such a
way of spreading the faith is altogether contrary to the
spirit of the Gospel. But the Mussulman who fights
against the infidel till he makes his choice between
the old alternatives of Koran or Tribute is simply
obeying the most essential precept of his religion.
This duty of spreading the faith by the sword, which
the Koran enforces on all Mussulmans, at once places
the Mahometan religion in a specially hostile position
towards all other religions. And furthermore the
whole character of that religion makes it the special
rival of Christianity. Without going into questions
of theological dogma, one main cause of this special
rivalry between Christianity and Islam is because
those two religions have so much in common. The
Christian would say of the Mahometan, and the Mahometan would say of the Christian, that in each case
the creed of the other had more of truth in it than
there was in any other creed which was not the whole
truth. As compared with heathen religions, the strife
between Christianity and Mahometanism has the proverbial bitterness of the strifes of kinsfolk. A few
plain facts show the special rivalry of the two religions.
Many heathen nations have embraced Christianity,
and many have embraced Mahometanism. They
have done so in both cases, sometimes freely, sometimes by force. And in both cases they have, by
embracing either Christianity or Mahometanism,

raised themselves in every way, moral, social, and
religious.   The advantage has been so clearly on the
side of the Christian or Mahometan teacher that the
heathens themselves have come to perceive it.   But no
Christian nation has ever embraced Mahometanism;
no Mahometan nation has ever embraced Christianity.
For they are distinctly rival religions, and not only
rival religions, but religions which represent rival
systems of social and political life.   Each holds itself
to be theologically the one truth ; each believes itself
to represent a higher and better civil and social system.
And the Mahometan further believes that his civil
and social system is directly of divine authority.   The
Christian does not hold that the Gospel is a legal code
for all times and places; the Mahometan does hold that
the Koran is such a code.   Here, as Christians and
all who are not Mahometans hold, lies the great fault
of the Mahometan system.   Precepts which were
admirable in the time and place where they were
first given, precepts which were a great reform when
Mahomet first preached them to the Arabs of the
seventh century, have been forced, wherever the
Mahometan power has spread itself, upon all nations
for all time.   Hence, while a Christian government is
simply bound to shape its conduct according to the
moral precepts of the Gospel, a Mahometan government is bound to enforce the Koran as the law of the
land.   Hence too, while the Gospel is altogether
silent about the relations between the spiritual
and temporal powers, while Christian nations have
therefore settled that question in different ways at
different times, the Mahometan religion settles it in
one way for all time.   Wherever the Mahometan
system is fully carried out, the spiritual power carries

the temporal power with it. The successor of the Prophet, the Caliph, is Pope and Emperor in one. In the Mahometan system there is no distinction between Church and State, no distinction between religious and civil duty. Every action of a good Mussulman is not only done from a religious motive, but is done directly as a religious act. From this spring both the best and the worst features of the Mahometan system. This carrying of religion into everything, the swallowing up, as one may say, of the secular life in the religious life, leads to much that is good in the relations of Mahometans towards one another. A good and earnest Mahometan, who carefully follows the precepts of his own law, must, at least towards men of his own faith, practise many of the moral virtues. The Mussulman too is never ashamed of his religion or of any of the observances which it enjoins. And this is certainly more than we can say of all Christians. In short, if Islam had never gone beyond Arabia, we might have reckoned Mahomet among the greatest benefactors of mankind. The only fault which could in such a case have been laid to the charge of his system would be that, in reforming the old evils of the Eastern world, polygamy and slavery, he had for ever consecrated them. The worst that we could have said of Islam within its own peninsula would have been that it was so great a reform as to make a still greater reform altogether hopeless.

But this very feature which brings out so much good in the relations of Mahometans to one another is the very one which, before all others, makes Mahometanism the worst of all religions in its relation to men of any other religion. The feeling of exclusive religious pride and religious zeal which it engenders is very like that spirit of exclusive patriotic zeal and pride which may be seen in the history of various nations. The Mahometan has something in common with the old Roman. The good and the bad features of the old Roman character sprang from the same source. The Roman commonwealth was to him what the creed of Islam is to the sincere Mahometan. For the Roman commonwealth he would freely give himself, his life, and all that he had. Towards his fellow citizens of that commonwealth he practised many virtues. But as he was ready to sacrifice himself to the commonwealth, so he was equally ready to sacrifice everything else. The rights of other nations, the very faith and honour of Rome herself, were as nothing in his eyes, if he deemed that the greatness of the commonwealth could be advanced by disregarding them. So it is with the Mahometan religion. No religion has ever called forth more intense faith, more self-sacrificing zeal, on the part of its own professors. But the one precept which corrupts all, the precept which bids the true believer to fight against the infidel, turns that very faith and zeal which have in them so much to be admired into the cruellest instruments of oppression against men of all other creeds.

At this stage it may very likely be asked, and that not unfairly, whether it is meant to charge all Mahometan nations and all Mahometan governments with the crimes which disgrace the rule of the Ottoman Turks. The answer is easy. If it is meant to ask whether all Mahometan nations and governments have been guilty of those crimes in the same degree, we may unhesitatingly answer, No. There is a vast difference between one Mahometan nation or govern-

ment and another, just as there is a vast difference
between one Christian or Pagan nation or government
and another. But it is none the less true that the
crimes which mark the Ottoman rule spring directly
from the principles of the Mahometan religion. They
show the worst tendencies of that religion carried out
in their extremest shape. There have been other
Mahometan powers under which those tendencies
have not been allowed to reach the same growth.
That is to say, there have been Mahometan governments which have been very far from being so bad
as that of the Ottoman Turks. But under every
Mahometan government those tendencies must exist
in some degree; therefore, while some Mahometan
governments have been far better than others, no
Mahometan government can be really good according
to a Western standard. For no Mahometan government which rules over subjects which are not
Mahometans can give really equal rights to all its
subjects. The utmost that the best Mahometan ruler
can do is to save his subjects of other religions from
actual persecution, from actual personal oppression;
he cannot save them from degradation. He cannot,
without forsaking the principles of his own religion,
put them on the same level as Mussulmans. The
utmost that he can do is to put his non-Mussulman
subjects in a state which, in every Western country
would be looked upon as fully justifying them in
revolting against his rule. And, as we have seen, the
tendencies to treat them worse than this are almost
irresistible. Among the Ottomans those tendencies
have reached their fullest development. A rude
people, a bigoted people, in its beginning a band of
adventurers rather than a nation, rose to power under

a line of princes who were endowed with unparalleled gifts for winning and keeping dominion, but who had but a small share in those qualities which make dominion something other than a mere rule of force. The Ottomans have been simply a power. They have been a power whose one work has been the subjugation of other nations, Mahometan as well as Christian, a power whose sole errand has been that of conquest, and which therefore, as soon as it ceased to conquer, sank into a depth of wickedness and weakness beyond all other powers. The Ottoman Turk, a conqueror and nothing more, has had no share in the nobler qualities which have distinguished many other Mahometan nations which have been conquerors and something else as well. He has no claim to be placed side by side with the higher specimens of his own creed, with the early Saracens or with the Indian Moguls. It would be a blessed change indeed if the lands of South-eastern Europe could be transferred from the rule of the corrupt gang at Constantinople to a rule just, if stern, like that of the first Caliphs. But, even under the rule of the first Caliphs, they would still be in a case which would cause any Western people to spring to arms. No Mahometan ruler, I repeat, can give more than contemptuous toleration; he cannot give real equality of rights. One Mahometan ruler tried to do so, and not only tried but succeeded. But he succeeded only by casting away the faith which hindered his work. Akbar was the one prince born in Islam who gave equal rights to his subjects who did not profess the faith of Islam. But he was also the one prince born in Islam who cast away the faith of Islam. To do his work, the noblest work that despot ever did, he had to cast aside the trammels of a creed under which his work could never have been done. No fact proves more clearly that under Mahometan rule there can be no real reform than the fact that the one Mahometan prince who wrought a real reform had to cease to be Mahometan in order to work it.(³)

So again with regard to another point. It may be asked, Is the Mahometan religion necessarily inconsistent with proficiency in literature, art, and science? Here too a different answer may be given according to the different standard which we take. The East has its own literature, art, and science, apart from those of the West: the East has its own civilization apart from that of the West. We may deem that the East is inferior to the West in all these things, and history proves that it is so. But the real point is, not that one is inferior or superior to the other, but that they are essentially distinct. Our position is that the Turk has never won for himself any share in the common intellectual possessions of the West. Even in the East, no one would place him in these respects on a level with either the Arab or the Persian. But our point is wholly with regard to his share in the intellectual possessions of the West. In those possessions we may say that no Mahometan nation has ever had a full share, and that the Ottoman Turk has had no share at all. The Saracen, both of the East and of the West, has his distinct place in the history of art and science; the Ottoman Turk has none. What the real share of the Saracens in these matters is I have tried to show elsewhere. I need here only repeat that those who speak of the Spanish Saracens as ever having at any time had learning, art, and science all to themselves simply show that they are themselves in the blackness of darkness with regard to the history of Christendom generally, and specially with regard to the history of the Eastern Rome.(⁴)

We have gone off somewhat from the main track of our argument to mark how far the special evils of Ottoman rule are shared by Mahometan governments in general, and how far they are directly owing to the Mahometan religion. The answer is that they are directly owing to the Mahometan religion, that they must in some measure affect every Mahometan government, but that the special character and position of the Ottoman Turks has aggravated the worst tendencies of the Mahometan religion, and has made their rule worse than that of any of the other great Mahometan powers of the world.(⁵) We now come back to the fifth point of difference between the state of South-eastern Europe under the Turk and the state of the nations of Western Europe under their several national governments. It follows from all that has gone before that the nations of Western Europe, saving those small exceptions which have been already spoken of, have national governments of their own, but that the nations of South-eastern Europe have not. Let us once more compare the Bulgarian and the Ottoman Turk. The Bulgarians came in as heathen invaders. They embraced Christianity, and were lost among their Christian neighbours and subjects. Their government then became a national government. The Turks came in, not as heathen but as Mahometan invaders. They have not embraced Christianity. They have always remained distinct from their Christian neighbours and subjects. Their government has never become a national government to any but the invading race themselves. It is a string of causes and effects. The rule of the Bulgarian could become a national government, because he embraced Christianity, and he was able to embrace Christianity because he came in as a heathen. The rule of the Ottoman Turk has never become a national government, because the Turk has never embraced Christianity, he could not embrace Christianity because he came in as a Mahometan. It is a fact well worthy of remembrance that both the Bulgarians, and somewhat later the Russians, when they became dissatisfied with their own heathen religion, had Mahometanism and Christianity both set before them, and that they deliberately chose Christianity. Had either of those nations chosen otherwise, the history of Europe would have been very different from what it has been. The rule of the Bulgarian would have been what the rule of the Turk has been. The state of things which began in the South-eastern lands in the fourteenth century would have begun in the ninth. We need not stop to show how different the whole history of the world would have been, if the heathen Russians, instead of adopting Christianity, had adopted Mahometanism. As it was, both nations made a better choice, and the history of the Bulgarian, as compared with that of the Ottoman Turk, has given us the most instructive of lessons. The heathen conquerors could be turned into Christian brethren ; the Mahometan conquerors could not. And, remaining Mahometans, they could not give a national government to those of the conquered who remained Christians. Now among those who so remained were the bulk of the conquered nations, the nations themselves as nations. Many individuals everywhere, in some lands large classes, embraced, as was not very wonderful, the religion of the conquerors, and so rose to the level of the conquerors. But the vast majority clung stedfastly to the faith whose continued profession condemned them to be bondmen in their own land. Thus the distinction of religion marked off the two classes of conquered and conquerors, subjects and rulers, the people of the land and the strangers who held them in subjection. Had it been merely the distinction of conqueror and conquered, that might have died out as it has died out in so many lands. The Turk might by this time have been as thoroughly assimilated as the Bulgarian. But the distinction of religion kept on for ever the distinction between conquerors and conquered. The process of conquest, the state of things directly following on conquest, still goes on after five hundred years.

Thus the rule of the Mahometan Turk is not, and cannot be, a national government to any of his Christian subjects. This must be thoroughly understood, because so many phrases which we are in the habit of using are apt to lead to error on this point. We said in an earlier chapter that many words which have one meaning when we apply them to the state of things in Western Europe, have another meaning or no meaning at all when we apply them to the state of things in South-eastern Europe. If in speaking of things in South-eastern Europe we use such words as "sovereign," "subject," "government," "law," we must remember that we are using them with quite another meaning than they bear when applied to the same things in Western Europe. Thus in common language we speak of the power which is now established

at Constantinople as the Turkish "government" or
the Ottoman "government." We speak of the
Sultan as the "sovereign" of Bulgaria, Bosnia, Thessaly, or Crete. We speak of the Christian inhabitants
of those countries as the Sultan's "subjects." His
subjects they undoubtedly are in one sense; but it is
in a sense quite different from that which the word
bears in any Western kingdom. The word "subject"
has two quite different meanings when we speak of a
Turkish subject and when we speak of a British subject. When we call an Englishman a British subject,
we mean that he is a member of the British state, and
we call him subject rather than citizen simply because
the head of the British state is a king or queen and
not a republican magistrate. Every British subject
is the member of a body of which the Queen of
Great Britain and Ireland is the head. But if we
call a Bulgarian an Ottoman subject, it does not
mean that he is the member of a body of which the
Ottoman Sultan is the head. It means that he is the
member of a body which is held in bondage by the
body of which the Ottoman Sultan is the head. It
does not simply mean that he is a subject of the
Grand Turk as a political ruler. It means that he
is also subject to all the lesser Turks as his daily oppressors. If we speak of "government," the "Turkish
government," and the like, the words are apt to sug-
gest, often unconsciously, that they have the same
meaning when they are applied to Eastern Europe
as they have when applied to Western Europe.
What we understand by "government" in Western
Europe is the administration of the law. The government is the body which protects those who obey the
law, and which punishes those who break it. And in

all the countries of Western Europe, whether they are called kingdoms or commonwealths, the nation itself has some share, more or less perfect, more or less direct, in appointing and controlling both those who make the law and those who administer it. When this is the case, it matters nothing for our purpose whether the state is called a kingdom or a common- wealth, whether the mass of the nation are spoken of as "subjects" or as "citizens." For our purpose, for the comparison between Eastern and Western Europe, "subject" and "citizen" mean the same thing. We speak of a British "subject" and we speak of a French "citizen;" but the use of the two different words simply marks the difference of the form of the executive in the two countries. "Subject" and "citizen" alike mean a man who is a member of a political community, and who has, or may by his own act acquire, a share in the choice of those who make and who administer the law. The duties of the sovereign and of the subject are correlative. The subject owes allegiance to the sovereign who gives him protection ; the sovereign owes protection to the subject who lives under his allegiance. All this applies in its fulness to all con- stitutional states, whether they are called kingdoms or commonwealths. It applies in a less degree even to despotic states, so far as the despotic sovereign is really the head of the nation and has interests and feelings in common with the nation. But in South- eastern Europe, under the rule of the Turk, there is nothing which answers to the state of things which we have just been describing. If therefore we use words like "government," "sovereign," "subject," to describe a state of things which does not exist in those lands, we must remember in what sense we

are using them. As far as the Turks themselves
are concerned, the Turkish government is a government, though a despotic one. To the Turks the
Sultan is their sovereign, the head of their nation.
As members of that nation, they are his subjects.
A Turk is a subject of the Sultan, if not in the sense
in which an Englishman is the subject of his Queen,
yet at least in the sense in which a Russian is the
subject of his Emperor. But the Christian subjects
of the Sultan, that is the people of the lands in which
the Sultan and his Turks are encamped as strangers,
so far from being the Sultan's subjects in the English
sense, are not even his subjects in the Russian sense.
He is not the head of their nation, but the head of a
foreign nation, a nation whom they look on as their
bitterest enemies. They are not his subjects, because
he does not give them that protection which is involved
in the relation of sovereign and subject, that protection
which the Russian receives from his despotic sovereign
no less than the Englishman from his constitutional
sovereign. They are not his subjects in the English,
or even in the Russian sense, because, as he gives them
no protection, they owe him no allegiance. He is
not their sovereign, but a stranger who holds them
down by force. They are not his subjects, except in
the sense of being held down by force. If we apply
the word "sovereign" and "subject" to the relation
between the Turkish Sultan and the Christian nations
which are under his power, we must remember that
we use those words in a sense in which we might
speak of a burglar who has broken into a house as the
"sovereign" of that house, and the owner of the house
and his family as the "subjects" of the burglar.

The rule of the Turk in short over the Christian

nations which are under his power is a rule of mere force and not a rule of law. This must be so whenever a Mahometan government bears rule over subjects of any other religion ; but it is so in a truer and fuller sense when the Mahometan government is the government of the Ottoman Turk. The rule of a Mahometan power cannot be a rule of law to its subjects of any other religion ; for them no law, strictly speaking, exists. They have not, as the people have in a constitutional state, any share, however indirect, in making the law. So far from having a share in making the law, the law is not even made in their interest or for their benefit, as it may be even in a despotic state, when the despot is really the head of the nation. In a Mahometan state the only law is the Koran, the sacred book of Mahomet ; or rather it is not the Koran itself, but what the Koran has been made into by successive expounders and commentators. But the law thus made is a law made wholly in the interest of the Mahometan rulers, not at all in that of their Christian subjects. The Christian is in strictness out of the pale of the law ; the utmost that he can do is to purchase certain rights, the security of his life, his property and the exercise of his religion, by the payment of tribute. The law is not made for him, and the law is not administered for him. So far as he is in theory entitled to its protection, that protection is a mere name, because the witness of an infidel cannot by the Mahometan law be taken against the true believer. The Christian is thus absolutely without protection. Even supposing the court to deal quite justly according to its own rules, to punish all crimes which are proved according to its own rules, still a crime done by a Mahometan against a Christian can hardly ever be punished, because it can hardly ever be proved. If it be done in the presence of any number of Christian witnesses, but of Christian witnesses only, their witness cannot be taken and the crime cannot be punished. Such is the theory of the Mahometan law. Its practice has been better and worse in different times and places. Under the Turkish rule now it is for the most part very hard to get justice done for a crime committed by a Mahometan against a Christian, unless the Christian can both bribe the judge and hire Mahometan witnesses. Practically then a Mahometan may do what he choses to a Christian with very little fear of being punished for it. It is plain that to apply the words "law" and "government" to a state of things like this is a mere abuse of words. For the Christian subject of the Turk law and government do not exist. The thing which usurps their names is not law and government, but simply a system of organized brigandage.

The utter difference between the meaning of the word government, as applied to Western and to South-eastern Europe, will be best understood if we look at it in this way. We have seen that among the nations of Western Europe, unless in a few exceptional corners, no one wishes to get rid of the government of his country, though he may wish to modify and improve it in many ways. The Swiss, the Englishman, the Russian, live under very different forms of government; and it is possible that this or that man among those three nations may think that the form of government which he sees in one of the other nations is better than his own. He may wish to reform his own government according to the model of the other. But, at the utmost, all that he wishes is to reform the government of his country, not to get rid of it. All alike wish to remain members of a political community which shall be Swiss, English, or Russian. But the Christian subject of the Turkish government does not wish to reform the Turkish government; he does not wish to re-construct it after the model of some other government; he simply wishes to get rid of it altogether. He is not a member of a Turkish political community; for, while he is under the power of the Turk, he stands outside all political communities. Nor does he wish to become a member of a Turkish political community; for he is not a Turk, and he does not look on Turks as his countrymen. What he wishes is to become a member of a political community of his own nation, which shall have nothing to do with the Turk. He knows nothing of the so-called Turkish "government," or of his so-called "sovereign" the Sultan, except so far as he is compelled by force to know something of them. They are not the heads of his own nation, but the heads of a foreign and hostile nation. These are the plain facts as to the state of South-eastern Europe; and, if we do not wish to use words which are altogether misleading, we must adapt our language to the facts; otherwise we shall fall into strange mistakes. Thus it has sometimes been said that, if the Christians of the East have grievances, they ought to lay them before "their own government," and not to listen to "foreign intriguers." In so saying, not only are the facts of the case altogether misstated, but the words themselves are used in a misleading sense. As a matter of fact, the subject nations have, over and over again, laid their grievances before the power

which calls itself their government, and they have got
no redress by so doing. It is impossible that they
could have redress by so doing, for the power to
which they applied was not their own government, nor any government at all. That power
could not redress their grievances, because to redress their grievances would be to destroy itself.
For the existence of that power, that falsely called
"government," is itself the greatest of their grievances, the root and cause of all lesser grievances.
Those again who are spoken of as foreign intriguers
are, in the eyes of the subjects of the Turk, not
foreigners but countrymen. They are that part of
their countrymen who have kept or won their freedom,
while they themselves are left in bondage. The
English statesman who gave that piece of advice
spoke as if the Turk was the countryman of the
Bosnian Christian, as if the Turkish government was
his government, as if the Servian or the Montenegrin
was a foreigner to him. In truth, the Bosnian Christian
looks on the Servian or Montenegrin as his countryman ; he looks on the Turk as a foreigner. He does
not look on the Turkish government as his government
at all ; for it does not discharge the common duties
of government. But he would gladly be under any
government, Servian, Montenegrin, or any other,
which would discharge those duties. So we often
hear of the "interests of Turkey," "the friends of
Turkey," "the enemies of Turkey." If by "Turkey"
is meant the land and people over which the Turks
rule, as we should mean if we spoke of the "interests,"
the "friends," the "enemies," of England or France,
then those phrases are used in a sense which is utterly
misleading. People talk of the "interests of Turkey,"

meaning the "interests of the Turks." But whatever
is for the real interest of Turkey is against the
interest of the Turks: for the interest of the Turk is
to keep Turkey in bondage ; the interest of Turkey
is to get free from the bondage of the Turk. So the
enemies of the Turks are the friends of Turkey ; the
friends of the Turk are the enemies of Turkey. At
the late Conference at Constantinople we sometimes
heard of the "representatives of Turkey," meaning two Turks who were allowed to sit with the
European ambassadors. Now all those European
ambassadors might in a sense be called "representatives of Turkey ;" for it is to be hoped that they
were all trying to do something for the good of the
land and people of Turkey. But the two Turks were
in no way "representatives of Turkey ;" for they
were doing all that they could against the land and
people of Turkey by striving to prolong their own
wicked dominion over them.

So again at the same Conference there was talk
about a "foreign occupation" of this or that province
of the land which we call Turkey. By a "foreign
occupation" was meant the presence of civilized
troops who should protect the people of the land.
But those who used that phrase seemed to forget
that those lands are already under a foreign occupation, a foreign occupation of the worst kind. The
Turks, as has been often said, are simply an army
of occupation in a conquered country. They have
been so for five hundred years, and they remain so
still. They are encamped on the lands of other
nations, where they hold down the rightful owners
by force. They are essentially an army ; for every
Turk is armed, while the Christian is unarmed. The

only objection to calling them an army is that in
an army there is discipline, and a soldier who does
wrong may be punished, while in the Turkish army
of occupation there is no discipline. For every Turk
may do whatever wrong he chooses to the people of
the land, and he is never punished for so doing.
Wherever the armed Turk is, whether he is enlisted
as a regular soldier of the Sultan or not, there is
the foreign army of occupation. What was really
proposed was, not to bring in a foreign occupation as something new, but to change one foreign
occupation for another. It was proposed to put a
friendly foreign occupation instead of a hostile
one; it was proposed to take away the Turkish
army of oppressors, and to put instead an European
army of protectors. It was proposed to take away
the army which killed and robbed the people of the
land at pleasure, and to put instead of them an army
which should save the people of the land from being
killed and robbed. That the army of foreign robbers
themselves disliked such a proposal was only natural :
but it was very strange to hear, as we often heard,
that such a measure was against the dignity, the
independence, or the interests of "Turkey." The
Turk of course did not want to be put aside, and
to put him aside might be said to be against his
interest ; but to put him aside was the very thing
which the interest of Turkey, its land and people,
demanded above all things.

This way of talking about "Turkey" and "the Turks"
as if they meant the same thing comes from our
Western way of looking at things. As England is the
land of England, as France is the land of the French,
we get almost unwittingly into a way of speaking

as if Turkey were the land of the Turks. And if we allow ourselves to speak in a misleading way, we can hardly fail to get in some degree confused in our thoughts as well as in our words. We cannot too constantly remember, we cannot too often repeat, that the Turks in the land which we call Turkey are not the people of the land, but simply an army of occupation encamped among them. They are an army of foreign invaders, towards whom the people of the land have only one interest and one duty, namely to free themselves from the foreign yoke as soon as they can. The words "army of occupation" so exactly express the truth of the case that there are no words which the friends of the Turks—that is, the enemies of the land and people of Turkey—so greatly dislike to hear. Those words exactly set forth the truth of the case; they bring out strongly that the Turk, though he has been so long in the land, is as much a stranger as he was when he first came, that his rule which began in force has been kept on by sheer force ever since. It was a foreign army which entered the land five hundred years back, and it is a foreign army which keeps the land in bondage still. The Turk who occupies the Greek and Slavonic lands is still as much a stranger in those lands, as much a mere foreign invader, as the Germans were in France, when a few years back they held part of France as an army of occupation. In one case the foreign occupation lasted only for a year or two; in the other case it has gone on for ages; but it has not changed its nature by length of time. Only between the two cases there was this great difference, that France was occupied by a civilized and disciplined army, acting according to

G

the rules of civilized warfare, while the Greek and Slavonic lands are occupied by a barbarian army which knows no rules of discipline at all. The regular soldiers of the Sultan are doubtless the least mischievous part of the army of occupation, for they are under some kind of discipline. The worst part of the army of occupation is made up of the armed Turks scattered through the whole land, who are under no discipline, and who do whatever evil they may think good. To call them an army of occupation is not, as the friends of the Turks often say, a figurative or rhetorical way of speaking. It is the soberest and truest way of setting forth the past history and the present state of the Turk, and of the lands which he holds under his yoke.

We have seen now what the Turk is, and we have seen that it is mainly his religion that has made him what he is. From all this another point follows. A system of this kind, a system under which the bondage of the mass of the people of a country is enforced by their rulers as a matter of religious duty, is incapable of reform. It can be got rid of; it cannot be reformed. It may be got rid of in three ways; first, by the rulers embracing the religion of their subjects ; secondly, by the subjects embracing the religion of their rulers; or thirdly, by transferring power to hands under which contending races and religions may be put on a level of real equality. The two former alternatives do not come within the range of practical politics. The general conversion of the Mahometans to Christianity is out of the question. It is barely possible in some special districts under special circumstances.([6]) The general conversion of the Christians to Mahometanism is equally out of the question ; and, even setting purely theological feelings aside, it is a solution which no one in Western Europe could wish for. The only means of putting an end to the state of things which necessarily follows on Mahometan rule is to put an end to the Mahometan rule itself. Schemes of reform lie as much out of the range of practical politics as any general conversion either way. A Mahometan government cannot really reform ; it cannot get rid of the inherent evils of Mahometan society ; nor can it get rid of the unjust relations in which in every Mahometan country Mahometans must stand towards men of other religions. Christianity has got rid of the two great evils of polygamy and slavery. Mahometanism cannot get rid of them, because they are allowed and consecrated by the Mahometan law. So too a Mahometan government cannot really reform the relations between its Mahometan and non-Mahometan subjects. It cannot give its non-Mahometan subjects the benefits which they have a right to demand. It cannot put them on a level with its Mahometan subjects : it cannot put them on a level with the inhabitants of countries where the government is not Mahometan. For it is the first principle of the Mahometan religion not to do any of these things. One Mahometan government may be, as we have seen, very much better than another ; but none can be really good. The utmost that any Mahometan government can do is to protect its non-Mahometan subjects from actual persecution, from actual personal oppression. It cannot do more than this. Do what it will, it cannot, as long as it remains Mahometan, make its non-Mahometan subjects other than a subject class in their own land. It therefore cannot reform, in the sense in which reform is understood in Western Europe. It cannot give the people of Eastern Europe what they seek for and what they have a right to demand, namely a condition equal to that of the people of Western Europe. Any scheme which expects that which is impossible lies without the range of practical politics. The expectation of reforms from the Turk, as expecting what is beyond all things impossible, lies preeminently without that range. The only solution which comes within that range is the transfer of the power of the Turk to other hands.

We have thus seen who the Turk is, and what he is. We have seen in what he differs from the nations of Europe, and why he can never really enter into the fellowship of the nations of Europe. We have seen that the Turks are a people alien to the blood, language, civilization, and religion of Western Europe. They have made conquests ; but they have never legitimated their conquests in the way that other conquerors have. They have never either assimilated the conquered nor yet been themselves assimilated by them. They have always remained a distinct race, holding the people of the land in bondage. The people under their rule have no national government ; what calls itself a government is simply a dominion of strangers ruling by force. Their Sultan gives no protection to his Christian subjects ; therefore his Christian subjects owe him no allegiance. And this state of things is one which cannot be mended, because it is a state of things which the religion of the Turks enforces as a religious duty. They are Mahometans, and a Mahometan government is bound to treat its subjects of other religions as a conquered race, and not to put them on a level with Mahometans. As long therefore as that Mahometan government lasts, there can be no real reform. If the people of South-eastern Europe are to be made really free, if they are to be raised to the level of the people of Western Europe, the great hindrance which keeps them from so doing must be taken out of the way. That hindrance is the power of the Turk. The power of the Turk must therefore pass away.

We have thus, in these three chapters, traced in a general way, the nature of the Ottoman power in Europe. We will now go on in the following chapters to trace out somewhat more fully what the Ottoman Turks have done in the European lands in which they are encamped. That is, we will go on to trace out the leading features in the history of the Ottoman power in Europe, how it began, how it rose to greatness, how it sank to the state of utter corruption and degradation in which we see it now.

NOTES.

(1, p. 58.) After the Castilian Conquest of Granada, the nations of Western Europe had nothing to do with any Mahometan people in Western Europe itself. But, besides the Ottoman Turks, they had a good deal to do with the Mahometan powers of Africa, that is they suffered a good deal at their hands in the way of piracy, but most of these African powers were at least nominally under the supremacy of the Ottoman Sultan. Their history therefore of some centuries back is rather a part of that Ottoman history than a part of the history of the European power of the Saracens.

(2, p. 61.) All that can be said on Mahometanism as a missionary religion will be found in the introductory lecture of Mr. R. B. Smith's "Mohammed and Mohammedanism." Mr. Smith seems to have got up very carefully all that can be said on the Mahometan side ; unluckily he does not seem to have bestowed the same care on any part of the history of Christendom. Like most panegyrists of Mahometanism, especially of Saracenic art and learning, he forgets that whatever the Saracens knew they learned from the abiding home of civilization at New Rome.

(3, p. 68.) On Akbar see History and Conquests of the Saracens, p. 114.

(4, p. 69.) History and Conquests of the Saracens, p. 155—159.

(5, p. 69.) I am not called on to inquire whether South-eastern Europe or Persia has at this moment the worst government. In Persia the Mahometans are the nation ; Christians and Fire-worshippers—if any Fire-worshippers be left—are small minorities. The main question there lies between Mahometan and Mahometan. As regards Mahometans, the Persian government may possibly be worse than the Turkish. So may the Egyptian government. But, as regards Mahometans, the Persian government is not inherently incapable of reform ; it may conceivably be brought to the best Mahometan standard. The great feature of Ottoman rule in Europe is that it is primarily and essentially a rule of Mussulman over non-Mussulman. So to be is the nature of its whole being. This the government of Persia is only to a very small extent, and, as regards Christians, we might say quite incidentally.

(6, p. 82.) On the possibility of reconversion in Bosnia and the Mahometan parts of Albania I shall find something to say further on.

CHAPTER IV.

THE RISE AND GROWTH OF THE OTTOMAN POWER.

WE have thus traced out the distinguishing characteristics of Eastern and of Western Europe. We have seen what are the great races which have from the beginning inhabited the South-eastern peninsula. We have shown the special position of the Turks among them, and the points in which they stand aloof from the European nations. We have seen also what is the nature of their rule over those European nations which they have brought into bondage, and how impossible it is that their rule can ever be mended. Thus far we have done this only in a general way; we have seen what, according to the laws of cause and effect, could hardly have failed to happen. We have now to see more fully how the working of those causes and effects has been carried out in fact. We have seen what the Turks, being what they were, could not fail to do. We must now see more minutely, by the help of history, what the Turks have really done.

Our immediate subject is not the history of all the Mahometan nations, not even the history of all the Turkish dynasties, but more specially the history of the Ottoman Turks, and mainly the

history of their doings in the lands which they
have conquered in Europe. Of the first Mahometans, that is the Arabs or Saracens, and of the
earlier Turkish dynasties, I have said something
in another book, and I will repeat as little as I
can of what I have said there. At the same time,
in treating the special history of the Ottoman Turks,
it will be necessary to draw certain distinctions.
For some of the things which we may have to say
about the Ottoman Turks will apply to Mahometan
powers in general, and some will not. It is quite
certain, as has already been shown, that no Mahometan government can ever rule over men of another
religion in a way which any one in Western Europe
would call ruling well. It is quite certain that no
Mahometan nation can ever rise to the highest point
of civilization. Still there are great differences, which
ought not to be forgotten, between one Mahometan
nation and another, just as there are differences between
one Christian nation and another. Some Mahometan
nations have been much more civilized than others,
and the rule of some Mahometan governments over
men of other religions has been milder than that of
others. In speaking of the Ottoman Turks, we must
carefully distinguish what is common to them with all
other Mahometan nations and what is peculiar to
themselves. We must distinguish the Turks from the
Saracens, and we must further distinguish the Ottoman Turks from other Turks. We may safely say
that no Mahometan nation—we are almost tempted
to say no other nation—ever produced so long a series
of great rulers as the Ottoman Turks. That is, if by
greatness we understand the power of carrying out
a man's purposes, good or bad. No people can show

so long a succession of rulers who were at once wise statesmen and skilful captains as the early Ottoman Sultans. Their business was to conquer; as long as they went on conquering they were great; when they ceased to conquer they fell into utter decay and degradation. Again, as regards what we call civilization, as distinguished from political and military success, the Ottoman Turks will be found to stand above some and below others of the chief Mahometan nations. But what specially distinguishes them is that no other Mahometan people has ever had so great a dominion over men of other religions. It follows that the worst feature of the Mahometan religion, its treatment of the unbeliever, comes out on a greater scale and in a worse form in their history than in any other.

The Ottoman Turks, it must be remembered, are only one branch out of many of the great Turkish family, which is one of the most widely spread among the families of mankind. There were several dynasties of Mahometan Turks before the Ottomans arose, and there are to this day vast nations of Turks, some of them mere savages, who have never embraced Mahometanism. It must always be borne in mind that all Mahometans are not Turks, and that all Turks are not Ottomans. The Turks with whom we have to do are those Turks who learned the Mahometan religion at the hands of the Saracens, and specially with that body of them which made their way into Europe and founded the Ottoman dominion there. The Turks and Saracens first came to have dealings with one another at the moment when the Saracen dominion which the Turks were to supplant was at the height of its power. This was in the year 710, seventy-eight years after the death of Mahomet. It was in that year that the Saracens passed from Africa into Spain, and made the beginning their greatest conquest in Europe. In the same year they first crossed the Oxus, and began to make converts and subjects among those Turks who lived between that great river and the Jaxartes. In the next year the conquest of Sind gave the Saracen dominion the greatest extent that it ever had. This last possession however was not long kept, and the great Mahometan conquests in India, conquests with which we have now no concern, did not begin till long afterwards. But it is worth noticing that it was almost at the same moment that the Mahometan religion and the Mahometan power made their way into India, into Western Europe, and into the land which was then the land of the Turks. The Caliph or successor of the Prophet, the temporal and spiritual chief of all who profess the Mahometan creed, now ruled over lands washed by the Atlantic and over lands washed by the Indian Ocean. The word which went forth from his palace at Damascus was obeyed on the Indus, on the Jaxartes, and on the Tagus.

While the whole Mahometan world was thus under one ruler, the Christian nations were divided among many rulers. But there were two Christian powers which stood out above all others. The Roman Empire still had its seat at Constantinople, and still held, though often in detached pieces, the greater part of the European coast of the Mediterranean Sea. The Saracens had lopped away Syria, Egypt, and Africa ; the Slaves had pressed into the South-eastern peninsula ; the Bulgarians had settled south of the Danube, and the Lombards had conquered great part of Italy.

Still both the Old and the New Rome obeyed the one Roman Emperor, and the Roman Empire was still the first of Christian powers, and still kept the chief rule of the Mediterranean. The other great Christian power was that of the Franks in Germany and Gaul, the power which was, at the end of the century, to grow into a new Western Empire with its seat at the Old Rome. Thus the Roman power still went on, only cut short and modified in various ways by the coming in of the Teutons in the West and of the Slaves in the East. And herein comes a very instructive parallel. For, as soon as the Saracens began to conquer and convert the Turks, the Turks begin to play a part in the history of the Saracen dominion in Asia which is much like the part which was played in Europe by the Teutons towards the Western Roman Empire and by the Slaves towards the Eastern. The Turks appear under the Caliphs as slaves, as subjects, as mercenaries, as practical masters, as avowed sovereigns, and lastly, in the case of the Ottomans, as themselves claiming the powers of the Caliphate. The dominions of the Caliphs gradually broke up into various states, which were ruled for the most part by Turkish princes who left a merely nominal superiority to the Caliph. It is not our business here to go through all of them. But one must be mentioned, that out of which the Ottoman dynasty arose. This was the Turkish dynasty of the house of Seljuk, which was the greatest power in Asia in the eleventh century. Their early princes, Togrul Beg, Alp-Arslan, and Malek Shah, were not only great conquerors, but great rulers after the Eastern pattern. They had many of the virtues which are commonly found in the founders of dynasties and their immediate successors. The Seljuk Turks pressed their conquests to the West, and so had more to do with Christians than any of the Turkish dynasties before them had. And it should carefully be noticed that it is from this time that a more special and crying oppression of the Christians under Mahometan rule begins. The Turks, even these earlier and better Turks, were a ruder and fiercer people than the Saracens, and they were besides full of the zeal of new converts. Doubtless, even under the Saracen rule, the Christian subjects of the Caliphs had always been oppressed and sometimes persecuted. But it is plain that, from the time when the power of the Turks began, oppression became harder and persecution more common. It was the increased wrongdoings of the Turks, both towards the native Christians and towards pilgrims from the West, which caused the great cry for help which led to the crusades. There were no crusades as long as the Saracens ruled ; as soon as the Turks came in, the crusades began.

In the latter part of the eleventh century began those long continued invasions of the Eastern Roman Empire by the Turks which led in the end to the foundation of the Ottoman power in Europe. There is no greater mistake than to think that the whole time during which the Eastern Empire went on at Constantinople was a time of mere weakness and decline. Such a way of talking at once shows its own folly. A power which was beset by enemies on all sides, in a way in which hardly any other power ever was, could not have lived on for so many ages, it could not have been for a great part of that time one of the chief powers of the world, if it had been all that

time weak and declining.   The Eastern Emperors are
often said by those who have not read their history
to have been all of them weak and cowardly men.
Instead of this, many of them were great conquerors
and rulers, who beat back their enemies on every
side, and made great conquests in their turn.   The
great feature in the history of the Eastern Empire
is not constant weakness and decline, but the alterna-
tion of periods of weakness and decline followed by
periods of recovered strength.   In one century provinces are lost ; in another they are won back again,
and new provinces added.   It was in one of these
periods of decline, following immediately after the
greatest of all periods of renewed power, that the
Turks and Romans first came across one another.
I say Romans, because the people of the Eastern
Empire called themselves by no other name, and the
nations of Asia knew them by no other name.   The
Eastern Empire was indeed fast becoming Greek,
as the Western Empire may be said to have already
become German.   But the Emperors and their subjects
never called themselves Greeks at any time, and the
time has not yet come when it becomes convenient
to give them the name.

The Turkish invasion of the Empire came just
after a time of brilliant conquest and prosperity
under the Macedonian dynasty of Emperors.   This
dynasty began in the ninth century and went on
into the eleventh.   Under it the Empire gained a
great deal, and lost comparatively little.   At the
very beginning of the period, in 878, the Saracens
completed the conquest of Sicily, which had been
going on for about fifty years.   A hundred years
later, in 988, Cherson, an outlying possession in

the Tauric peninsula or Crimea, was taken by the
Russian Vladimir. On the other hand, the power of
the Empire was vastly increased both in Europe and
in Asia. The dominions of the Emperors in Southern
Italy were increased ; Crete was won back ; the great
Bulgarian kingdom was conquered, and the other
Slavonic states in the Eastern peninsula became
either subject or tributary to the Empire. In Asia
large conquests, including Antioch, were made from
the Saracens ; Armenia was annexed, and the power of
the Empire was extended along the eastern shores of
the Euxine. The greatest conquests of all were made
in the reign of Basil the Second, called the Slayer of
the Bulgarians, who reigned from 976 to 1025. A
dominion of this kind, which depends on one man, is
something like a watch, which, if wound up, will go
for a while by itself, but will presently go down, if it
is not wound up again. So, as after Basil no great
Emperor reigned for some while, the Empire began
again to fall back, not at once, but within a few years.
About the middle of the eleventh century came one
of the periods of decline, and the Empire was cut
short by the Normans in Italy and by the Turks in
Asia. The Seljuk Sultan Alp-Arslan invaded Asia
Minor, a land which the Saracens had often ravaged,
but which they had never conquered. He overthrew
the Emperor Rômanos in battle, and treated him personally with marked generosity. This was in 1071,
and from this time dates the establishment of the
Turks, as distinguished from the Saracens, in the lands
which had been part of the Roman Empire. All the
inland part of the peninsula was now occupied by the
Turks, and, when in 1092 the great Seljuk dominion
was broken up, the city of Nikaia or Nice, the place

of the famous council, became the capital of a Turkish dynasty. The map will show how near this brought the Turks to Constantinople. And it might hardly have been thought that three hundred and sixty years would pass before the Turks entered the imperial city. But, as ruling over a land conquered from the Roman Empire, the Sultans who reigned at Nikaia called themselves Sultans of *Roum*, that is of *Rome*. It was this great advance of the power of the Seljuk Turks which caused the Christian nations of the West to come to the help of their brethren in the East.

The history of the crusades concerns us here only so far as, by affecting both the Eastern Roman Empire and the power of the Seljuk Turks, they did in the end pave the way for the advance of the Ottomans. The effect of the first crusade was to drive back the Turks from their position at Nikaia which was so threatening to the Empire. The Emperors who now reigned, those of the house of Komnênos, were for the most part either wise statesmen or good soldiers. Under their reigns therefore came another period of renewed strength, though the Empire never again became what it had been under the Macedonians. We are most concerned with their advance in Asia. There, following in the wake of the crusaders, they were able to win back a great part of the land, and the capital of the Seljuk Sultans fell back from Nikaia to Ikonion. The dominion of these Sultans gradually broke up after the usual manner of Asiatic powers, and so paved the way for the coming of a mightier power of their own race. But meanwhile events were happening in Europe which equally paved the way for the growth of new powers there. After the time of revival under the Komnenian Emperors came another time of decline, in the latter years of the twelfth century. The Bulgarians threw off the Roman yoke, and formed a restored Bulgarian kingdom which cut the Empire short to the north-west. At the other end of the Empire, a separate Emperor set himself up in the isle of Cyprus. A time of utter weakness and disunion had come, when it seemed as if the Empire must fall altogether before any vigorous enemy.

And so in some sort it happened. A blow presently came which may be looked on as really the ending of the old Roman Empire of the East. In 1204 Constantinople was taken by a band of crusaders who had turned away from the warfare to which they were bound against the Mahometans in Asia, to overthrow the eastern bulwark of Christendom in Europe. Now begins the dominion of the Franks or Latins in Eastern Europe. The Christians of the West were known as Latins, as belonging to the Western or Latin Church which acknowledged the authority of the Bishop of Rome. And they were called Franks, as Western Europeans are called in the East to this day, because most of them came from countries where the French tongue was spoken. But along with the French-speaking crusaders came the Venetians, who had a great trade in the East, and who had already begun to establish their power in Dalmatia. Constantinople was taken, and Baldwin Count of Flanders was set up as a Latin Emperor. So much of *Romania*, as the Eastern Empire was called, as the Franks and Venetians could get hold of was parcelled out among the conquerors. But they never conquered the whole, and Greek princes kept several parts of the Empire. Thus what really happened was that the Empire was split up into a number of small states, Greek and Frank. We now cannot help using the word Greek; for, after the loss of Bulgaria, the Empire was wholly confined to Greek-speaking people, and we need some name to distinguish them from the Franks or Latins. But they still called themselves Romans; and it is strange, in reading the Greek writers, to hear of wars between the Romans and the Latins, as if we had gone back to the early days of the Old Rome and the Thirty Cities of Latium. Latin Emperors reigned at Constantinople for nearly sixty years. For a few years there was a Latin kingdom of Thessalonica, and there were Latin princes at Athens and in Peloponnêsos, while the commonwealth of Venice kept the great islands of Corfu (¹) and Crete, and allowed Venetian families to establish themselves as rulers in several of the islands of the Ægæan. On the other hand, Greek princes reigned in Epeiros, and two Greek Empires were established in Asia. One had its seat at Trapezous or Trebizond on the south-east coast of the Euxine, while the other had its seat at Nikaia, the first capital of the Turkish Sultans of Roum. This last set of Emperors gradually won back a considerable territory both in Europe and Asia, and at last, in 1261, they won back Constantinople from the Latins. Thus the Eastern Roman Empire in some sort began afresh, though with much smaller territory and power than it had before the Latin conquest. It was threatened on all sides, by Bulgarians, Servians, Latins, and Turks; and no great Emperors reigned in this last stage of the Empire. Yet, even in these last days, there was once more something of a revival, and the Emperors gradually won back nearly the whole of all Peloponnêsos.

H

Thus a way was opened for a new race of conquerors both in Europe and Asia, by the breaking up of the power of the old Emperors who, even as late as the eleventh century, had reigned at once in Italy and in Armenia.   Instead of the old Eastern Empire, there was now only a crowd of states, two of which, at Constantinople and Trebizond, kept on the titles of the old Empire.   None of them were very great, and most of them at enmity with one another.   The thirteenth century too, which saw the break-up of the Empire in Europe, saw also the break-up of the older Mahometan powers in Asia and the beginning of the last and the most abiding of all.   This was in fact the time when all the powers of Europe and Asia seemed to be putting on new shapes.   In the thirteenth century the Western Empire in some sort came to an end as well as the Eastern.   For after Frederick the Second the Emperors kept no abiding power in Italy.   In Spain the Mahometan power, which had once held nearly the whole peninsula, was shut up within the narrow bounds of the kingdom of Granada. Castile now took its place as the leading power of Spain, and France was in the like sort established as the ruling power of. Gaul.   And, while great Christian powers were thus established in the western lands which had been held by the Mahometans, the Caliphate of Bagdad itself was overthrown by conquerors from the further lands of Asia.   I have said in an earlier book that at this time in the middle of the thirteenth century, Islam seemed to be falling back everywhere.   But in truth the blow which seemed the most crushing of all, the overthrow of the Caliphate by the Moguls, was part of a chain of events which brought on the stage a Mahometan power more terrible than all that had gone before it. We have now come to the time of the first appearance of the Ottoman Turks.

I have spoken elsewhere of the conquests of the Moguls both in Europe and in Asia. We have here to deal with them only so far as, in the course of their attacks on all other powers Christian and Mahometan, they began also to cut short the power of the Seljuk Sultans of Roum. But these last found unlooked-for helpers. The tale runs that, in a battle between the Turks and the Moguls, the Turks, as the weaker side, were being worsted, when an unknown company of men came to their help. These proved to be a wandering band of Turks from the far East, who, in the confusions of the times, were seeking a settlement under their leader Ertoghrul. Through their help the Seljuk Sultan overcame his enemies. The strangers were rewarded with a grant of lands, and those lands, step by step, grew into the Ottoman Empire. At this time the Latin Empire still lingered at Constantinople, but the Greek Emperors at Nikaia had won back large territories both in Asia and in Europe. Partly at the expense of the Greeks, partly at the expense of other Turkish Emirs or princes, Ertoghrul and his son Othman or Osman gradually grew in power. Warriors flocked to the new standard, and Othman became the most powerful prince in Western Asia. From him his followers took the name which it has ever since borne, that of Osmanli or Ottoman.

Our strictly Ottoman history now begins, and one characteristic feature of Ottoman history may strike us from the very beginning. The house of Othman arose on the ruins of the house of Seljuk; but

H 2

whatever our own day may be destined to see, no other
power has yet arisen on the ruins of the house of
Othman. No other Eastern power has had such an
abiding life. The Bagdad Caliphate lasted as long by
mere reckoning of years; but for many ages the Bagdad
Caliphate was a mere shadow. Other Eastern powers
have commonly broken in pieces after a few generations. The Ottoman power has lasted for six hundred
years; and, stranger than all, when it seemed for a
moment to be going the way of other Eastern dynasties, when the power of the Ottoman Turk seemed to
be breaking in pieces as the power of the Ghaznevid
and the Seljuk Turk had broken in pieces before him,
the scattered fragments were again joined together,
and the work of conquest and rule again began. But
by means of this very abiding life, by prolonging the
rule of a barbarian power in the midst of modern
civilization, the rule of the Ottoman has shewn us, in
a way in which the earlier Turkish dynasties could
not shew us, what a power of this kind comes to in
the days of its long decay. An Eastern dynasty,
above all a Mahometan dynasty, is great and glorious
according to an Eastern standard as long as it
remains a conquering dynasty. The Ottoman Turks
remained a conquering dynasty longer than any
other. Their power was thus so firmly established
that it has been able to outlive the causes which
broke up earlier dynasties. But, by having its being
thus prolonged, it has lived on to give an example of
corruption and evil of every kind for which it would
be hard to find a parallel among the worst of earlier
dynasties.

The Ottoman Turks have never been, in any strict
sense, a nation. They were in their beginning a

wandering horde, and even in the time of their
greatest dominion they kept up much of the character of a wandering horde.   They have nowhere really
become the people of the land.   Where they have
not borne rule over Christians, they have borne
rule over other Mahometans, and they have often
oppressed them nearly as much, though not quite in
the same way, as they have oppressed their Christian
subjects.   They have been, we may say, a ruling
order, a body ready to admit and to promote any
one of any nation who chose to join them, provided
of course that he accepted the Mahometan religion.
In this has lain their strength and their greatness ;
but it has been throughout, not the greatness of a
nation, but the greatness of a conquering army, bearing rule over other nations.   Stripping conquest and
forced dominion of the false glory which surrounds
them, we may say that the Ottomans began as a band
of robbers, and that they have gone on as a band of
robbers ever since.   To a great part of their history,
especially to their position in our own times, that
description would apply in its fulness.   But it would
not be wholly fair to speak in this way of the early
Ottomans.   The settled and self-styled civilized Turk
is really more of a robber than the wandering barbarian under whom his power began.   When conquest
simply means transfer from one despot to another,
the conquered often gain rather than lose.   The rule
of the conquering despot is stronger than that of
the despot whom he conquers, and a strong despot
usually comes nearer to a good ruler than a weak
one.   That is to say, he does a kind of justice in
his dominions.   However great may be his own
personal crimes and oppressions, he puts some check

on the crimes and oppressions of others. As long
therefore as the Ottoman rulers were strong, as long
as they were conquerors, there was a good side to
their rule. Most of the Sultans were stained with
horrible crimes in their own persons ; but most of
the early Sultans had many of the virtues of rulers
and conquerors. It was when their power began to
decay that the blackest side of their rule came out.
The oppression of the Sultans themselves became
greater. To oppression was added the foulest corruption, and the weak Sultans were not able, as the strong
ones had been, to keep their own servants in some
kind of order. In short, the Ottoman rulers were
the longest, and the early Ottoman rulers were the
greatest, of all lines of Eastern despots. Because of
their greatness, their power has been more long lived
than any other. Because it has been more long lived,
it has in the end become worse than any other.

We must be prepared then from the beginning to
find in the Ottoman rulers much that is utterly repulsive to our moral standard, much that is cruel, much
that is foul, joined with much that may fairly be
called great. They were in any case great soldiers.
If we may apply the name statesmanship to carrying
out any kind of purpose, good or bad, they were also
great statesmen. And it is not till they have passed
into Europe that their worst side distinctly prevails.
And he who was at once the greatest of all and the
worst of all was he who fixed his throne in Constantinople. As long as they remained in Asia, the
Ottomans might pass for one among many Asiatic
dynasties. It is their establishment in Europe which
gave them their special character.

It is hardly for me to settle how far the exploits

of the patriarch of the new dynasty, of Ertoghrul himself, belong to legend or to history. Both he and his son Othman were merely Asiatic rulers. They were not even avowed sovereigns ; they still respected the nominal superiority of the Seljuk Sultan at Ikonion. Othman bears a high character among Eastern rulers ; yet he murdered his uncle simply for dissuading him from a dangerous enterprise. The slaughter of brothers and other near kinsfolk has always been a special feature of Ottoman rule. Othman however at least slew his uncle in a moment of wrath ; later Sultans sacrificed their brothers by wholesale out of cold-blooded policy. Othman enlarged his dominions at the expense of the Emperors, and just before his death, in 1326, his armies took Brusa, which became the Asiatic capital of the Ottomans. It is with Othman's son Orkhan that the Ottoman Empire really begins. He threw off his nominal allegiance to the Sultan, though he still bore only the title of Emir. And in his time the Ottomans first made good their footing in Europe. But while his dominion was still only Asiatic, Orkhan began one institution which did more than anything else firmly to establish the Ottoman power. This was the institution of the tribute children. By the law of Mahomet, as we have seen, the unbeliever is allowed to purchase life, property, and the exercise of his religion, by the payment of tribute. Earlier Mahometan rulers had been satisfied with tribute in the ordinary sense. Orkhan first demanded a tribute of children. The deepest of wrongs, that which other tyrants did as an occasional outrage, thus became under the Ottomans a settled law. A fixed proportion of the strongest and most promising boys among the conquered Christian nations were carried off for the service of the Ottoman princes. They were brought up in the Mahometan faith, and were employed in civil or military functions, according to their capacity. Out of them was formed the famous force of the Janissaries, the new soldiers, who, for three centuries, as long as they were levied in this way, formed the strength of the Ottoman armies. These children, torn from their homes and cut off from every domestic and national tie, knew only the religion and the service into which they were forced, and formed a body of troops such as no other power, Christian or Mahometan, could command. In this way the strength of the conquered nations was turned against themselves. They could not throw off the yoke, because those among them who were their natural leaders were pressed into the service of their enemies. It was not till the practice of levying the tribute on children was left off that the conquered nations shewed any power to stir. While the force founded by Orkhan lasted in its first shape, the Ottoman armies were irresistible. But all this shews how far the Ottomans were from being a national power. Their victories were won by soldiers who were really of the blood of the Greeks, Slaves, and other conquered nations. In the same way, while the Ottoman power was strongest, the chief posts of the Empire, civil and military, were constantly held, not by native Turks, but by Christian renegades of all nations. The Ottoman power in short was the power, not of a nation, but simply of an army. The Ottomans began, and they have gone on ever since, as an army of occupation in the lands of other nations.

By the end of Orkhan's reign the Ottoman power was fully established in Asia Minor. Its Emirs had spread their power over all the other Turkish settlements, and nothing was left to the Christians but a few towns, chiefly on the coast. Above all, Philadelphia and Phôkaia long defended themselves gallantly after everything else was lost. The chief Christian power in Asia was now no longer the Roman or Greek Emperor at Constantinople, but the more distant Emperor at Trebizond. Besides their possessions on the south coast of the Euxine, these Emperors also held the old territories of the Empire in the Tauric Chersonêsos or Crimea. The Turks had now the whole inland part of Asia Minor. And this inland part of Asia Minor is the only part of the Ottoman dominions where any Turks are really the people of the land. The old Christian population has been quite displaced, and Anadol or Anatolia, the land of the East, is really a Turkish land. Yet it can hardly be said to be an Ottoman land. There the ruling body have borne sway over the descendants of the old Seljuk Turks. The Ottomans in short are strangers everywhere. They are strangers bearing rule over other nations, over Mahometans in Asia, over Christians in Europe.

The Ottoman rule over Christians in Europe began in the last years of Orkhan. The state of South-eastern Europe in the fourteenth century was very favourable for the purposes of the Turks. We have seen how utterly the old Empire was broken up, and how the Greek-speaking lands were divided among a crowd of states, Greek and Frank. A new power had lately arisen in the Ægæan through the occupation of Rhodes and some of the neighbouring islands

by the Knights of St. John.   A military order is not
well fitted for governing its dominions ; but no power
can be better fitted for defending them, and the
Knights of St. John at Rhodes did great things
against the Turks.   The power of the Emperors at
Constantinople, cut short by the Turks in Asia, was
cut short by the Bulgarians in Europe.   It was only
in Peloponnêsos that they advanced at the cost of the
Latins.   Just at the time before the Turks crossed
into Europe, a new power had arisen, or rather an
old power had grown to a much greater place
than it held before.   Stephen Dushan, King of
Servia, who took the title of Emperor, had established a great dominion which took in most part
of Macedonia, Albania, and Northern Greece.   But
the Greek Emperors kept Constantinople and the
lands round about it, with detached parts of Macedonia and Greece, including specially the great city
of Thessalonica.   Had the Servian Emperor been
able to win Constantinople, a power would have been
formed which might have been able to withstand the
Turks.   Servia would have been the body, and Constantinople the head.   As it was, the Turks found in
Servia a body without a head, and in Constantinople
a head without a body.   The Servian Empire broke
up on the death of its great king, and the Greeks were
divided by civil wars.   Thus, instead of Servians and
Greeks together presenting a strong front to the
Turks, the Turks were able to swallow up Greeks,
Servians, and all the other nations, bit by bit.

The Ottomans did not make their first appearance
in Europe as avowed conquerors.   They appeared,
sometimes as momentary ravagers, sometimes as

mercenaries in the Imperial service or as allies of
some of the contending parties in the Empire. Thus
in 1346 the Emperor John Kantakouzênos called in
the Turks to help him in civil war. From this time
we may date their lasting presence in Europe, though
they did not hold any permanent possessions there
till in 1356 they seized Kallipolis in the Thracian
Chersonêsos. This was the beginning of the Ottoman
dominion in Europe. From this time they advanced
bit by bit, taking towns and provinces from the
Empire and conquering the kingdoms beyond the
Empire, so that Constantinople was quite hemmed in.
But the Imperial city itself was not taken till nearly a
hundred years after the first Turkish settlement in
Europe. It must always be remembered that the
Turks overcame Servia and Bulgaria long before they
won Thessalonica, Constantinople, and Peloponnêsos.
Their first conquests gathered threateningly round
Constantinople; but they did not as yet actually
attack it. Nor did they always at once incorporate
the lands which they subdued with their immediate
dominions. In most of the lands of which the Turks
got possession, the process of conquest shews three
stages. There is, first, mere ravage for the sake of
plunder, and to weaken the land which was ravaged.
Then the land is commonly brought under tribute or
some other form of subjection, without being made a
part of the Sultan's immediate dominions. Lastly,
the land which is already practically conquered becomes a mere Ottoman province. In this way it is
worth noticing that, as we shall see further on, a large
part of the European dominions of the Turk, though
they were subdued long before the taking of Constantinople, were allowed to keep on some shadow

of separate being under tributary princes till after Constantinople was taken.

The first lasting settlement of the Turks on European ground was made, as we have seen, while Orkhan still reigned. But it was in the reign of Murad or Amurath the First, the successor of Orkhan, that the first settlement at Kallipolis grew into a compact European power. In a very few years from their first occupation of European territory, the Turks had altogether hemmed in what was left of the Empire. As early as 1361 Amurath took Hadrianople, which became the European capital of the Ottomans till they took Constantinople.([2]) Nothing was now left to the Empire but the part of Thrace just round Constantinople, with some of the cities on the Euxine, together with the outlying possessions which the Emperors still kept in Macedonia and Greece. Among them were the greater part of Peloponnêsos and the Chalkidian peninsula with Thessalonica. In Asia all that remained to the Empire was a little strip of land just opposite Constantinople, and the two cities of Philadelphia and Phôkaia, which might now almost be looked on as allied commonwealths rather than as parts of the Empire. But Amurath not only cut the Empire short, he also carried his arms into the Slavonic lands to the north. They lay as temptingly open to conquest as the Greek lands. The power of Servia went down at once after the death of Stephen Dushan, and Bulgaria a few years later was split up into three separate kingdoms. Amurath's first important conquest in this direction was the taking of Philippopolis in 1363. That city had changed masters several times, but it was then Bulgarian. Bulgaria

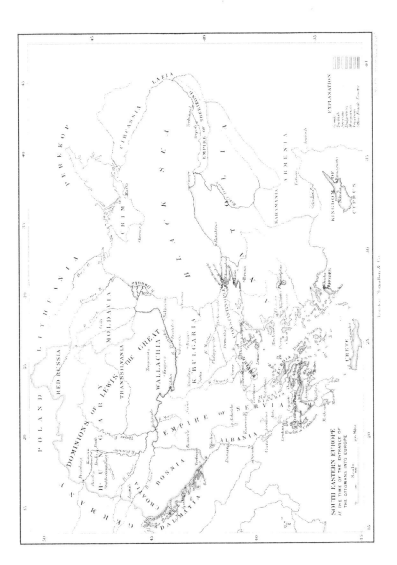

SOUTH EASTERN EUROPE
AT THE TIME OF THE ENTRANCE OF
THE OTTOMANS INTO EUROPE

EXPLANATION

Greeks
Turkish
Slavonic
Bulgarians
Roumanians
Hungarian
Other French Country

London Stanford & Co.

just now, besides her own divisions, had wars with Hungary to the north and with the Empire to the south. Yet amid all this confusion, several powers did unite to withstand the Turks ; and it was only gradually, and after several battles, that either Servia or Bulgaria was conquered. It seems to have been about 1371 that the chief Bulgarian kingdom, that of Trnovo, became tributary. But while Servia and Bulgaria were breaking in pieces, Bosnia to the north-west of them, which lay further away from the Turks, was growing in power. A great Slave confederation was formed under the Bosnian King Stephen, and Bosnians, Croats, and Servians for a little while won some successes over the Turks. But at last a great confederate army, Bosnian, Servian, Bulgarian, and Wallachian, was utterly defeated by the Turks at Kossova in 1389. Amurath himself was killed, not in the battle, but by a Servian who pretended to desert. But he was at once succeeded by his son Bayezid or Bajazet, who reaped the fruits of the victory. In the course of two or three years after the battle, Servia and Wallachia became tributary, and the greater part of Bulgaria was altogether conquered.

It is from the battle of Kossova that the Servians, and the Southern Slaves generally, date the fall of their independence. Bosnia, in its corner, still re-mained but little touched; it was ravaged, but not yet conquered. But all the lands which had made up the great Servian and Bulgarian kingdoms of former times were now either altogether conquered by the Turk, or made tributary to him, or else driven to maintain their independence by ceaseless fighting. And as the lands which the Turks subdued were made into tributary states before they were fully annexed, the

Turks were able to use each people that they brought
under their power as helpers against the next people
whom they attacked. Thus at Kossova Amurath
had already Christian tributaries fighting on his side.
From this time till Servia was completely incorporated with the Turkish dominions, the Servians had
to fight in the Turkish armies against the other Christian nations which the Turks attacked. In this way
the strength of the Christian nations was used against
one another, till the Turk thought the time was come
more directly to annex this or that tributary land. In
this the policy of the Ottomans was much the same
as the policy of the Romans in old times. For they
also commonly made the lands which they conquered
into dependent states, before they formally made
them into Roman provinces. In either case it may
be doubted whether the lands which were left in this
intermediate state gained much by not being fully
annexed at once. Still the way by which the Ottoman Empire came together suggests the way by
which it ought to fall asunder. Some of the tributary
lands have always kept a certain amount of separate
being. Some have, after a long bondage, come back
again to the tributary state. In short, experience
shews that the natural way for restoring these lands
to their ancient independence is by letting them pass
once more through the intermediate state. Only this
time it must be with their faces turned in the direction of a more thorough freedom, not of, as in ages
past, in the direction of a more thorough bondage.

The accession of Bajazet marks a distinct change
in the history of Ottoman conquest. Up to this time
the Ottoman princes had shewn themselves—except
in the exaction of the tribute children—at least not

worse than other Eastern conquerors. With Amurath's successor Bajazet the darker side of the Ottoman dominion comes more strongly into view. He was the first to begin his reign with the murder of a brother out of cold policy. Under him too that foul moral corruption which has ever since been the distinguishing characteristic of the Ottoman Turk came for the first time into its black prominence. Other people have been foul and depraved ; what is specially characteristic of the Ottoman Turk is that the common road to power is by the path of the foulest shame. Under Bajazet the best feature of the Mahometan law, the almost ascetic temperance which it teaches, passed away, and its worst features, the recognition of slavery, the establishment of the arbitrary right of the conqueror over the conquered, grew into a system of wrong and outrage of which the Prophet himself had never dreamed. Under Bajazet the Turk fully put on those parts of his character which distinguish him, even more than other Mahometans, from Western and Christian nations. Yet amid all this corruption, Bajazet could sometimes exercise a stern Eastern justice, and the mission of his race, the mission of warfare and conquest, still went on ; Bajazet was surnamed the Thunderbolt, and he was the first of the Ottoman princes to exchange the humbler title of Emir for that of Sultan. Yet, after Bajazet had consolidated the results of the victory of Kossova by his Bulgarian and Servian conquests, the actual dominion of the Ottomans did not make such swift advances under him as it had made under his father Amurath. It was rather distinguished by a scourge worse than that of actual conquest, by constant plundering expeditions, carried on chiefly for the sake of booty and slaves—the slaves being specially picked out for the vilest purposes. These ravages spread everywhere from Hungary to Peloponnêsos. But the most remarkable conquest of Bajazet was in Asia. Philadelphia still held out, and its citizens still deemed themselves subjects of the Emperors at Constantinople. Yet, when Bajazet thought proper to add the city to his dominions, the Emperor Manuel and his son were forced, as tributaries of the Sultan, to send their contingent to the Turkish army, and to help in the conquest of their own city.[3] But enemies presently came against Bajazet both from the West and from the East. His enemy from the West he overthrew ; but he was himself overthrown by his enemy from the East. A large body of crusaders came to the help of Sigismund King of Hungary, the same who was afterwards Emperor of the West. But Bajazet, at the head of his own Turks and of his Christian tributaries who were of course forced to serve with them, overthrew Sigismund and his allies in the battle of Nikopolis in 1396. A number of Christian knights from the West were massacred after the battle, and others were put to ransom ; among these last was one whose name connects Eastern and Western history, John Count of Nevers, afterwards Duke of Burgundy, the second of those dukes of Burgundy who play so great a part in the history of France, England, and Germany. Bajazet also was the first of the Sultans who directly attacked Constantinople. Things looked as if the last traces of the Eastern Empire were now about to be wiped out. But the Ottoman conqueror was presently met by a still more terrible conqueror from the further East. The conquests of Timour, the famous Tamerlane, which

spread slaughter and havoc through Mahometan Asia,
gave a moment's respite to Christian Europe. Of his
career I have said somewhat elsewhere.(4) What concerns us now is that Bajazet was overthrown and taken
captive by Timour at Angora in 1402. No such blow
ever fell on any Ottoman prince before or after.

After the defeat and captivity of Bajazet, things
looked as if the Ottoman dominion had run the
common course of an Eastern dominion, as if it
was broken up for ever. And, as I before said, the
most wonderful thing in all Ottoman history is that,
though it was broken up for a moment, it was able
to come together again. The dominions of Bajazet
were for a while divided, and their possession was
disputed among his three sons. At last they were
joined together again under his son Mahomet the
First. Still the time of confusion was a time of relief
to the powers which were threatened by the Turks,
and, even after Mahomet had again joined the
Ottoman dominions together, he was not strong
enough to make any great conquests. Thus the
European power of the Ottomans made but small
advances during his reign. It was otherwise under
his son Amurath the Second, during whose reign of
thirty years, from 1421 to 1451, the Turkish power,
notwithstanding some reverses, greatly advanced.
He failed in an attack on Constantinople; but he
took Thessalonica, which had lately passed from the
Empire to the Venetians. So in his wars with
Hungary he underwent several defeats from the great
captain Huniades; but his defeats were balanced by
victories. And in one battle it must be allowed that
the Turk was in the right and the Christian in the
wrong. In a triumphant campaign, the Hungarian

I

army had reached the Balkan.   By the peace which
followed, Servia again became independent, and
Wallachia was ceded to Hungary.   Then Wladislaus,
King of Hungary and Poland, was persuaded to break
the treaty, but he was defeated at Varna and the Ottoman power was again restored.   Still the crowning of
all, by the taking of the Imperial city and the complete subjugation of the lands on the Danube, was
not the work of Amurath, but was reserved for the
days of his son.

   This son was Mahomet the Second, surnamed the
Conqueror.   We may take him as the ideal of his
race, the embodiment in their fullest form of Ottoman
greatness and Ottoman wickedness.   A general and
statesman of the highest order even from his youth,
a man who knew his own purposes and knew by what
ends to achieve his purposes, no man has a clearer
right to the title of great, so far as we can conceive
greatness apart from goodness.   We hear of him also,
not merely as soldier and statesman, but as a man
of intellectual cultivation in other ways, as master of
many languages, as a patron of the art and literature
of his time.   On the other hand, the three abiding
Ottoman vices of cruelty, lust, and faithlessness
stand out in him all the more conspicuously from
being set on a higher pedestal.   He finished the work
of his predecessors ; he made the Ottoman power
in Europe what it has been ever since.   He gave a
systematic form to the customs of his house and to
the dominion which he had won.   His first act was
the murder of his infant brother, and he made the
murder of brothers a standing law of his Empire.
He overthrew the last remnants of independent

Roman rule, of independent Greek nationality, and
he fixed the relations which the Greek part of his
subjects were to bear both towards their Turkish
masters and towards their Christian fellow-subjects.
He made the northern and western frontiers of his
Empire nearly what they still remain.   The Ottoman
Empire, in short, as our age has to deal with it, is,
before all things, the work of Mahomet the Conqueror.
The prince whose throne was fixed in the New Rome
held altogether another place from even the mightiest
of his predecessors.

Mahomet had reigned two years, he had lived
twenty-three, on the memorable day, May 29th 1453,
when the Turks entered the city of the Cæsars and
when the last Emperor Constantine died in the breach.
The last ruling prince of his house, he was also the
worthiest.   The degradation of the last hundred years
of the Empire is almost wiped out in the glory of its
fall.   The Roman Empire of the East, which had
lasted so long, which had withstood and outlived so
many enemies, whose princes had beaten back the
Persian and the Saracen, the Avar, the Bulgarian,
and the Russian, now at last fell before the arms of
the Turk.   The New Rome, so long the head of the
Christian and civilized world, became the seat of
Mahometan and barbarian rule.   The Sultan took
the place of a long line of Cæsars.   And the great
church of Saint Sophia, the most venerated temple of
the whole Eastern Church, the seat of Patriarchs and
the crowning-place of Emperors, has been, from
Mahomet's day to our own, a mosque for Mahometan worship.   And now that the Imperial city was
at last taken, Mahomet seemed to make it his policy
both to gather in whatever remained unconquered,

and to bring most of the states which had hitherto
been tributary under his direct rule. Greece itself,
though it had been often ravaged by the Turks, had
not been added to their dominions. The Emperors
had, in the very last days of the Empire before the
fall of Constantinople, recovered all Peloponnêsos,
except some points which were held by Venice.
Frank Dukes also reigned at Athens, and another
small duchy lingered on in the islands of Leukas
and Kephallênia and on the coasts of Akarnania.
The Turkish conquest of the mainland, again saving
the Venetian points, was completed by the year
1460, but the two western islands were not taken
until 1479. Euboia was conquered in 1471, when
the Venetian governor Erizzo, who had stipulated
for the safety of his head, had his body sawn
asunder. No deeds of this kind are recorded of the
earlier Ottoman princes ; but by Mahomet's time
the Turks had fully learned those lessons of cruelty
and faithlessness which they have gone on practising
ever since. The Empire of Trebizond was conquered
in 1461, and the island of Lesbos or Mytilênê in
1462. There was now no independent Greek state
left. Crete, Corfu, and some smaller islands and
points of coast, were held by Venice, and some of
the islands of the Ægæan were still ruled by Frank
princes and by the Knights of Saint John. But, after
the fall of Trebizond, there was no longer any independent Greek state anywhere, and the part of the
Greek nation which was under Christian rulers of any
kind was now far smaller than the part which was
under the Turk.

While the Greeks were thus wholly subdued, the
Slaves fared no better. In 1459 Servia was reduced

from a tributary principality to an Ottoman province, and six years later Bosnia was annexed also. The last Bosnian king, like the Venetian governor in Euboia, was promised his life ; but he and his sons were put to death none the less. One little fragment of the great Slavonic power in those lands alone remained. The little district of Zeta, a part of the Servian kingdom, was never fully conquered by the Turks. One part of it, the mountain district called Tsernagora or Montenegro, has kept its independence to our own times. Standing as an outpost of freedom and Christendom amid surrounding bondage, the Black Mountain has been often attacked, it has been several times overrun, but it has never been conquered. In a ceaseless warfare of four hundred years, neglected, sometimes betrayed, by the Christian powers of Europe, this small people, whose whole number does not equal the population of some of our great towns, has still held its own against the whole might of the Turkish power. First under hereditary princes, then under warrior bishops, now under hereditary princes again, this little nation of heroes, whose territory is simply so much of the ancient land of their race as they are able to save from barbarian invasion, have still held their own, while the greater powers around them have fallen. To the south of them, the Christian Albanians held out for a long time under their famous chief George Castriot or Scanderbeg. After his death in 1459, they also came under the yoke. These conquests of Mahomet gave the Ottoman dominion in Europe nearly the same extent which it has now. His victories had been great, but they were balanced by some defeats. The conquest of Servia and Bosnia opened the way to endless inroads into Hungary, South-eastern Germany, and North-eastern Italy. But as yet these lands were merely ravaged, and the Turkish power met with some reverses. In 1456 Belgrade was saved by the last victory of Huniades, and this time Mahomet the Conqueror had to flee. In another part of Europe, if in those days it is to be counted for Europe, Mahomet won the Genoese possessions in the peninsula of Crimea, and the Tartar Khans who ruled in that peninsula and the neighbouring lands became vassals of the Sultan. The Ottomans were thus brought into the neighbourhood of Poland, Lithuania, and Russia. The last years of Mahomet's reign were marked by a great failure and a great success. He failed to take Rhodes, which belonged to the Knights of Saint John ; but his troops suddenly seized on Otranto in Southern Italy. Had this post been kept, Italy might have fallen as well as Greece ; but the Conqueror died the next year, and Otranto was won back.

Thus two Empires, and endless smaller states, came out of the power of the Ottomans under the mightiest of their Sultans. Greeks, Slaves, Albanians, all came under the yoke. But it must not be forgotten that it was by the arms of men of Greek, Slave, and Albanian blood that they were brought under the yoke. For the Janissaries formed the strength of the Ottoman armies, and the Janissaries were formed of the kidnappéd children of the conquered nations. Thus the Christian nations of South-eastern Europe had their own strength turned against them, and were overcome by the arms of their own children. And presently the far-seeing eye of Mahomet found out that their wits might be turned against them as well

as their arms. He saw that the Greeks had a keener
wit, either than his own Turks or than the other
subject nations, and he saw that their keen wit might,
in the case of a part of the Greek nation, be made an
instrument of his purposes. By his policy the
Eastern Church itself was turned into an instrument
of Turkish dominion. Speaking roughly, the lower
clergy throughout the conquered lands have always
been patriotic leaders, while the Bishops and other
higher clergy have been slaves and instruments of
the Turk. Greek Bishops bore rule over Slavonic
churches, and so formed another fetter in the chain
by which the conquered nations were held down. In
course of time the Sultans extended the same policy
to temporal matters. The Greeks, not of Old Greece,
but of Constantinople, the Fanariots, as they came to
be called, became in some sort a ruling race among
their fellow-bondmen. Their ability made them useful, and the Turks learned to make use of their
ability in many ways. In all conquests a certain
class of the conquered finds its interest in entering the service of the conqueror. As a rule, such
men are the worst class of the conquered. They
are commonly more corrupt and oppressive than
the conquerors themselves. It therefore in no way
lessened but rather heightened the bitterness of
Ottoman rule, that it was largely carried on by Christian instruments. The Slavonic provinces had in fact
to bear a two-fold yoke, Turkish and Greek. But
this it should be remembered only applies to the
Greeks of Constantinople. The Greeks of Greece
itself and the rest of the Empire were no better off
than the other subjects of the Turk. It must be
remembered too that, after all, the Fanariot Greeks

themselves were a subject race, cut off from all share
in the higher rule of their country. That was reserved
for men of the ruling religion, whether native Turks
or renegades of any nation. And lastly it should be
remembered that, under the rule of Mahomet the
Conqueror, every man, Turk, Christian, or renegade,
held his life and all that he had at the pleasure of
Mahomet the Conqueror.

The Turkish rule was now fully established over a
considerable part of Europe, over nearly the whole of
the lands between the Hadriatic and the Euxine.
Save where the brave men of Zeta still held out on
the Black Mountain and where the city of Ragusa
still kept its freedom, no part of those lands was
under a national government. The few islands and
pieces of coast which had escaped the Turk were
under the rule either of Venice or of other Frank
powers. From that day, till in our own century Servia
and Greece became free, all those lands have been in
bondage. The greater part of them remain in bondage still. Their people have not only been subjects
of a foreign prince; they have been subjects of a
foreign army in their own land. The rule of law has
for all those ages ceased in those lands. The people
of the land have had only one way of rising out of
their state of bondage, namely by embracing the
religion of their conquerors. This many of them
did, and so were transferred from the ranks of the
oppressed to the ranks of the oppressors. In some
parts whole classes did so. This happened specially
in Bosnia. There the mass of the land-owners embraced Islam in order to keep their lands, while the
body of the people remained faithful. These renegades

and their descendants have ever since formed an oligarchy whose rule has been worse than that of the Turks themselves. The same thing happened in Bulgaria to some degree, though to a much less extent than in Bosnia. It was only in Albania that the Mahometan faith was really adopted by the mass of the people of large districts. In Albania a large part of the country did become Mahometan, while other parts remained Christian, some tribes being Catholic and some Orthodox. But, as a rule, throughout the European lands which were conquered by the Turk, the mass of the people clave to their faith, in defiance of all temptations and all oppressions. Rather than forsake their faith, they have endured to live on as bondsmen in their own land, under the scorn and lash of foreign conquerors, while apostasy would at any moment have raised them to the level of their conquerors. They have endured to live on, while their goods, their lives, the honour of their families, were at the mercy of barbarians, while their sons were kidnapped from them to be brought up in the faith of the oppressor and to swell the strength of his armies. In this state of abiding martyrdom they have lived, in different parts of the lands under Turkish rule, for two, for four, for five hundred years. While the nations of Western Europe have been able to advance, they have been kept down under the iron heel of their tyrants. And because they have not been able to advance as the nations of Western Europe have advanced, men in Western Europe are not ashamed to turn round and call them degraded and what not, as though we should be any better if we had lived under a barbarian yoke for as many ages as they have lived.

It may however be asked with perfect fairness, how came the Ottoman Turks, starting from such small beginnings and having at first such small power, to make such great conquests, and to win and to keep so many lands, both Christian and Mussulman? With regard to the conquests of the Ottomans over other Mussulmans, there is nothing wonderful in their making them; the wonderful thing is that they were able to keep them. Their rise to power was exactly like the rise to power of many other Eastern dynasties. Only, while other Eastern dynasties have commonly soon broken in pieces, this one kept on unbroken. Or it would be truer to say, what is really more wonderful, that, after the fall of Bajazet, the Ottoman power did break in pieces for a moment, but that it was able to come together again. The continued succession of able princes in the House of Othman, the firm administration which they established, their excellent military discipline, and above all the institution of the Janissaries, will account for a great deal. And before long we shall see that the Ottoman Sultans won a further claim to the religious allegiance, not only of their own subjects, but of all orthodox Mussulmans. With regard to their conquests over Christians, the state of the South-eastern lands at that moment gave them many advantages. The Ottomans were a power— *nation* is hardly the word—in the full freshness of youth and enthusiasm, military and religious. Every Janissary, it must be remembered, brought to his work the zeal of a new convert. As yet the Ottomans were in their full strength, under princes who knew how to use their strength. They found in South-eastern Europe a number of disunited powers, jealous of one another, and many of them having no real basis of national life. The Eastern Empire was worn out. The vulgar talk about its weakness and degradation, which is mere vulgar talk when it is applied to the whole time of the Byzantine history, ceases to be vulgar talk if it is confined to the last hundred and fifty years of Byzantine history. It would seem as if the strength of the Greeks had been worn out by winning back Constantinople. Certain it is that the Emperors who reigned at Nikaia in the thirteenth century were far better and more vigorous rulers than the Emperors who reigned at Constantinople in the fourteenth century. Certain it is that the greatness of Constantinople, its strength and its great traditions, helped to prolong the existence of a power whose real day was past, and thereby to hinder the growth of the more vigorous Slavonic nations which might otherwise have stepped into its place. The Frank powers, save Venice, were small and weak, and they were nowhere national. We may believe that their rule was nowhere quite so bad as that of the Turks; still it was everywhere a foreign rule. The Greeks who were under Venice and under the Frank princes, were under rulers who were alien to their subjects in speech, race, and creed. There could be no loyalty or national feeling felt towards them. It is not very wonderful that the Turkish Sultans, with their stern determination and their admirably disciplined armies, could swallow up these powers, disunited and some of them decaying, one by one. Again the fashion of making their conquests for a while merely tributary, instead of at once fully annexing them, helped the purpose of the Turk by enabling him to employ the forces of one nation to help

in subduing the nation next beyond it. So did
the fashion of harrying and plundering lands before their actual conquest was attempted. Men
might be tempted to doubt whether regular bondage
to the Turk might not be a less evil than having
their lands ravaged and their children carried away
into slavery.

As most things in history have their parallel, it
may be well to notice that the cause which brought
the Ottoman power nearer to destruction than it ever
was brought at any other time was essentially the
same as one of the causes which most promoted its
success. Any two sects of Christians, any two sects
of Mahometans, are really separated from one
another by a difference which should seem very slight
compared with the difference which separates both of
them from men of the other religion. Yet in practice
it is not always so. The Eastern Empire was saved
from Bajazet, and its existence was prolonged for
fifty years, because Timour, who belonged to the
Shiah sect of Mussulmans, waged a religious war on
the Ottomans, who have always belonged to the
Sonnite sect. And in exactly the same way, nothing
helped the Ottomans so much as the dissensions
between the Eastern and Western Churches, the
members of which could be got heartily to act with
one another. Many of the Greeks said that they
would rather see the Turks in Saint Sophia than the
Latins, and they lived to see it. And the Latins,
with a few noble exceptions, could never be got to
give any real help to the Greeks. All this illustrates
the law that the quarrels of near kinsfolk are the
most bitter of any. And it is after all another
instance of this same law which, as has already been

said, makes Christianity and Islam rival religions above all others.

The Turkish dominion in Europe was now thoroughly formed. For some years after the death of Mahomet the Conqueror, it was hardly at all enlarged. The next Sultan, Bajazet the Second, who reigned from 1481 to 1512, was not a man of war nor in any way a man of genius like his father. His character was an odd mixture of sensuality and religious mysticism, two things which, under the Mahometan system, are not incompatible. His wars were confined to winning a few points from Venice, and to constant ravages of Hungary and the other Christian lands to the north. Here we may mark how evil deeds produce evil. The horrible cruelties of the Turks in these incursions provoked equal cruelties on the part of the Christians, and so a black strife of retaliation went on. Such a reign as this was naturally unsatisfactory to the ruling race. Bajazet was deposed, and, after the manner of deposed princes, he speedily died. Then came the eight years' reign of his son Selim, called the Inflexible. His was a reign of conquest, but of conquest waged mainly against Mahometan enemies beyond the bounds of Europe. Syria and Egypt were added to the Ottoman dominion, and the Sultan added to that secular title the spiritual authority of the Caliphate. The real Caliphs of the Abbasside house had come to an end when Bagdad was taken by the Moguls; but a line of nominal Caliphs, who had no temporal power whatever, had gone on in Egypt. From the last of these phantoms Selim obtained a cession of his rights, and ever since the Ottoman Sultans have been

acknowledged as chiefs of their religion by all orthodox Mussulmans, that is all who belong to the Sonnite
sect and admit the lawfulness of the first three Caliphs.
The Persians and other Shiahs of course do not acknowledge the religious supremacy of the Sultan, any
more than the Orthodox and the Reformed Churches
in Christendom acknowledge the supremacy of the
Pope. The Caliph, it should be remembered, is
Pope and Emperor in one. For one who was already
Sultan thus to become Caliph was much the same as
if, in the West, one who was already Emperor had
also become Pope.

The rule of the new Caliph was in some things
worse than that of any of the Emirs and Sultans who
had gone before him. In systematic blood-thirstiness,
whether towards Christians, towards heretical Mahometans, or towards his own ministers and servants,
Selim outdid all who had gone before him. But here
comes out one of the special features of Ottoman rule.
The one check on the despot's will is the law of the
Prophet. What the law of the Prophet bids on any
particular matter the Sultan must learn from the
official expounders of that law. And it must be
said, in justice to these Mahometan doctors, that, if
they have sometimes sanctioned special deeds of
wrong, they have also sometimes hindered them. So
it was in the reign of Selim. The Mufti Djemali,
whose name deserves to be remembered, several
times turned the Sultan from bloody purposes. At
last he withstood Selim when he wished to massacre
all the Christians in his dominions and to forbid the
exercise of the Christian religion. Now such a purpose was utterly contrary to the text of the Koran,
and the act of Djemali in hindering it was the act of a

righteous man and an honest expounder of his own law. But be it remembered that, if the question had been, not whether Christians should be massacred, but whether they should be admitted to equality with Mahometans, Djemali must equally have withstood the Sultan's purpose. The contemptuous toleration which the Koran enforces equally forbids massacres on the one side and real emancipation on the other.

The next reign was a long and famous one, that of Suleiman—the name is the same as *Solomon*—called the Magnificent and the Lawgiver, who reigned from 1520 to 1566. Mahomet had established the Empire; Suleiman had to extend it. But Suleiman was a nobler spirit than Mahomet. Under any other system, he would have been a good as well as a great ruler. And allowing for some of those occasional crimes which seem inseparable from every Eastern despotism—crimes which in his case chiefly touched his own ministers and his own family—we may say that he was a good prince according to his light. The Ottoman Empire was now at the height of its power. Its army was the strongest and best-disciplined of armies. But the Christian nations were now growing up to a level with their Mahometan enemies. Even the long and cruel wars among the Christian powers themselves, while they hindered those powers from joining together to withstand the Turk, schooled them in the end severally to cope with him. Suleiman took Rhodes early in his reign, and the Knights withdrew to Malta. He again besieged them at Malta in the last years of his reign, but this time without success. But the greatest of Suleiman's victories and the most instructive for our purpose, are those which he won in Hungary. At the beginning of his reign, in 1521, he took Belgrade. Five years later, the last of the separate Kings of Hungary—those I mean who were not also Archdukes of Austria—Lewis the Second, died in battle against the Turks at Mohacs. After that the crown of Hungary was for a long while disputed between rival Kings. Thus at once on Lewis' death, John Zapolya, Prince of Transsilvania, and Ferdinand of Austria, who was afterwards Emperor, were both chosen by different parties. Suleiman found it to his interest to support Zapolya ; he even besieged Vienna, though in vain. The end was that the Emperors kept that part of Hungary which bordered on Austria and their other dominions, while princes who were vassals of the Turk reigned in Transsilvania and the eastern part of the kingdom. But the Turk himself took a larger share of Hungary than either, and a pasha ruled at Buda as well as at Belgrade. Here too the progress of the Turks was helped by disunion among the Christians. Just as further south the Turks profited by the dissensions between the Catholics and the Orthodox, so in Hungary they profited by the dissensions between the Catholics and the Protestants. These last were of various sects, but all alike were persecuted by the bigotted Austrian Kings. It was no wonder then that the Protestants preferred the alliance, and even the sovereignty, of the Sultan to the rule of a Catholic sovereign. This fact has often been made a strange use of by the partisans of the Turks. No doubt the contemptuous toleration which the Turk gives to his Christian subjects was better than actual persecution, and men who were actually persecuted might well think that they gained by becoming his subjects. It

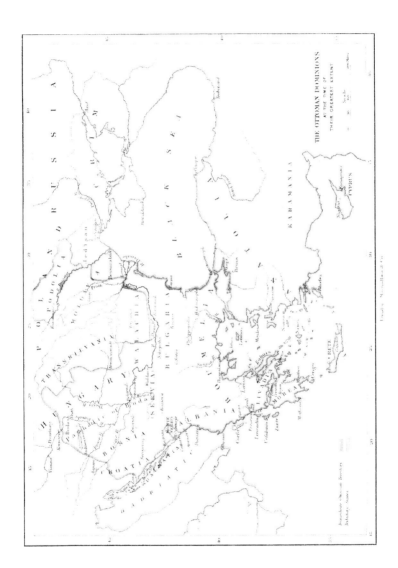

THE OTTOMAN DOMINIONS
AT THE TIME OF
THEIR GREATEST EXTENT

would be so even now. A man who was forbidden to exercise his religion under pain of death or bonds would even now gain by becoming a subject of the Turk. He would have to put up with degradation; he would have to take his chance of irregular oppression, oppression which might sometimes amount to robbery or murder; but no sentence of law would condemn him to death or bonds or banishment, simply for the practice of his religion. And if it is so even now, much more was it so in the time of Suleiman, when oppression was not so great as it is now, and when it was the policy of the Sultan to attach one party in the Hungarian nation to himself, that they might act as his allies against the other party. But this does not prove that the Turk is, or ever was, really tolerant, as toleration is now understood in the West. Their toleration was always contemptuous, or at most politic. And, though it is certain that in Suleiman's day any English Roman Catholic or Hungarian Protestant would have gained by becoming the subject of Suleiman, it is still more certain that neither of them would gain by becoming a subject of the Sultan now.

Besides the conquests of Suleiman in Hungary, the relations between the Turk and the two Rouman principalities of Wallachia and Moldavia were now definitely settled. They were to be vassal states, paying tribute; but the Sultan was to have no part in their internal government. No Turk was to live in the country, and the princes were to be freely chosen by the nobles and clergy of the principalities. This system lasted from 1536 to 1711. Then the Sultans took to appointing and deposing the princes at pleasure. They appointed Fanariot Greeks; and so,

K

strangely enough, the Greeks, bondmen in their own
land, became rulers in another.

Splendid as was the character and the rule of
Suleiman, still it is from his day that both Turkish
and Christian writers date the decline of the Turkish
power. Suleiman ceased to manage all state affairs
so directly as earlier Sultans had done. The power of
the Viziers and the influence of the women increased.
The taxes were farmed out to Jews, Greeks, and others,
a system which always at once lessens the revenue of
the sovereign and increases the burthens of the subject.
Conquest, we are told, brought with it luxury, love
of ease, love of weath. The soldiers fought less for
victory than for plunder. Certain it is that, while up
to Suleiman's time the Ottoman power had steadily
advanced, after his time it began to go down. The
Turkish lords of New Rome, like their Roman and
Greek predecessors, had their times of revival, their
days of unexpected conquest. But, on the whole, the
Ottoman power now steadily declined.

After Suleiman came a second Selim, known as the
Drunkard, a name which marks the little heed which
he paid to the precepts of his own law. His short reign,
from 1566 to 1574, was marked by the first great reverse of the Ottoman arms. This was the overthrow
of the Turkish fleet by the fleets of Spain and of
Venice in the great fight of Lepanto in 1571. It has
been often said, and said with perfect truth, that though
the Turk was defeated in the battle, yet he had really
the better in the war. For the Turk lost only his fleet,
which might be replaced, while the Venetians lost the
great island of Cyprus, which has ever since formed
part of the Turkish dominions. But the battle of

Lepanto none the less marks the turning-point in the history of the Ottoman power. It broke the spell, and taught men that the Turks could be conquered. Hitherto, though they had failed in particular enterprises, their career had been one of constant advance. Now, for the first time, they were utterly defeated in a great battle. And, with the military power of the Ottomans, their moral power decayed also. The line of the great Sultans had come to an end. Several of the later Sultans were men of vigour and ability; but the succession of great rulers which, unless we except Bajazet the Second, had gone on without a break from Othman to Suleiman the Lawgiver, now stopped. The power of the Sultans over their distant dominions was lessened, while the power of the Pashas grew. The discipline of the Ottoman armies was relaxed, and the courts of most Sultans became a scene of corruption of every kind. Early in the seventeenth century men marked the decay of the Turkish power, and expected that it would presently fall to pieces. Why did it not fall? The growth of the Turkish power is easily explained. A succession of such men as the early Sultans, wielding such a force as the Janissaries, could not fail to conquer. Why their power lasted so long after it began to decay may seem, at first sight, less easy to explain. But the causes are not very far to seek. The preservation of the same ruling family, and that a family whose head is not only Sultan of the Ottomans, but is deemed by orthodox Mussulmans to be the Caliph of the Prophet, alone counts for a good deal. More important still has been the possession of the Imperial city. New Rome, under her elder lords, held on under greater dangers than have ever threatened their Ottoman successors.   In quite late times the Turkish power has been propped up by the wicked policy of the governments of Western Europe.   But, long before that policy began, men had begun to ask why the Ottoman power did not fall.   The possession of Constantinople is of itself perhaps reason enough.   In the case of the later Byzantine Emperors, the possession of Constantinople prolonged the existence of a power which otherwise must have fallen, and whose prolonged existence did no good to the world.   The case is exactly the same with the dominion of the Ottomans.

We have thus traced the growth of the Ottoman power, from its first small beginnings till it had swelled into a vast dominion, first in Asia and then in Europe.   It had grown to that extent of power by the great qualities of a long succession of princes, whose skill in the craft of conquerors and rulers sometimes goes far to make us forget their crimes. And, in the case of the Ottoman Sultans, it is not merely their personal crimes that we are tempted to forget.   Their personal crimes may be paralleled in the history of other times and other nations.   But there has never been in European history, perhaps not in the history of the whole world, any other power which was in everything so thoroughly a fabric of wrong as the power of the Ottomans.   There has been no other dominion of the same extent lasting for so long a time, which has been in the same way wholly grounded on the degradation and oppression of the mass of those who were under its rule.   Others among the great empires of the world have done much wrong and caused much suffering ; but they have for the most part done something else besides doing wrong and causing suffering. Most of the other powers of the world, at all events most of those which play a part in the history of Europe, if they had a dark side, had also a bright one. To take the great example of all, the establishment of the Roman dominion carried with it much of wrong, much of suffering, much wiping out of older national life. But the Empire of Rome had its good side also. If Rome destroyed, she also created. If she conquered, she also civilized ; if she oppressed, she also educated, and in the end evangelized. She handed on to the growing nations of Europe the precious inheritance of her tongue, her law, and her religion. The rule of the Ottoman Turk has no such balance of good to set against its evil. His mission has been simply a mission of destruction and oppression. From him the subject nations could gain nothing and learn nothing, except how to endure wrong patiently. His rule was not merely the rule of strangers over nations in their own land. It was the rule of the barbarian over the civilized man, the rule of the misbeliever over the Christian. The direct results of Turkish conquest have been that, while the nations of Western Europe have enjoyed five hundred years of progress, the nations of South-eastern Europe have suffered five hundred years of bondage and of all that follows on bondage. The rule of the Turk, by whatever diplomatic euphemisms it may be called, means the bondage and degradation of all who come beneath his rule. Such bondage and degradation is not an incidental evil which may be reformed ; it is the essence of the whole system, the groundwork on which the Ottoman power is built. The power which

Othman began, which Mahomet the Conqueror firmly established, which Suleiman the Lawgiver raised to its highest pitch of power and splendour, is, beyond all powers that the world ever saw, the embodiment of wrong. In the most glorious regions of the world, the rule of the Turk has been the abomination of desolation, and nothing else. Out of it no direct good can come ; indirect good can come of it in one shape only. The natives of South-eastern Europe came under the yoke through disunion. Greek, Slave, Frank, could not be brought to combine against the Turk. Orthodox and Catholic could not be brought to combine against the Mussulman. If the long ages during which those nations have paid the penalty of disunion and intolerance shall have taught them lessons of union and tolerance, they may have gained something indirectly, even from five hundred years of Turkish bondage. We have thus far traced the steps by which they came under the yoke. We have now to trace the steps by which, on the one hand, the yoke was made harder, while, on the other hand, hopes began to dawn which promised that the yoke might one day be thrown off. We have in this chapter traced the gradual course of the growth of the Ottoman power ; in the next chapter we must go on to trace the gradual course of its decline.

NOTES.

(1, p. 97.) Corfu is the island which called itself *Korkyra*, but which in Attic and modern Greek is called *Kerkyra*. It is better to use the real Greek names of Greek places than their Turkish or Italian names. But Corfu is a case where one Greek name has been changed for another. It comes from κορυφαί, *peaks*, or perhaps from κόρφος-κόλπος, the gulf.

(2, p. 108.) The dates of the death of Orkhan and of the taking of Hadrianople seem not to be quite certain. I have followed Von Hammer and Finlay, who place the death of Orkhan in 1359, and the taking of Hadrianople in 1361. But it seems that there are other authorities according to which Orkhan did not die till 1362, and Hadrianople was taken the next year. See Jirecek, *Geschichte der Bulgaren*, p. 319.

(3, p. 112.) The different dates given to the taking of Philadelphia range from 1374 to 1391 ; but it seems to have been taken during the reign of Bajazet.

(4, p. 113.) See History and Conquests of the Saracens, p. 181.

CHAPTER V.

THE difference between the time which we have just gone through and the time to which we have now come is well marked in this way. Thus far it is easy for any one who follows the history, even in the most general way, to carry in his head the names and order of the Ottoman Emirs and Sultans. Each of them has a character of his own; the reign of each is marked by some special event, commonly by some conquest, which is the prince's own doing. The reign of Othman is marked by the establishment of the Ottomans as an Asiatic power. Under Orkhan they pass into Europe. Under the first Amurath Hadrianople is taken ; the Eastern Empire is hemmed in ; Servia becomes tributary. Bajazet, the first Sultan, defeats the great crusade from the West at Nikopolis. Mahomet the First restores the Ottoman power after its overthrow by Timour. Amurath takes Thessalonica and overthrows Wladislaus at Varna. Mahomet the Conqueror wins the city of the Cæsars ; he gives his dominions their lasting extent, and organizes as well as conquers. The second Bajazet, the first Sultan who was deposed, seems like a shadow from the second period cast back into the first. But the few years of Selim nearly double the extent of the

Ottoman dominion, and crown its master with the sacred honours of the Caliphate. Under Suleiman the Ottoman power reaches its highest point. Even the second Selim, unworthy of remembrance in himself, lives in the memory as the prince in whose days Cyprus was won and Lepanto lost. Thus far it is easy to go, even without book. But to remember the Sultans after Selim needs an effort. A few of them stand out through some special point in their character. Amurath the Fourth (1623-1640) stands forth as the most bloody, Ibrahim (1640-1648) as the most brutally sensual, of the line. Suleiman the Second (1687-1691) and Mustafa the Second (1695-1703) were men of some force of character, who might have played a greater part than they did, if they had lived in days when their empire was rising instead of falling. Of course any one who studies the Ottoman history minutely will be able to remember the Sultans of this time, just as he may remember the Kings of England or France, great and small. The difference is that no one who reads the general history of the world with any thoughtfulness will fail to re-member the order of the Sultans for the first two hundred years or more, while for the next two hundred years he may follow the general course of events, and the general relations of the Ottomans to other powers, without always remembering who was Sultan at any particular time. No one can help remembering that Amurath died at Kossova and that Mahomet took Constantinople. But it is easy to remember the second siege of Vienna, and to remember what terri-tories were lost and won by the peace of Carlowitz and the peace of Passarowitz, without remembering who was Sultan when each of those events happened.

At one part of the history, namely the second half of the seventeenth century, the ministers stand out rather than the sovereigns. In an Eastern despotism, where all alike are the slaves of the prince, there can hardly be such a thing as an hereditary aristocracy. A man may rise from the lowest place, even from slavery itself, to the highest offices in the empire. It is rare then in the Ottoman empire, or in any other Eastern despotism, to find anything like a succession of power in the same family. But in the seventeenth century there was an exceptional case of this kind in the family of Kiuprili. Several members of that house were chief ministers of the Sultans ; they were all men of ability, and some of them were really better and more tolerant rulers than the common run either of the Sultans or their ministers. But, as a rule, through the whole of this period, such a sketch as this may deal with events and with the general course of things, without having so much to say as before about particular men. In short, the time of the great Sultans has passed away, and the time of the small Sultans has begun.

Allowing, as has been already said, for occasional fits of revived energy, the Ottoman power went steadily down after the time of Suleiman the Lawgiver. It went down in two ways. Though territory was still sometimes won, yet on the whole the Ottoman frontiers fell back. After Suleiman no lasting conquests of any importance were made, except those of the islands of Cyprus and Crete. The frontier on the north towards Hungary, and in later times towards Russia, though there have been considerable fluctuations and winnings back of territory, has on the whole steadily gone back. And, last of all, in our own age

large parts of the Ottoman territory have been
separated from it to form distinct states, either
tributary or wholly independent. In these ways the
extent of the Ottoman dominion on the map has
lessened wonderfully indeed since the days of Suleiman. And, during the greater part of the times with
which we are dealing, the power of the Sultans was
getting less and less in the dominions which were left
to them. The central administration got more and
more corrupt, more under the influence of ministers,
favourites, and women than under the authority of the
Sultans themselves. The Pashas or governors of provinces got more and more independent, and in some
cases they made their offices practically hereditary. In
some parts indeed, especially toward the end of the
last century, when the power of the Sultans was at·its
lowest, there was utter anarchy without any control
of any kind. Through the seventeenth century especially, we may mark the short reigns of the Sultans, as
contrasted with the long reigns of most of the great
Sultans. Many of them were deposed and murdered,
as they have again begun to be in our own times.
Nor must we forget, as one cause of decay, the
wretched education, if we may so call it, of the Sultans themselves. Kept in a kind of imprisonment till
they came to the throne, with every means of enjoying
themselves, but with no means of learning the duties
of rulers, they came forth from prison to be clothed
with absolute power. One is really inclined to wonder
that they were not even worse than they were, and
that any of them shewed any sign of virtue or ability
of any kind.

This may pass as a general picture of the character of Ottoman rule during the days of the decay of

the Ottoman power. But it concerns us more to know what was the effect of this state of things on the nations which the Turks held in bondage. It must not be thought that the decay of the power of the Sultans brought any direct or immediate relief to the subject nations. Some indirect advantages they did gain from it; but in the main the weakening of the power of the Sultans, the general decay of their empire, meant not lessened but increased oppression ; it meant, not lighter, but heavier bondage to be borne by their Christian subjects. The great Sultans, as a rule, were not men who delighted in oppression for oppression's sake. Their personal crimes mainly touched those who were personally near to them; they had wisdom enough to see that they would gain nothing by making the bondage of the conquered nations intolerable. In all despotisms there is more chance of justice and mercy from the head despot than from his subordinates, and many a tyrant has deemed tyranny a privilege of the crown which no subordinate might share. As the power of the Sultans grew weaker, the subject nations lost their one chance of redress. In such a state of things grinding local oppression at the hands of a crowd of petty tyrants takes the place of the equal, if stern, rule of the common master of all. Under such grinding local oppression, lands were untilled, houses were uninhabited, the population of the country sensibly lessened. But, as the demands both of central and of local rulers did not lessen, the burthens of those who survived were only made the heavier. Such, with a few moments of relief, has been the general state of things in South-eastern Europe since the decline of the empire began. There have been exceptions.

One of the viziers of the house of Kiuprili, Zade Mustafa, who became vizier in 1689, was an exceptional case of a Turkish ruler who did every justice to the Christians which the Mahometan law allowed. He thereby for the while did much for the truest prosperity of his master's dominions. Other ministers of the same family had the wisdom to follow the same course; but the beginning of better times, or at least of brighter hopes, for the subject nations, which may be dated from the latter years of the seventeenth century, was mainly owing to quite different causes.

Those causes were chiefly two, the remission of the tribute of children and the advance of the Christian powers at the expense of the Turk. As was before said, as long as the tribute of children was levied, the subject nations really could not stir. From the time when it ceased, even when there was no actual improvement in their condition, there was the beginning of hope. There was a stirring of national life, such as there could not be as long as their best strength was taken from them. And every success gained by any Christian power against their masters raised the hopes and heightened the spirit of those who were under the yoke. Herein comes out the main difference between a national government and the rule of strangers. When any Christian power was at war with the Turk, the enslaved nations looked on the enemies of the Turk, not as their enemies, but as their friends. Every failure on the part of their masters, every danger that threatened their masters, gave them a hope of deliverance. In any Western country we should deem it treason for any man to help, or wish success to, the enemies of his country.

But to the Christians under the Turk, it was the Turk
who seemed the enemy of their country. Those who
made war on the Turk seemed, not the enemies of
their country, but its friends. And so it ever will be,
as long as, instead of being under a government of
their own, they are left under the yoke of strangers.
The subject nations have often been very badly
treated by Christian powers who professed to be
their friends. Hopes have often been kindled, promises have often been made, which were never
fulfilled. Still, all these causes joined together to
stir up men's minds, and to raise them from the state
of utter wretchedness and despair under which they
had been bowed down for so many generations.

From the middle of the seventeenth century the
Turks had constant wars with the neighbouring
Christian powers, wars in which, though the Turks
sometimes won victories and recovered provinces,
their dominion on the whole went back. The chief
powers with which they had to strive up to the latter
part of the seventeenth century were the commonwealth of Venice and the kingdom of Hungary, then
held by the Emperors of the House of Austria. They
had also wars with Poland, when the Polish kingdom,
in the sixteenth and seventeenth centuries, stretched
much further to the south-east than it did before or
after. And lastly, they have had wars with Russia,
which, for a long time past, have been of greater
moment than any of the others. But, in the latter
part of the sixteenth and the greater part of the
seventeenth century, the chief wars were those with
Venice and with the Emperors in their character
of Kings of Hungary. Both the Venetian and the

Hungarian wars greatly affected the interests of the subject nations.   The Hungarian wars chiefly affected the Slaves, and to some extent the Roumans.   The Venetian wars mainly affected the Greeks, and to some extent also the Slaves.   The possessions of Venice in the East consisted of islands and points or lines of coast.   These might easily be lost and won, as they often were, without the loss or gain of one settlement greatly affecting any other.   But the kingdom of Hungary had, before the time of Suleiman, lain as a compact mass, with a continuous frontier, to the north of the Ottoman dominions.   And, as the Ottoman frontier went back, Hungary gradually took that character again.   Along the Danube and its great tributaries, sometimes the power of the Emperors, sometimes the power of the Sultans, advanced. But on the whole the Ottoman frontier fell back.   It will be seen by the map how great a territory has been won back from the Turks since the days of Suleiman.   On the other hand, though the Venetians gained some successes, though they often won back lands which they had lost and sometimes even won new lands, still, on the whole, the Venetian power fell back, and the Ottoman power advanced.   In both cases, the change of frontier between the Turk and Venice or between the Turk and the Emperor was, for the Greek and Slavonic inhabitants of the disputed lands, a mere change of masters.   Still there was the difference between civilized and barbarian masters. The rule of Venice in her distant possessions was bad, and often oppressive.   It could awaken no kind of national or loyal feeling on the part of the subjects of the commonwealth.   Still it was not brutal and bloody, like that of the Turks.   And, on the

Hungarian frontier, when the Austrian kings ceased to persecute, instead of Hungarian Protestants welcoming the Turk as a deliverer, the Christian subjects of the Turks welcomed every success of the Imperial arms as bringing deliverance to themselves.

It may be as well to sketch, as far as may be, in one continuous story the chief gains and losses of territory, especially among the islands, which happened in the long wars between the Venetians and the Turks. At the time when the Turks took Constantinople, Venice had a dominion in Dalmatia, the boundaries of which had often fluctuated in the wars between Venice and the Kings of Hungary, and which afterwards no less fluctuated again in the wars between Venice and the Turks. Many of the Dalmatian towns in this way changed masters over and over again; but it would be impossible to tell their story except at great length. But the commonwealth of Ragusa, by contriving to keep on good terms with the Turks, kept on its independence throughout. When Mahomet took Constantinople, besides her Dalmatian dominion, Venice held some territory to the south on the Albanian coast, and also several points on the coasts both of Northern Greece and of Peloponnêsos, Argos and Nauplia. She also held the great islands of Crete, Euboia, Corfu, and Cyprus. The first three of these she had kept continuously from the Latin taking of Constantinople. Euboia and Crete she kept till they were conquered by the Turks, while Corfu she kept till the end. The other islands off the west coast of Greece, commonly called the Ionian Islands, were tossed to and fro over and over again between Venetians, Turks, and Frank princes. But in the end Venice got them all, and kept them till the time of her own fall. Several of the islands of the Ægæan were also held either by the commonwealth of Venice or by Venetian families. In 1489 the Venetians got possession of the island of Cyprus, which had hitherto been a Frank kingdom. The Venetian possessions in Peloponnêsos, Euboia, and most of those in the smaller islands of the Ægæan, were gradually conquered by the Turks from the reign of Mahomet the Conqueror to that of Suleiman. Thus, at the time when the decay of the Ottoman Empire began, Venice had lost a great part of her Eastern territories, but she still kept a large insular dominion. She had Cyprus, Crete, Corfu and the other Ionian Islands, and a few points on the western coast and in the Ægæan. In all these she was a ruler over Greeks, or, in some of the northern points, over Albanians. In Dalmatia she ruled over Slaves, except so far as the coast towns had largely become Italian.

We have already seen how Cyprus was lost in the reign of Selim the Second. In the next century Crete was lost also. The Turks attacked the island in 1645, and the war went on till 1669, when Crete was lost. This is called the war of Candia, from the long siege of the town of Candia, which was most gallantly defended by the Venetians, with the help of many volunteers from Western Europe. It must be remembered that, though the island has sometimes got to be called Candia, from the town of Candia and its memorable siege, yet the island itself has never changed its name, but has always been called Crete both by Greeks and Turks. This great island now passed under Turkish bondage. The mass of the people remained faithful, and sank to the usual lot of the subject nations, or rather to a worse lot than most of them. For a good many of the

L

inhabitants became Mussulmans, so that there are Greek-speaking Mussulmans in Crete, just as there are Slavonic-speaking Mussulmans in Bosnia. And the result was the same as it was in Bosnia, and as it was everywhere. These renegades and their descendants were more oppressive to their Christian fellow-countrymen than the Turks themselves. In Cyprus, on the other hand, the exactions of the Sultan's government were even greater than in most other parts; but Turks and Christians in the island were on better terms than usual. It is important to remember these distinctions; for it is easy, by drawing inferences which apply to one time or place only, and applying them to other times and places to fall into great mistakes. The Christian subjects of the Turk were everywhere in bondage; they were everywhere in a case which in Western Europe would be held to justify them in revolting. But it is not wonderful that bondage was lighter in some places and heavier in others; nor is it wonderful that, as a rule, renegades and their descendants were worse oppressors than the natural Turks. For the conqueror can afford to shew some kind of mercy, if it be only contemptuous mercy. The renegade is full of a mean spite towards better men than himself.

These were the chief changes of territory with regard to those great islands which were at different times held by Venice in the East of Europe. Corfu alone was always held by the Republic for nearly six hundred years, from the Latin taking of Constantinople to her own fall. But besides the wars in the islands and the wars in Dalmatia, Venice had also important wars with the Turks on the mainland of Greece. But these wars had a great deal to do with wars which were carried on at the same time by other European powers. It will therefore be well to go back a little in our story, in order to understand the general position in which the Turkish power stood in the latter part of the seventeenth century. Though, as we have seen, several of the Sultans of this time were men of some vigour, though they were often served by able ministers, still decay and corruption had greatly advanced, and the Ottoman power was going down on every side. It was during this century that the tribute of children was gradually left off. The Janissaries were now no longer what they had been, and the tables were now altogether turned in military matters between the Turks and the nations of Europe. Mahomet the Conqueror had commanded armies such as no European power could put in the field against him. In the two centuries which had passed since his time, the military system of every European power had improved, while the system of the Turks had gone back. They had lost their own old discipline, and they had not learned the discipline of European armies. Thus the latter part of the seventeenth century was a general time of loss to the Ottoman power. Besides Venice and Hungary, the Turks had wars with Poland and Russia, of which we shall say more presently. Notwithstanding some occasional successes, the Turkish power gave way at all these points. During this period wars with the Turks were going on at various points from Peloponnêsos to the mouth of the Don. But the war in Hungary formed the centre of all. This was now the region where the great struggle between Turks and Christians was waged, and in that region at this time the Turkish frontier steadily went back. The wars of this time were like a vast battle, in which Venice at one end, Poland and Russia at the other, were attacking and defending this and that outpost, while the main struggle went on in the lands upon the Danube.

We have seen that the conquests of Suleiman left only a small part of Hungary to its nominal king the Emperor. The greater part of the land was ruled by a Turkish Pasha, while Transsilvania and part of Hungary itself formed a vassal principality. The state of things in these lands often changed, and there were several wars in the sixteenth and seventeenth centuries. But, on the whole, the Turks kept their predominance in Hungary. In the latter half of the seventeenth century things began to change. In 1663, while the siege of Candia was still going on, when Mahomet the Fourth was Sultan and Leopold the First was Emperor and King of Hungary, a war began in which for the first time the Imperial arms decidedly had the better. The war was famous for the great battle of Saint Gotthard, fought in 1664, in which the Imperial general Montecuculi won a great victory over the Turks under the Vizier Kiuprili. This battle was by land much the same as Lepanto was by sea. It was the first great overthrow of the Turks ; it therefore marks a turning-point in their history. Or rather it was really of much greater moment than Lepanto. For, though Lepanto broke the spell of Turkish success, it really did no material harm to the Turkish power. But Saint Gotthard was really the beginning of a long series of victories over the Turks on the part both of the Emperors and of other Christian powers. Yet it was like Lepanto in this, that, as the victory of Lepanto was accompanied by the loss of

Cyprus, so the victory of Saint Gotthard was very soon followed by the loss of Crete. The battle was followed by a truce for twenty years between the Emperor and the Turks. Meanwhile the affairs of the Cossacks, the wild people of the border-lands between Poland, Russia, and the Turkish vassal states north of the Euxine, led to wars both with Poland and Russia. The Polish war lasted from 1672 to 1676. In this, though the famous John Sobieski won several brilliant victories both before and after his election to the Polish crown, yet Poland lost the strong town of Kaminiec, and the whole province of Podolia. This should be noticed, as it was the last time that the Turks won any large territory from any Christian power, as distinguished from merely winning back territory which they had held before. In this war both Sultan Mahomet and his minister Kiuprili had a share. Its issue is instructive. Sobieski won battles, but the Turks kept Podolia. For the Turks were just now ruled, in the person of Kiuprili, by a single wise and strong will, while, though the Poles are one of the bravest nations on earth, yet the weak and disorderly nature of their government made them constantly lose in other ways what they won in fighting. In the Russian war, the first war of any moment between Russia and the Turk, the Sultan, who had just won a superiority over the Cossacks of Ukraine from the Poles, lost it again to the Russians. But the real beginnings of the struggle between Russia and the Turk come a few years later, though still within the times with which we are dealing. It will be better to go back to what were at the time the more important wars in Hungary and Greece.

We have already seen that the religious intolerance of the Austrian Kings in Hungary gave a great advantage to the Turks, and that it often made the Protestants of Hungary think, with good reason, that the rule of the Turk was the less heavy bondage of the two. No king did himself and his subjects more harm in this way than the Emperor Leopold the First. His persecutions, and the revolts to which they led, laid not only Hungary but the Empire itself open to the Turks. Mahomet the Fourth was still Sultan; but he had lost his wise minister Kiuprili, and the present vizier Kara Mustafa was fond of planning enterprises too great for his power to carry out. It was he who had conducted the unsuccessful war with Russia; now in 1682 he undertook, not only to complete the conquest of Hungary, but once more, like Suleiman, to invade Germany itself. In 1683 the Turks again besieged Vienna, and the city was saved, not at all by the Emperor, but by John Sobieski and his Poles. Austria and Hungary were in truth delivered from the Turk by the swords of a Slavonic people, the people of a kingdom which, within a hundred years, Austria helped to dismember. A war now went on, which lasted till 1698. The Turks were gradually driven out of Hungary. In this war Sobieski at the beginning, and Prince Eugene of Savoy in its later stages, won some of their most famous victories. It might at the time be doubted whether Hungary gained much by being delivered from the Turk, only to be put under such a king as Leopold. No doubt Hungary has had much to complain of at the hands of her Austrian Kings; but the same rule applies here as everywhere else. The Christian government

can amend and reform ; the Mahometan government cannot. During the reign of the next Sultan,
Suleiman the Second, came the administration of
another Kiuprili, the one who has been already
mentioned as one of the very few Turkish rulers who
ever really thought of the welfare of the Christians
under Turkish rule. At the time, it was doubtless
better to be a Christian under Kiuprili than to be a
Protestant under Leopold. But mark the difference
in the long run. Hungary was freed from the Turk ;
Bosnia and Bulgaria remained under his yoke. No
subject of the Hungarian crown, not even in those
Slavonic lands which have good reason to be discontented with Magyar supremacy, would now wish
to change places with a Christian subject of the Turk.
But it is hard that a people like the Magyars, who
owe their freedom to Slavonic help, should grudge
their Slavonic neighbours the same freedom which
they themselves enjoy.

While the centre, as we may call it, of the general
Christian army was thus victoriously bearing the
main brunt of the strife in Hungary, much was also
done by what we may call the two wings, the ancient
power of Venice, the seemingly new, but really only
revived, power of Russia. It was now that Venice,
whose island dominion had been cut so sadly short
by the loss of Crete, suddenly began to play a great
part on the mainland of Greece. We have seen that
Peloponnêsos had wholly fallen into the hands of the
Turks, the greater part under Mahomet, and the
little that was left by him under Suleiman. But
in some of the wilder parts of the country, as in
the peninsula of Maina, the Christians long kept a
rude independence. It was not till 1614 that the

people of Maina were compelled to pay the *haratch*, the tribute by which the non-Mussulman buys the right to toleration at the hands of the Mussulman. The Greek coasts were often visited by Spanish and other European ships in their wars with the Turk, so that the Greek inhabitants really suffered instead of their masters. At last, in the year after the siege of Vienna, when the Turkish power was giving way in Hungary, it seemed a good time for Venice to strike a blow. So in 1684 the great Venetian commander Francesco Morosini, who was chosen Doge in the course of the war, began the conquest of the peninsula. It was thought that Peloponnêsos would be more easily held than Crete. The Venetian forces, with help from other parts of Europe, conquered all Peloponnêsos. The war also went on in Attica and Euboia: Athens was taken, and it was in this siege that the Parthenôn, the great temple of Athênê, was ruined. It had been a church under the Emperors and under the Frank Dukes; but the Turks had turned it into a powder magazine, and a falling shell caused an explosion which broke it down. But the Venetians were not able to keep anything beyond the isthmus; Peloponnêsos itself they did keep for a while. Thus a large part of Greece was placed under a government which, if not national, was at least civilized. The Greeks at this time had no hope for anything better than a change of masters. But the Venetian was at least a better master than the Turk: Peloponnêsos passed under political bondage to the republic; but its people were saved from personal oppression and degradation.

But meanwhile events were happening in what we may call the other wing of the great battle, events which, though they seemed less at the time than either the Hungarian or Venetian wars, were the beginning of much that has gone on with increasing importance down to our own time. This is the beginning of those long wars between Russia and the Turk at which we have already glanced. Russia, it should not be forgotten, though it is less than two hundred years since she began again to play a part in European affairs, is really a very old power. Russia is a nation which made a start, so to speak, early in life, which then received a great check, and which began a second career some ages after. In the ninth century the Russians, a Slavonic people, though under rulers of Scandinavian descent, threatened the Eastern Empire, just as the Bulgarians and afterwards the Servians did. Only, while the Bulgarians and Servians came by land, the Russians for the most part came by sea. They crossed the Euxine, and tried to take Constantinople, and afterwards they had wars with the Emperors on the Danube. Presently Russia became Christian; Vladimir, its first Christian prince, had as I have already said, deliberately preferred Christianity to Islam. The Russians got their Christianity from Constantinople, and thus, being both Slavonic in race and Orthodox in creed, they had a closer tie to the nations who were under the Turk than any of the nations of Western Europe. The Church of Russia was for several ages dependent on the Church of Constantinople; but for several ages too Russia had no means of taking any share in the affairs of South-eastern Europe, or indeed in the general affairs of Europe at all. Two things joined to keep Russia back. First, the great Russian power of the ninth and tenth centuries broke up into several smaller states. Then, in the thirteenth century, the power of Russia was altogether overthrown by those same Mogul invasions which, by overthrowing the Seljuk Turks and the Bagdad Caliphate, had made the ground ready in Asia for the first growth of the Ottomans. On these Moguls, better known by the name of Tartars, Russia was dependent for more than two hundred years. Thus the Russians, like the people of South-eastern Europe, had in some sort Mahometan masters. They had not indeed, as the Greeks, Bulgarians, and Servians had, a body of oppressors scattered through their whole land. They were rather like Wallachia and the other lands which were tributary to the Turk. Still they had felt bondage at the hands of Mahometan masters. They had therefore a traditional hatred of Mahometan rule ; and, as members of the Orthodox Church, they had a tie of special fellowship with the South-eastern Christians. The history of Russia answers in some points to the history of Spain. In both these lands at the extreme east and west of Europe, Mahometan masters had to be driven out, and there are some points of likeness in the processes by which they were driven out in the two cases.

At the time which we have now reached, two of the great seats of the Tartar power, at Kasan and at Astrakhan, had long been held by Russia. But the Tartars of Crim, that is of the peninsula of Crimea and the neighbouring lands, still remained. And, as long as they remained, Russia, whose fleets had in old times sailed over the Euxine to attack Constantinople, was even more thoroughly cut off from that sea than Castile had been cut off from the Mediterranean by the Saracens of Granada. The Khans of Crim

had been vassals of the Sultans ever since the time of
Mahomet the Conqueror, and their affairs, and those
of the Cossacks to the north of them, led to disputes
between Russia, Poland, and the Turks. The wars
between Russia and the Turks began in the middle
of the seventeeth century, and we have already spoken
of a war somewhat later, in which Russia won the
land of Ukraine. But in the reign of Peter the Great,
under whom Russia first began to play any great
part in European affairs, the wars between Russia
and the Turks put on a new character. Hitherto the
Euxine had been wholly under the power of the
Turks, and was chiefly used for their trade in slaves.
No European nation had had any commerce there
since Mahomet the Conqueror had taken the Genoese
possessions in Crimea. The object of Russia was
now for a long time to get free access to the sea,
which the Turks of course tried to keep to themselves.
This strife was begun when Peter the Great took Azov
in 1696. For a long while after that time the possession of Azov, as the key of the Euxine, was the great
point of contention between Russia and the Turks.
It was disputed with fluctuating success during a
great part of the next century.

Thus, at the end of the seventeenth century, the
Turks had been at war with all their Christian neighbours, and they had lost territory at all points except
one. They had gained Podolia; but they had lost
Peloponnêsos, Hungary, and Azov. Most of these
territories they formally gave up by treaties in 1699
and 1700. The peace of Carlowitz in 1699 marks a
point in the history, or more truly in the decline, of
the Ottoman power. Up to this time the Sultans had
deemed themselves the superiors of all European

princes, and had treated them and their ambassadors with great haughtiness. Sometimes they imprisoned ambassadors, and dealt in other ways contrary to the received law of nations. Strictly following the law of their own Prophet, they would not make peace with any Christian power; they would only grant truces. Now, in the reign of Mustafa the Second, they were driven to treat with European powers on equal terms, and formally to give up territory. They formally ceded Peloponnêsos to Venice, and gave back Podolia to Poland. But, oddly enough, it was not a peace for ever, but only a truce for twenty-five years, which was concluded between the Turk and the power which had won most back from him. By this truce the Turks gave up all Hungary, except the district called the Banat of Temesvar, with Transsilvania and the greater part of Slavonia. This treaty, it should be remarked, was concluded under the mediation of England and the United Provinces. This shows that we have now got to the beginnings of modern diplomacy. Russia was not a party to the Peace of Carlowitz; but she concluded an armistice for two years, which in the next year was changed into a thirty years' truce. By this truce Russia kept Azov.

The Turkish power thus received one of the heaviest blows that was ever dealt to it. From that blow it has never really recovered. The power of the Turk has never again been what it was before the wars which were ended by the Peace of Carlowitz. But we have already said that the Ottoman power, just like the Byzantine power before it, had times of revival, which alternated with times of decay. So, through a great part of the eighteenth century, the

Turks were still able to win victories, and, though they won no new ground, they sometimes won back a good deal of what they had lost. There soon were wars again between the Turks and all their European enemies, except Poland, whose day of greatness has now come quite to an end. War with Russia broke out again in 1711, and this time the Turks had the better. By the Treaty of the Pruth, Azov was restored to the Turk. Here was one success, and this was followed by the Turkish conquest of Peloponnêsos, Tênos, and whatever else Venice held on the Eastern side of Greece in 1715. The Turks went on to threaten Corfu and Dalmatia; but in 1716 the Emperor Charles the Sixth, who of course was also King of Hungary, made an alliance with Venice. Charles the Sixth was more powerful than any Emperor had been since Charles the Fifth. Men began to hope that the Turks might be altogether conquered, and that a Christian Emperor might again reign at Constantinople. This indeed did not happen; but the Imperial armies, under Prince Eugene, made large conquests from the Turks. The small part of Hungary and Slavonia which the Turks kept was won back, and Belgrade, with a large part of Servia, a small strip of Bosnia, and the western part of Wallachia, became part of the dominions of the House of Austria. Things were now different from what they had been under Leopold. Every inch of territory won from the Turk was so much won for civilization and comparative good government, and the Imperial armies were welcomed as deliverers by the people of the lands which they set free. By the Peace of Passarowitz, in 1718, made for another term of twenty-five years, all these conquests were confirmed to the Emperor. But he shamefully neglected the interests of Venice, and Peloponnêsos was again confirmed to the Turk, when there were hopes of winning it back. Venice now, as a power, passes out of our story, though we shall hear again of the fate of what was left of her Eastern possessions. Through the rest of the eighteenth century Austria and Russia are the powers which keep up the struggle ; in the nineteenth century it is Russia only.

There is no need to go through every detail of war and diplomacy in these times, but only to mark those events which form real landmarks in the decline of the Turkish power. Thus it has no bearing on our subject, though we may mark it for its very strangeness, that in the latter days of Peter the Great the Czar and the Sultan joined together to make conquests from Persia. And when the war again began in Europe, the tide seemed at first to have turned to the side of the Turks. Russia was eager to get back Azov, and the Emperor Charles was ready to go on with the conquests which had begun early in his reign. War began again on the part of Russia in 1735, and of Austria in 1737. The Russians made conquests, but did not keep them ; and, now that the Emperor Charles had no longer a great general like Eugene, he lost much of what he had won in the earlier war. By the peace of Belgrade, in 1739, Belgrade, with all that had been won in Servia, Bosnia, and Wallachia was given back by the Emperor to the Turk. We read of this and other like things very calmly, as this or that clause of a treaty, and we sometimes forget what they really mean. To give up those lands to the Turk meant that the people of those lands were taken from under a government which was not

a national government, which doubtless had many
faults according to the standard of our times, but
which still was a Christian and civilized government
having some notion of right and wrong, and were put
once more under the cruel bondage of Mahometan
tyrants. How the people of these lands felt as to the
change, we see by the way in which, whenever they
had a chance, they helped the Imperial armies against
the Turks. We see this specially in the next war
between Austria and the Turk, which was waged in
the last years of the Emperor Joseph the Second.
Belgrade was again taken, and other conquests were
made ; but nearly all was given back by the Emperor
Leopold the Second at the Peace of Sistova in 1791,
when the Turk again got Belgrade. In this last war
the Servians fought most gallantly on the Imperial side,
and learned much military discipline. But, as usual,
they were made the playthings of policy in other
directions, and were shamefully given up to their cruel
masters. But a great deal came out of the taste of
civilized government and civilized discipline which
Servia had in these wars.

The war which was ended by the Peace of Sistova
was the last of the wars between the Turks and the
Emperors of the House of Austria for the possession
of Hungary, Servia, and the other lands on the Danube,
wars which had gone on, with breaks from time to time,
ever since the battle of Mohacz. The result of all these
wars was that Hungary was freed from the Turk,
but that Servia and Bosnia were left in his clutches.
But it must always be borne in mind that all these
lands alike, Hungary, Servia, and the rest, have
been lost and won again in exactly the same way.
The frontier which now divides the Hungarian

kingdom from the Turk is simply the result of the successive victories and defeats of the Austrian arms, from the deliverance of Vienna in 1683 to the betrayal of Belgrade in 1791. There is no reason but the accidents of those wars, the accident that Charles the Sixth had a great general early in his reign and had no great general in his later years, to account for the fact, that part of the lands on the Danube are now under a civilized government, while part are left under the Turk. In the days of Sobieski and Eugene, men had not learned to talk about the integrity and the independence of the Ottoman Empire, or to think it a good thing for Christian nations to be held in Turkish bondage. Whatever may have been the mixture of generous and merely politic motives in the minds of the men of those times, they at least did not openly profess the doctrine that certain nations should be deprived of the rights of human beings for the sake of the supposed interests of some other nation. The great powers of those days, Austria and Russia alike, cruelly deceived and forsook the nations that were under the Turks. But they at least did not tell them that their bondage was to be maintained as if it were something for the general good of mankind. The ministers of the despotic governments of those days were not ashamed to use the subject nations for their own purposes, and then to betray them. But they would have been ashamed to stand up and either to deny that those subject nations had wrongs, or to make those wrongs a matter of mockery.

The wars between Austria and the Turk are thus ended. They ended in establishing the frontier which

remains still, except so far as one of the lands which
were given up to the Turk has won its freedom
for itself. But the wars between the Turk and
Russia still went on. As long as the Austrian wars
went on, there was commonly a Russian war at the
same time, while there were other wars with Russia
in which Austria had no share. Thus, at the Peace of
Belgrade in 1736, when Austria gave up so much, it
was agreed that the fortifications of Azov should be
destroyed, and that Russia should be shut out from
the Euxine. It was not till the reign of Catharine
the Second that the real advance of Russia began.
The first war of her reign began with the declaration
of war by the Turk in 1768, and it was ended by the
famous treaty of Kainardji in 1774. Two points are
specially to be noticed in the wars which now begin.
This first war had a special effect in stirring up the
Greeks to revolt. A Russian fleet appeared in the
Ægæan, and the Greeks of Peloponnêsos rose against
their oppressors. They were badly used by Russia,
just as the Servians were by Austria; they were by
no means backed up as they ought to have been
against the Turks, or protected from their vengeance.
Still it was a great thing for the Greeks again to feel
that their masters had powerful enemies, and that
they themselves could do something against their
masters. And now too the people of Montenegro
begin to play a part in all the wars against the Turk.
They had always kept their own independence by
endless fighting. Their land had been often overrun,
but it was never really conquered. Montenegro was
now under the rule of its Bishops, who, somewhat
strangely according to our notions, acted also as civil
and military chiefs. Russia had long given the

M

Montenegrins a certain measure of help and encouragement, and in all the wars from this time, Montenegro,
as an Orthodox land always at war with the Turk,
was found an useful ally.

The treaty of Kainardji, which finished this war,
marks an important stage in the history, just as the
Peace of Carlowitz marked another. The Peace of
Carlowitz taught the Turk that he was no longer to
deal with the Christian nations of Europe as if he
were their superior. The Peace of Kainardji taught
him the further lesson that he was not really their
equal. The Ottoman power was now for the first time
brought into some measure of dependence. By this
treaty Russia at last gained the long disputed possession of Azov, with some other points on the Euxine,
and the Tartars of Crim were recognized as a state
independent of the Turk. It is worth notice that,
by the treaty, the spiritual authority of the Sultan,
as Caliph of the Prophet, was fully recognized on
behalf of these Tartars, at the same time that they
were released from his temporal authority. The
principalities of Wallachia and Moldavia were restored to the Turk, on condition of his observing their
ancient privileges and at the same time acknow-
ledging a right in Russia to remonstrate in case of
any breach of them. Russia was acknowledged by
this treaty as the protector of the Christian subjects of the Turk; in truth the principle was proclaimed, though not in so many words, that Turkish
rule was something different from anything that
we understand by government. It was practically
proclaimed that those whom he called his subjects had need of the protection of another power
against the man who called himself their sovereign.

Both at the time and ever after, this treaty has been looked on as the beginning of the fall of the dominion of the Turk. For it did in truth make the Ottoman power in some sort dependent on Russia, and ever since the power of the Turk has steadily gone down and the power of Russia has steadily advanced.

At the same time it must be remembered that whatever good Russia did at this time to the enslaved nations was wholly indirect. More than once Russia stirred them up to revolt, and then left them in the lurch. The truth is that, in those days, the more generous emotions which, in our days, have stirred whole nations, especially the feeling of sympathy between men of kindred race, hardly existed. It was not, as now, the Russian people who were stirred to help their oppressed brethren ; it was merely the rulers of Russia who carried out their own schemes of policy. Still, with every step that the power of the Turk went back, the nations that were still under his yoke took fresh heart. At no time have they really wished for annexation by Russia, though doubtless at any time, if they had been driven to choose between the rule of the Turk and the rule of the Russian, they would have chosen the rule of the Russian. But every time that the power of their masters was weakened, they saw fresh hopes of deliverance, whether by the help of Russia, or, better still, by their own right hands. We must therefore set down every advance made by Russia at the cost of the Turk as, indirectly at least, a step towards the deliverance of the subject nations.

After the Treaty of Kainardji those steps pressed fast upon one another. In 1783 the land of Crim was altogether incorporated with Russia, which thus at last got a great sea-board on the Euxine. This was one of those things which could not fail to happen. The Tartars of Crim could not possibly keep on as an independent state. It was something like Texas, which, when it was cut off from Mexico, could not fail to be joined to the United States. Russia, a growing power, could not be kept back from the sea. The next war, from 1787 to 1791, was the last in which Austria shared, that which was ended by the Peace of Sistova, when Belgrade was last given back to the Turk. It almost seemed as if, between the two Christian powers, the Turk would have been altogether crushed. But, as we have seen, the Emperor Leopold drew back, and the loss of the Austrian alliance, together with the general state of affairs in Europe, caused Russia to draw back also. Still this war gave Russia the famous fortress of Oczakow, and advanced the Russian frontier to the Dniester. Russia thus gained, but Christendom lost. For this increase of the territory of Russia did not mean the deliverance of any Christian people, while the surrender of Belgrade was the betrayal of a Christian city to the barbarians. It did not perhaps much matter when Russia ended a war in which Montenegro had helped her without making stipulations on behalf of Montenegro. For the Montenegrins could help themselves, and could keep their own borders. It was different when Greeks and Servians, who had helped Russia and Austria, were again left under the rule of the Turk. Still the whole course of events helped to raise the hopes of the subject nations, and to make them feel their strength. Before the next war between Russia and the Turk began, one of the subject nations had done great things for its own deliverance.

We have now reached another marked stage in our tale. We have gone through the history of the decline of the Ottoman power, so far as that decline was the work either of its own vices or of warfare with enemies beyond its borders. The two causes had worked together. Each cause of decline had strengthened the other, and the two together had called a third cause into being. Up to this time, our tale of warfare has been mainly a tale of external warfare. So far as we have had any revolts of the subject nations to record, they have not gone beyond help given by the subject nations to the external enemies of the Turk. From this point the character of the story changes. The main interest will now gather round the efforts of the subject nations to free themselves. The external wars of the Turk now stand in a certain relation in the general history of the world; they stand in a special relation to the struggles of the subject nations themselves. The wrongs of those nations are the cause or the pretext or the occasion for every war. Something for their good or for their harm is contained in every treaty. We may therefore fittingly draw a line at this point; we may end our history of the mere decline of the Ottoman power, and begin a new chapter with the revolts of the subject nations.

CHAPTER VI.

THE REVOLTS AGAINST THE OTTOMAN POWER.

WE have now reached our own century. We have to tell the history of things of which the latest are still going on, while the earliest happened so near to our own times that a few old people can still remember them. The wars of the seventeenth and eighteenth centuries had taught the subject nations their own strength, and they now began to strive to win freedom for themselves. Both the two great races have had their share in the work. The Slaves began ; the Greeks followed ; in later times the Slaves have again been foremost. The history is a continuous tale, so far as that there has hardly been a moment during the present century when revolt against the Turk has not been going on in some corner or other of his dominions. But, for that very reason, because different nations have revolted at different times and in different places, the story is in another sense not continuous. The greatest of the Slavonic revolts and the greatest of the Hellenic revolts were going on at the same time, without having much directly to do with one another. It will therefore be well, first to tell the story of the deliverance of Servia, then the

story of the deliverance of Greece, and then the story
of the revolts, partly Greek but mainly Slavonic,
which have happened since Europe betrayed the
subject nations to the Turk by the treaty of Paris in
1856.

The surrender of Belgrade to the Turk was the last
and the most shameful act of the wars between the
Turk and the Emperors. Yet this betrayal of the
Servians by their Christian allies did very directly
help towards the freedom of Servia. It taught the
Servians that they might, by their own right hands,
win something better than either of the two things
which as yet had been their only choice. They
learned that they might cease to be the subjects
of the Sultan without becoming the subjects of
the Emperor. As soon as the Servians were given
back to the Turk after a taste of civilized government, they found themselves worse off than ever. The
Emperor, in giving up Belgrade, did indeed stipulate
for an amnesty for the Servians who had acted on his
side ; but just at that moment amnesties and stipulations of any kind did not count for much. It would
have been a hard fate, if men who had been once set
free had been given back to one of the great Sultans,
or even to one of the Saracen Caliphs. But a harder
fate than either was in store for the Servians whom
the Peace of Sistova gave back to the Turk. The
greater part of the Ottoman dominion was now in a
state of utter anarchy. The authority of the Sultan
went for nothing. Servia was now in the hands of
local military chiefs, the leaders of the rebellious
Janissaries. In some parts bands of men which might
be called armies went about taking towns and ravag-
ing the country at pleasure.(1)   Brave men among

the Christians took to a life of wild independence, throwing off, for themselves at least, the Turkish yoke altogether. In other parts the Sultans found it necessary to allow the Christians to bear arms, in defence alike of themselves and of the Sultan's authority against Mussulman rebels. Thus, in all these ways, the subject nations were gaining courage and were learning the use of arms. And it must be remembered that now the bravest and strongest of their children were no longer taken from them, but were left to grow up as leaders of their countrymen. In such a state of things as this, the rule of the Sultan, where it was to be had, was the least of many evils. We therefore sometimes actually find an alliance between the Sultan and the Christians against their local oppressors. This was the case in Servia. The Servians, under the yoke of their local oppressors, cried to the Sultan for help, and the Sultan was for a while disposed to favour their efforts against his rebellious officers. But the war against local oppressors gradually swelled into a war against the chief oppressor himself. Herein is an instructive lesson. A Sultan may for a while, for his own purposes, favour his Christian subjects against local Mahometan oppressors. But such an alliance can never be lasting; it can last only so long as the interests of the Sultan and the interests of the Christians remain the same; and that can only be for a very short time. The two may act together as long as they have a common enemy; as soon as that common enemy is overthrown, their interests part asunder. The yoke of the Sultan will often be lighter than that of the local tyrant; but men who have thrown off the heavier yoke will not be willing to put their necks under the lighter yoke. They will rather be stirred up by their success to cast off every yoke, heavy or light. On the other hand, though a Sultan may find it for his momentary interest to favour Christians against Mahometans who are in rebellion against himself, he will not find it for his interest to do anything which may stir up a general spirit of resistance in the Christians against the Mahometans. The alliance between a despot and a people is always dangerous and precarious; because such an alliance can only be founded on interest, and the interest of a despot and of a people can never be the same for any long time together. And this, which is true in any case, becomes tenfold more true when the despot is Mahometan and the people are men of any other religion. So it was with Servia. The war which began in 1804 with an appeal to the Sultan against local oppressors grew in the next year into war with the Sultan himself, which led in the end to the deliverance of Servia.

By this time the affairs of Servia, and of the subject nations generally, were getting mixed up, in a way in which they had not been before, with the general affairs of Europe. It was not now merely the powers whose dominions bordered on those of the Turk, but Western powers like France and England, which came to have a direct share in the affairs of the South-eastern lands. We have seen something like the beginning of this at the Peace of Carlowitz. where England and the United Provinces acted as me-diators. And, long before that, French Kings, both Francis the First and Lewis the Fourteenth, were not ashamed to give help and comfort to the Turks in their wars with the Emperors. Lewis the Fourteenth,

while he was persecuting Protestants in his own kingdom, was not ashamed to pretend to be the protector
of the Protestants in Hungary and Transsilvania. But,
from the last years of the eighteenth century onwards,
the affairs of the South-eastern lands began to have a
much more direct connexion with the affairs of Europe
in general. The French Revolution had begun before
the Emperor Leopold had given up Belgrade to the
Turk. The wars which sprang out of that revolution
began soon after; and they were at their full height
when the Servians were fighting for their freedom.

After the surrender of Belgrade, but before the
Servian revolt really began, Russia and the Turk
had become allies. The revolutionary French, under
Buonaparte, had in 1798 attacked Egypt, and this
led the Turk into an alliance with Russia and
England. Oddly enough, one result of this alliance
between a Mussulman, a Protestant, and an Orthodox
power was to set up again for a little while the temporal dominion of the Pope which the French had
upset. At a later stage, in 1805, Russia again demanded a more distinct acknowledgement of the
Russian protectorate over the Christians. Sultan
Selim wept, and presently came under the influence
of France, which power, by annexing the Illyrian provinces of Austria, had become his neighbour. Selim
presently, Turk-like, broke his faith by deposing the
princes of Wallachia and Moldavia contrary to treaty,
and now England and Russia were both armed
against him. The barbarian bragged as usual, and
this time with more reason than usual. A Turkish
fleet was burned in the Propontis by the English;
a little more energy, and Constantinople might have
been taken, and Europe might have been cleansed of

Asiatic intruders. Later still, when Buonaparte and Alexander of Russia were for a while friends, there were further schemes for getting rid of the Turk altogether, and for dividing his dominions between Russia, Austria, and France. Such a division would doubtless have been an immediate gain for the subject nations. Any civilized masters, Russian, Austrian, or French, would have been better than the Turks, even under a reforming Selim. But for some at least of the subject nations better things were in store. They were, partly by their own valour, partly by help from Christian nations, to be raised to a state in which they had no need to acknowledge any masters at all.

The war between Russia and the Turk went on till it was ended in 1812 by the Peace of Bucharest. By that peace Russia kept Bessarabia and all Moldavia east of the Pruth, which river became the boundary instead of the Dniester. The war concerns us chiefly so far as its course influenced the course of the war between the Turk and the Servian patriots. Whenever Selim was frightened by the advance of Russia, he made promises to the Servians ; whenever he thought that he had a chance against Russia, he withdrew or broke his promises. Up to 1805 the Servian war was not strictly war against the Sultan, it was a war against the Sultan's rebellious enemies. Under their leader, Czerni, Kara, or Black George, the Servians fought valiantly against their local tyrants, but they tried to make favourable terms with the Sultan through the mediation of Russia. Selim, instead of granting any terms, attacked the men who had been fighting against his enemies. But Czerni George and the other Servian chiefs crushed his forces right and left, and the Russian army was on the march. Selim was cowed; he offered to let Servia go free in every thing, except payment of tribute and keeping a small Turkish garrison in Belgrade. But, as soon as Selim heard of the French successes against Russia, he backed out of his promises and went on with the war. Presently, in 1807, Selim was deposed and soon after murdered, as was also Mustafa who was set up in his stead. Then, in 1808, began the reign of the fierce Mahmoud the Second, another Turkish reformer, the nature of whose reforms are well remembered by the people of Chios. The war went on till the peace with Russia in 1812. That treaty contained some provisions on behalf of Servia which might have been more clearly expressed, but which certainly were meant to make Servia a tributary state, free from all Turkish interference in its internal affairs. But now the Turk no longer feared Russia; he feared her still less when Buonaparte was marching against her. Mahmoud therefore thought himself strong enough to break the treaty. Servia was attacked again; Czerni George lost heart, and took shelter in the Austrian dominions. Servia was conquered, and Mahmoud the reformer had it all his own way. The old tyranny was brought back again. The Turk did after his wont; every deed of horror which is implied in the suppression of an insurrection by Turkish hands was done in the suppression of the insurrection of Servia. When Belgrade submitted, the Turks promised to put no man to death. Turk-like, they beheaded and impaled the men to whom they had promised their lives. Men still live who remember seeing their fathers writhing on the stake before the citadel of Belgrade. For these good services Servia has been told by the man who rules the counsels of England that she ought to be grateful to the Turk.

Such was the first act of the Servian drama. Servia was conquered; her first deliverer had fled. But a new deliverer arose in Milosh Obrenovich. He was not a hero like Czerni George, and he was guilty of some great crimes, specially in procuring the death of George himself. Still he gradually won the freedom of the land, and in 1817 he was chosen Prince. Servian affairs dragged on for several years; this and that agreement was made with the Turk, but none were fully carried out. By the treaty of Akerman, in 1826, Mahmoud consented to Servian independence. The land was to be free, saving only the payment of tribute and the keeping of Turkish garrisons in certain fortresses. But Mahmoud thought but little of treaties. He massacred the Janissaries, he made himself a new army, and thought that he could defy all mankind. He was taught better, as we shall see when we come to the affairs of Greece, at Navarino and at Hadrianople. It was not till the treaty of Hadrianople in 1829 that the provisions for the independence of Servia were really carried out.

Since then Servia has been a separate state under its own princes; but more than one change of dynasty has taken place between Milosh and his descendants and the descendants of Czerni George. The land has flourished and advanced in every way, as it never could have done under Turkish masters. The Prince of Servia rules over a free people. But for a long time freedom was imperfect, as long as the Turks kept garrisons in Belgrade and other fortresses. In 1862

Servia had a proof that, where the Turkish soldier is allowed to tread, he will do as he has ever done. A brutal outrage of the usual Turkish kind on a young Servian was resisted ; the barbarian garrison presently bombarded Belgrade. Diplomacy dragged on its weary course; but at last, after five years, Servia was wholly freed from the presence of the enemy. The Turkish troops were withdrawn, and since then Servia has been wholly free, saving the tribute which goes, which sometimes does not go, from the purses of her free children, for the tyrant whose yoke she has thrown off to squander on his vices and follies.

Such has been the deliverance of Servia. We must now go back some years to begin the tale of the deliverance of Greece. And, though the deliverance of Greece itself did not begin till Servian freedom was nearly won, still the deliverance of Greece is closely connected with a chain of events which influenced the affairs of Servia. Down to the last years of the eighteenth century, no part of the Greek nation was even nominally free. That part of the nation that was not subject to the Turk was subject to Venice. The Venetian possessions now consisted of the Ionian Islands, and a few points on the coast of Albania and Epeiros. These last lay in detached pieces to the south of the dominion of Venice in Dalmatia. When Austria and France divided the Venetian possessions in 1797, these outlying possessions of Venice were to pass to France. But, when Russia and the Turk made an alliance in the next year, it was settled that the Turk should have the Venetian possessions on the coast, and that the islands should be formed into a nominal republic, which should be at once tributary to the Turk and under the protection of Russia. Of the points on the coast some were presently subdued by the famous Ali Pasha of Joannina, but Parga held over till after the general peace, and was then surrendered. As the acquisition of Podolia late in the seventeenth century was the last case in which the Turk extended his dominion over a considerable province which he had never before held, so this was the last time in which he extended his dominion by the acquisition of outlying points on the coast of one of his provinces. Both this and the supremacy over the islands might pass for an increase of the power of the Turk; but all these transactions were in effect a blow dealt to his power. The towns which were taken really passed, not to the Sultan, but to his rebellious vassal Ali, and the surrender of Parga against the will of its inhabitants stirred up a strong feeling everywhere. And the erection of the islands into a separate state was really a great step in the direction of Greek freedom. However nominal might be the freedom of a commonwealth which was put under the lordship of two despots, men saw in its foundation the beginning of better things for the Greek people. Part of the Greek nation had been declared free, and however shadowy their freedom might be, such a declaration could not fail to do much towards kindling the hopes of that part of the nation which was still under the yoke. Thus the Greeks at one end and the Servians at the other were stirred up at about the same time. The new commonwealth was presently swallowed up by France; but at the Peace in 1815 it was set up again, under a protectorate on the part of England which did not differ much from actual sovereignty. Still the Greeks who were subjects of the Turk saw by their side other Greeks who, if not really free, were at least under civilized instead of under barbarian masters.([2]) And this helped to keep up hope and a spirit of enterprise in the whole nation.

We are now coming near to the greatest events in the later history of the Turkish power and of the nations under the Turkish yoke. This is no other than the general uprising of the Greek nation against its barbarian lords, the liberation of part of the Greek nation, and the formation of the liberated part into a new and independent European state. The revolt of Servia began first; but the Greek and the Servian war were going on at the same time, and both were mixed up with the general affairs of Europe, especially with the wars between Russia and the Turk. It is only in this last way that the Greek and the Servian revolutions are at all brought together. Each was an indirect help to the other, by diverting a part of the Turkish force; but the two struggles could hardly be said to be carried on in concert. Many causes joined together to stir up the spirit of the Greek nation. When we speak of the Greek nation, we must remember that the Greeks and those Albanians who belong to the Orthodox Church have always had a strong tendency to draw together. A large part of Greece was at various times settled by Albanians, and among these should be specially mentioned the people of the small islands of Hydra and Spezza, because they did great things for the cause. But there are Albanians in other parts of Greece also, and it must

be remembered that the Albanians generally, both
Christian and Mahometan, have always kept up a
strong national feeling. Christians and Mahometans
alike have always been discontented, and often rebellious, subjects of the Turk. Some of them were able
to maintain their independence for a long time in
wild parts among the mountains. Such were the
people of Souli, Christian Albanians who were never
fully subdued till 1803, when they were overcome by
Ali of Joannina. This was a conquest of Christians
by Mahometans; but it was not a conquest of
Christians by Turks. It was in truth a conquest
of Albanians by Albanians. Ali was a cruel and
faithless tyrant; still he was not a Turk, but an
Albanian; he was a rebel against the Sultan, and
he was so far an indirect friend of the Sultan's
enemies. And, like many other tyrants, among all his
own evil deeds, he did a certain amount of good by
keeping smaller oppressors in order. Thus the most
opposite things joined together to weaken the Turkish
power and to stir up the spirit of the Greeks. The
way in which the Souliots withstood Ali, and the way
in which Ali withstood the Sultan, both helped. Just
at the end of his life, Ali, who had destroyed the
freedom of Souli and Parga, was actually in alliance
with the Greeks who had risen up to win their own
freedom.([3])

The Greek Revolution, or War of Independence,
began in 1821, and the first fighting was where one
would certainly not have looked for it, namely, in the
Danubian Principalities. It could hardly be said
that the Greeks had suffered any wrongs in that part
of the world; but the rule of Greek princes had
brought together a considerable Greek element in that

N

quarter, and it was there the war actually began. There was fought the first battle at Drageshan, where the Greeks showed that they could fight bravely, but where they were defeated by the Turks. The real Greek War of Independence was of quite another kind, and had quite another ending. It is most important to remember that the rising was in no way confined to the narrow bounds of that part of Greece which was set free in the end. The whole Greek nation rose in every part of the Turkish dominions where they had numbers and strength to rise. They rose throughout Greece itself, both within the present kingdom and in Epeiros, Thessaly, and Macedonia, in Crete too and Cyprus and others of the islands. In some parts they were too weak to rise at all; in some parts the rising was easily put down; and in some parts where there was no rising at all the Turk did as he always had done, as he always will do whenever he has the power. Wherever the Turk was strong enough, he did then exactly as he did last year. Fifty years and more ago men were shocked by the story of the massacres of Chios, Kassandra, and Cyprus, just as we have been shocked by the story of the massacres of Bulgaria. Sultan Mahmoud, whom it has been the fashion to praise, was guilty of exactly the same crimes as his predecessors and his successors. In Constantinople innocent men were slaughtered day by day by the Sultan's order. The Patriarch Gregory suffered martyrdom; and what should specially be noticed, good men among the Turks themselves who tried to stop the cruelties of Mahmoud and the Turkish populace were, in some places murdered, in others disgraced.(4) This also has happened again in our own time.

The effect of Mahmoud's cruelties was to put down the revolt in many places, but in many others, especially in the greater part of old Greece, the Christians were able to hold their own.   Truth forbids us to pretend that the Greek war was a scene of unmixed virtue and patriotism on the Greek side. No insurrection ever was or will be.   War is a fearful scourge, even when carried on by civilized armies; and it is, in the nature of things, something yet more fearful when it is carried on between barbarians and men who have long been held down by barbarians, and have therefore learned somewhat of barbarian ways.   The revolt of Greece against the Turk, like the revolt of the Netherlands against Spain, was marked by some ugly deeds on the part of the patriots as well as on the part of the oppressors.   And, as usual, jealousies and dissensions often weakened the patriot arms.   It could not be otherwise; men who had just escaped from bondage will carry about them some of the vices of the slave; it is only in the air of freedom that they can get rid of them.   But many great and noble deeds were done also.   Among the foremost in the struggle were the men of some of the islands, the Albanians of Hydra and Spezza, and the Greeks of Psara.   These islands were among the parts of the Turkish dominions which suffered least, or rather they did not directly suffer at all.   They contributed a quota of men to the Sultan's fleet, and beyond that were left to themselves.   Shallow people sometimes ask, Why should men who were so much better off than their neighbours be the foremost to revolt?   The reason is simply because they were better off than their neighbours.   Men who enjoy a partial freedom, who therefore have some knowledge of what freedom is, will be more eager to win perfect freedom, and will be better able to win it than those who are in utter bondage and who have neither heart nor strength to stir. Besides this, there are such things, though some people seem to think otherwise, as noble and generous feelings, which lead those who are free themselves to help those who are in bondage. Therefore great things were done in the War of Independence by those who were themselves nearest to independence. Such were the two foremost men of the War of Independence by sea, the Albanian Andrew Miaoulês of Hydra and the Greek Constantine Kanarês of Psara.

The Greek revolution was mainly the work of the Greeks themselves, counting among them the Christian Albanians. They had some help, but not very much, from the other subject nations. The Servians had their own war of independence going on ; but a few Bulgarian and Rouman volunteers did good service in Greece. But more was done by volunteers from England, France, and other western countries. Lord Byron's name is well known as one who in his latter days gave himself for the Greek cause, and much was done by other Englishmen, as Lord Cochrane, Sir Richard Church, General Gordon, and Captain Hastings, the worthy fellow of Miaoulês and Kanarês by sea. These are men whose names should be remembered in days like ours, when Englishmen sell themselves to the service of the barbarian. And great things were done by the Greeks and Albanians themselves, as by the Souliot hero Mark Botzarês, and by Alexander Mavrokordatos, who was not a military man, but a Fanariot of Constantinople, almost the only one of that class who did anything. He bravely defended Mesolongī against the Turks in one of its two sieges. In short, among many ups and downs, the Greeks, with such help as they had, were able to hold the greater part of Greece itself against the Turks. From European governments, Russian or any other, they had no help. Most powers were against them; none were for them; till at length things took such a course that Christian rulers could not for very shame keep themselves from stepping in.

After the war had gone on for some years, Sultan Mahmoud found that neither his massacres in other places nor the armies which he sent against Greece itself could break the spirit of the Greek people. Greece at one end, Servia at the other end, were too strong for him. He had to send for what was really foreign help. In the break-up of the Turkish power, Mahomet Ali, the Pasha of Egypt, had made himself practically independent of the Sultan, just as earlier Turkish Emirs had made themselves independent, at one time of the Saracen Caliphs, at another time of the Seljuk Sultans. Mahmoud, in order to bring back the Greeks under his yoke, had to humble himself to ask for help of his rebellious vassal. In a war against Christians, where plunder and slaves might be had, Mahomet Ali was ready to help; so he sent his son Ibrahim (Abraham) with an Egyptian force. The Greeks, who had held their ground against the Turks alone, found Turks and Egyptians together too strong for them. Ibrahim, who afterwards, like most tyrants, was honourably received in England, went on the deliberate principle of making the land a desert, by slaying or enslaving the whole Christian population. Thus he went on, committing every kind of crime

and fiendish outrage that even a Turk could think of
in Crete, Peloponnêsos, and elsewhere, from 1824 to
1827. At last the patience of Europe was worn out.

What followed is well worthy of our study
just now. The first movement on behalf of right
came from England, and England at once sought
for Russia as ally. The Minister of England, Mr.
Canning, did not write and tell the Turk to suppress
the insurrection; he did not forbid any help to be
given to the victims of the Turk; he did not think
that the liberation of Greece lay beyond the range
of practical politics. He saw well enough that there
were difficulties; but he knew that human duty chiefly
takes the form of overcoming difficulties. In short,
he was a man and an Englishman, with the heart of
a man and an Englishman, and he acted as such.
In 1826 England and Russia agreed on a scheme for
the liberation of Greece which was distinctly drawn
up, not in the narrow interests of England or of
Russia, but in the interests of humanity. Both
powers disclaimed any advantage for themselves; they
sought the advantage of others and of humanity in
general. Greece was to become a separate tributary
state, like Servia. Presently Mahmoud signed the
treaty of Akerman with Russia, which, as we have
seen, is an important stage in the history of all the
principalities on the Danube. But with regard to
Greece Mahmoud was obstinate; the wild beast would
not let go his prey till it was dragged out of his
jaws. In those days men knew the art, which seems
since to have been forgotten, of dealing with wild
beasts in such cases. The " rights," the " dignity," the
" susceptibility " of the barbarian went for very little
then. The sentimental admiration of the Turk had

not yet set in, nor did base talk about English interests then rule everything. Canning was guided by reason and humanity. In July 1827 England, France, and Russia signed the Treaty of London, by which they bound themselves to compel the Turk, by force, if it should be needful, to acknowledge the freedom of Greece. In November was fought the great battle of Navarino. Three great European powers, representing three great divisions of the Christian name, Orthodox Russia, Catholic France, Protestant England, joined their forces to crush the power of the barbarian and to set free his victims. The Turkish and Egyptian fleet was destroyed, and Greece was saved. But by that time the great English Minister was dead : the Treaty of London was his last work. Men succeeded him who could not understand his spirit or walk in his steps. The great salvation of Navarino was spoken of in the next King's speech as an "untoward event." England therefore had no share in the great works that followed. France had the glory of clearing Peloponnêsos from the Egyptian troops ; Russia had the glory of bringing the Turk on his knees at Hadrianople. Mahmoud himself had to yield, and by accepting the Treaty of London, to consent to the liberation of Greece.

Such was the wise and generous policy of England under a great Minister; such was the way in which she fell back under smaller men. Such was the way in which, fifty years back, three great European powers could join together to do righteousness. The pride of the Turk was utterly humbled; his power was utterly broken. A large part of his dominions was taken from him; that is, a large part of mankind was set free from his tyranny,

and again admitted to the rights of human beings.
Servia and Greece were now free; Greece became not
only free, but altogether independent. This last was
a special humbling of Mahmoud's pride. He had
insolently said that he would allow no interference
between him and those whom he called his subjects.
No one should interfere with his right to rob, massacre,
and do all other things that a Sultan does to his subjects. He was presently driven to acknowledge the
independence of those subjects, to deal with them
as an independent power, to receive a minister from
them, and to send a minister to them. And all this
was done simply by union, determination and vigour,
by dealing with the Turk, not after any sentimental
fashion, but as reason and experience teach us is the
only way to deal with him. Mahmoud bragged as
loud as any Turk can brag now; but his bragging
was stopped at Navarino and Hadrianople. And we
learn another lesson from this history. As long as
Mahmoud thought that he could have his own way, he
massacred whom he would, Christian and Mussulman.
After Navarino and Hadrianople he left off massacring.
To bring the Turk to reason only needs a will: the
way is perfectly plain. Canning not only knew the
way, but had the will. Any other Minister who has
Canning's will can easily find Canning's way.

Greece now became an independent state: but it
took some time for the powers exactly to settle its
boundaries and its form of government. Several
boundaries were traced out, one after another, and
at one time it was actually proposed to leave
all the western part of the present kingdom, Aitolia
and Akarnania, to the Turk. As it was, somewhat

more than this was set free; but still a large part
of the Greek nation was left in bondage, including some of the parts which had done and suffered most in the War of Independence.   Epeiros,
Thessaly, and Chalkidikê, Crete and Chios, and
Psara, the birthplace of Kanarês, were all left to
the barbarians.   It is hard to give any reason why, if
one part of the nation was to be freed, another part
was to be left in bondage.   And now that the Turk
was utterly cowed and weakened, it would have been
as easy to wrest a large territory from him as a small
one.   The truth is that the powers were beginning to
be afraid of their own work.   Nowhere in Europe
was there any man in power with a wise and generous
heart like Canning.   The crushing of a despot and
the setting up of a free people was something which
seemed new and strange.   It was something which
the powers of those days, as they could not wholly
back out of what they had already done, seemed
anxious to do as feebly and imperfectly as they could.
Mere diplomacy seems never to understand either
the facts of the past or the needs of the present.   For
mere diplomacy always thinks that it can settle
every thing by mere words and by signing papers; it
leaves the thoughts and wishes and feelings of nations
out of sight.   The diplomatists wished to cripple
Greece, and they did cripple it.   In so doing, they
did a great wrong to that part of the Greek nation
which they left in bondage, and they hindered that
part of Greece which was set free from flourishing
as it otherwise might have done.   All history shows
that, when a people has been set free, its impulse is
to extend itself and to enlarge its borders, either by
arms or by persuasion.   Greece was shut up in a

narrow boundary, and was strictly forbidden to extend itself. The policy of the powers with regard to Greece was as much as if, when the Swiss Confederation began, the powers of Europe had said that Uri, Schwyz, and Unterwalden might remain united, and might even admit Luzern, but that they might on no account admit Bern or Zürich. Happily in the fourteenth century there was no diplomacy, and nations were allowed to grow; in the nineteenth century there was diplomacy, and nations were not allowed to grow.

The folly of the narrow boundary given to the new state was soon shown in a marked way. Greece had as yet no settled form of government, and things were in a most confused and disorderly state. Servia had been more lucky; for her struggle had given her a prince of her own, who, though he did some evil deeds, was a man of energy and knew how to rule. But Count Capo d'Istria, who was now at the head of affairs in Greece, though a better man than Milosh, was less able to rule over a newly freed people. The great powers now settled that Greece should have a king, and a king of some foreign reigning family. Prince Leopold, afterwards King of the Belgians, accepted the crown ; but he presently resigned it, because he saw that no Greek state could flourish which was pent up in such a narrow frontier. Above all, he saw no good in a Greek kingdom which did not take in Crete. But no ; Crete was on no account to be free, and Greece thus lost the services of a prince who, as his reign in Belgium showed, was the wisest prince of his time. Capo d'Istria was murdered in 1831, and the confusions in Greece got worse. At last in 1833 the powers sent a young

Bavarian prince, Otho by name, as king, with a Bavarian regency. The regents did not know how to manage matters, and by their centralizing schemes they rooted out such traces of the old institutions of the country as had lived through years of Turkish bondage. Otho reigned as an absolute sovereign till 1843, when the kingdom became constitutional. In 1862 Otho was deposed, and was presently succeeded by another young foreign prince, George of Denmark. In 1864 the Ionian Islands, hitherto a nominal commonwealth under the protectorate of England, became part of the Greek kingdom.

It is the fashion to say that the experiment of Greek freedom has failed, and that its failure proves something against setting free other lands which are under the Turk. In a certain sense, it is true that free Greece has failed. That is, it has failed to answer the extravagant hopes which were formed by some Greeks and some friends of Greece when the War of Independence began. Some people thought that Greece was to be again all that Greece had been in days when Greece was in truth the whole of the civilized world. The history of the world never goes back in that kind of way. It is also perfectly true that the kingdom of Greece has not flourished so much as even more reasonable people hoped. Still Greece has gained greatly, and has advanced greatly, since she was set free. She is again a nation. She is free from the brutal and bloody yoke of the Turk. She is under civilized instead of barbarian rule. And her difficulties have been great, difficulties which were partly inherent in the case, partly the fault of the European powers. Greece might have succeeded better, if she had had no memories of days of past greatness, and if she had been less in sight of modern European civilization. She might then have grown steadily and healthily from the point which she had already reached. As it is, she has, in the very nature of the case, had unsuitable models set before her. Then again, in those parts of the world, those states seem to succeed best which are most left to themselves. Servia has succeeded better than Greece, because Servia has been less meddled with than Greece; Montenegro has succeeded better than Servia, because Montenegro has not been meddled with at all. But a great part of the failure of Greece, so far as Greece has failed, has been the fault of the European powers. She has been half cockered, half snubbed, neither of which are healthy ways of treating a young nation. The powers gave her an absurd frontier, and sent a prince instead of a man to rule her. If we look below the surface of modern affairs in Greece, we shall see that whatever is good in the state of Greece has been the work of the Greek people themselves, that whatever is bad is the work of foreigners, or of Greeks who have aped the ways of foreigners. Greece has done much and has gained much. At all events, no Greek could wish to exchange the present place of his country for the place of any province of the Turk. If the promising child has done less as a grown man than might have been hoped, it is largely because foolish nurses insisted on keeping him in swaddling clothes throughout the days of his youth.

After the final establishment of the Greek kingdom came a time of more than twenty years, an epoch in which men's minds changed in a wonderful way with regard to South-eastern Europe. Sultan Mahmoud, who had shewn himself one of the bloodiest tyrants in history, set up in his later days for a reformer. The man who had the blood of Chios on his hands put forth beautiful proclamations, as his successors have done since, promising all kinds of good government to his subjects of all religions. This kind of talk has taken many people in; but no Turkish reform has been ever carried out; no Turkish reform was ever meant to be carried out. The object is always simply to throw dust in the eyes of Europe. For the Turk is cunning, and he knows that he can always deceive some people, especially diplomatists and others who look to names instead of things. The only real reform that Mahmoud or any of his successors ever made is doubtless a reform from the point of view of the Turk, but it is no reform from the point of view of the nations which the Turk holds in bondage. That is, Mahmoud and his successors, while they have broken all their promises of good government to the subject nations, have improved and strengthened their army in order the better to keep the subject nations in bondage. And in this work officers of several European nations, to their everlasting shame, have not blushed to help them.

Then again, besides this foolish belief in Turkish reforms, a foolish fear of Russia grew up in men's minds during this time. No doubt it is wise for any power to be on its guard against any other power; but it is not wise to treat any power with unworthy suspicion, and to try to thwart the objects of that power, simply because they are the objects of that power. Gradually a strange notion has sprung up, that, because Russia was thought to be dangerous, therefore Russia is to be thwarted in every way, and the Turk is to be patched and bolstered up in every way. For fear lest Russia should get too much power, Englishmen became ready to support the Turk, and to give him greater power of oppression. Nothing could be more foolish. If we are afraid of Russia taking the South-eastern lands or gaining an exclusive influence in those lands, the true way to hinder it is for ourselves to gain influence in those lands, by showing ourselves the friends of the subject nations and helping them in every way to throw off the yoke. In all their struggles, in the Greek War of Independence and in every other, the hearts of the subject nations turned first to England. They turned to England, because they wished to be free, and they held that England, as a free country, would help them better than any other. For one moment under Canning, England acted a wise, a righteous, and a generous part. She made herself the protector of the oppressed, and the oppressed gave her their love and thankfulness. Since then we have gone back. We have thrust away the nations which asked our protection ; we have done all that we could to prop up the wicked power of their oppressors. In our foolish fear of Russia, we have done all that Russia could most wish us to do. We have taught the subject nations, whose impulse was to look to England for help, to look to Russia for help instead. And when we have done all this, we turn round and blame, sometimes Russia, sometimes the subject nations, for a state of things which is simply the result of our own foolish fears.

In the latter days of Mahmoud, while his pretended

reforms did little good to the Christians, they set his Mahometan subjects against him. There were Mahometan revolts in Bosnia, Albania, and other parts, and Mahomet Ali of Egypt, the same who had helped Mahmoud against the Greeks, began to found a dominion of his own. He founded a dominion at the expense of the Ottoman Turks, just as the first Ottomans had founded a dominion at the expense of the Seljuk Turks. He held Egypt and Crete, and presently conquered Syria. As usual, the rule of the new despot was not so bad as that of the old one. Mahomet was a tyrant of that kind which will not endure smaller tyrants; so, like Ali of Joannina, he established, if not really good government, at least something of stern order in his dominions. It was clearly the natural course of things for the new power to grow at the expense of the old ; and it was clearly the policy of the European powers to let the two barbarians struggle against one another, and only to keep them from doing any further wrong to any Christian people. But by this time men had begun to think that "English interests" called for the support of the Turk. So the power of England was used to take Syria from Mahomet, and to give it back to the Turk. That meant to take both Mahometans and Christians in Syria from a rule which was comparatively good, and to put them under the worst rule of all. Since then the Turk has had his way in Syria ; he has done his Damascus massacres and the like. Happily for once England did interfere to get a better government for Lebanon. Here again what was gained was gained by energy, by acts and not by words. It marks the difference between Lord Dufferin's interference and later cases of interference, that, instead of idle talk and compliments, a Turkish Pasha was hanged, and a large measure of freedom was given to his Christian victims.

These Asiatic affairs concern our subject only indirectly, nor have I told them at all at length. Nor need we here to go at length through the provisions of the several treaties which were made between the liberation of Greece and Servia and the beginning of the Crimean war.([5]) Nor yet is it needful to go through the history of that war. But it must be remembered that the disputes which led to that war arose, not with Russia, but with Louis-Napoleon Buonaparte. It was Buonaparte's evident policy to pick quarrels in succession with the great military powers of the continent, and each time to give his doings a respectable look, by getting some free nation to help him. He began with Russia, and altogether deceived England into a war with Russia, though Russia had done England no harm. He next attacked Austria, under pretence of helping Italy. But Italy was not deceived as England was; she was able to make use of Buonaparte against her enemy, and then to establish her own freedom in defiance of Buonaparte himself. Lastly, he attacked Prussia, expecting that he would deceive South Germany; but South Germany, as all the world knows, would not listen to him, and this third time he and his power were got rid of altogether. But the first time England was the dupe of his schemes, and plunged into a war with Russia on behalf of the Turk. Buonaparte began by getting up a quarrel about the Holy Places at Jerusalem on behalf of the Latins against the Orthodox. Then the Emperor Nicolas of Russia demanded a fuller acknowledgement of his rights as protector of the Orthodox, and he, on the Turk's refusal, occupied the Principalities. The Turk then declared war and was, after a while, helped by France and England, and, later again, by Sardinia. Few Englishmen perhaps now remember the noble appeals of the Russian Emperor to his subjects when he was thus attacked by two Christian powers who drew the sword to hinder the nations of South-eastern Europe from having the protection of a sovereign of their own faith against their oppressor. (6) The English declaration of war spoke of "coming forwards in the defence of an ally whose territory is invaded, and whose dignity and independence are assailed." It went on to speak of an ally, "the integrity and independence of whose empire had been recognized as essential to the peace of Europe." It even spoke of "the sympathies of the English people with right against wrong." The Turk then, whose power England had helped to crush in 1827, had in 1854 become the ally of England. To be the ally of the Turk could only mean to become the enemy of the Turk's enemies, that is, the enemy, not only of Russia, but of the nations which the Turk holds in bondage. It was declared that the "independence and integrity of the Ottoman Empire"—that is, the continuance of the bondage of those nations—was essential to the peace of Europe. It was declared that right was on the side of the barbarian power which existed only by trampling every form of right under foot. We went to war to maintain the dignity and independence of the common enemy of Christendom and humanity. It is hard to understand what was meant by the "dignity" of the chief of a barbarian horde encamped on the lands of other nations. This "independence," at any rate, could mean nothing but the uncontrolled power of doing evil at his own will.

In all these dealings with the Turk, it is most important to remember that the ordinary phrases of law and politics do not apply. There is no question of international right in any matter that touches the Turk; for the existence of the Turkish power is itself a breach of all international right. He exists only by the denial of all national rights to the nations which he keeps in bondage. The Russian Emperor was not interfering between a lawful government and its subjects; for the rule of the Turk is not a government, but a mere system of brigandage; and those whom the Turk calls his subjects are not his subjects but his victims. And if there was danger to Europe from Russia gaining an exclusive influence over the South-eastern nations, England had no one but herself to blame for that. It was the policy of England which had driven those nations to seek for a protector in Russia, when they would much rather have found a protector in England. In such a cause as this, in the cause of the independence of the Turk, that is, on behalf of his right to hold Christian nations in bondage, three Christian powers made war upon Russia. The armies of England, France, and Sardinia appeared as allies of the armies of the Turk. Free Greece was held down by force, lest she should give what help she could against the common enemy. And, as if to throw mockery upon titles and badges which once had a meaning, the Sultan, the successor of Mahomet, was admitted to the Order of the Garter, the Order of Saint George, and the Grand Cross of the Bath was given to Omar Pasha, a renegade of Slavonic birth, who had forsaken his nation and his religion for the pay of the Turk. This man had done the Turk's work against his countrymen in Montenegro and other Christian lands, and he was now commander of the barbarian army against Russia.

The war was ended by the treaty of Paris in 1856. The terms of that treaty are well worth studying. By its seventh article, the powers which signed it, France, Austria, Great Britain, Prussia, Russia, and Sardinia, declared that the Sublime Porte—that is, the Turk—was admitted to partake in the advantages of public law and the European concert. That is to say, the barbarian was, by a kind of legal fiction, to be treated as a civilized man. He was to be outwardly admitted to an European concert in which it was utterly impossible that he could have any real share. To admit the Turk to the advantages of public law is like giving the protection of the law to the robber and refusing it to those whom he robs. As applied to the Turk, the word law has no meaning; for the very existence of his power implies the wiping out of all law. To admit the Turk to the European concert was to give an European recognition to a power which is not and never can be European. It was to give the sanction of Europe to the position of the Turk; it was to give an European approval to the bondage of European nations held down under a barbarian yoke. Things had indeed strangely gone back since earlier times. It was a step in advance when the pride of the Turk was humbled at Carlowitz. It was a further step in advance when his pride was further humbled at Kainardji. Now the work of a century and a half was undone, when the barbarian was solemnly admitted into the fellowship of European and Christian powers. To admit the Turk to the advantages of public law and of European concert was in effect to declare that the South-eastern nations were shut out from the advantages of that law and that concert. The nations themselves, and the power which debarred those nations from the rights of nations, could not both enjoy them at the same time.

In the same spirit the powers further engaged to respect the "independence and territorial integrity of the Ottoman Empire" and they guaranteed the strict observation of this engagement. It is worth while to stop and see what these words mean. To guarantee the territorial integrity of the Ottoman Empire could only mean that the powers would hinder any part of the lands which were under the yoke of the Turk from being set free from his yoke, whether by becoming independent states or by annexation to any other power. It meant, for instance, that Thessaly, Epeiros, and Crete might not be joined to Greece. It meant that Bosnia, Herzegovina, or Bulgaria might not become independent states as Greece had become. It meant that no part of these lands might be added to Montenegro, or even put under the power of Austria. It was declared to be a matter of European interest that the Turk should keep what he had got. And it was further declared to be matter of European interest that the Turk should be allowed to treat all that he had got as he thought good. For the powers guaranteed the independence of the Ottoman Empire, which could only mean the right of the Sultan to do what he pleased; that is of course, to commit any oppression that he pleased. And this was made

clearer still by the ninth clause. Sultan Abd-ul-Medjid
had at the time of the treaty just put forth one of the
usual papers of lying promises, talking about his concern for all his subjects, and promising to do this and
that without distinction of race or religion. Reason
and experience should by·this time have taught men
that all promises of the kind were good for nothing.
But this empty talk of the Turk was treated by the
powers as if it had been something serious. The treaty
speaks respectfully of the "firman which had spon-
taneously emanated from the sovereign will of the
Sultan." The powers go on to say — one might
almost think that it was in irony—that they "accept
the value of this communication;" and they go on
to disclaim any right "collectively or separately" to
interfere with "the relations between the Sultan and
his subjects, or in the internal administration of his
empire." That is to say, if words have any meaning,
the powers pledged themselves to let the Turk do
what he would with the nations under his yoke, and
promised that they would do nothing to help them.
The "relations between the Sultan and his subjects"
could only mean the usual relations between the oppressor and the oppressed, between the murderer and
the murdered, between the robber and the robbed,
between the doer of every kind of outrage and the
sufferer of every kind of outrage. Those relations had
been for ages, as the powers must have known, the relations between the Sultan and those whom he called
his subjects. There was no guaranty, only the word
of a Turk, to make any one think that things were
likely to change. As a matter of fact, they have not
changed; things have gone on since Abd-ul-Medjid's
paper of false promises exactly as they went on before,

or, if anything, they have been worse still. The relations between the Sultan and his subjects, that is the
relations between the tyrant and his victims, have gone
on just as they went on before ; or, if anything, they
have become worse still. And with those relations the
Christian powers pledged themselves not to interfere.

There is of course no need to believe that the
European powers deliberately meant to do all this.
They may have really put faith in the false promises
of the Turk. To be sure the Turk had even then
broken his word so often that no wise man ought to
have trusted him ; still he had not then broken his
word so often as he has now. Or they may have
been simply led away by the misuse of names and
phrases. They may really not have fully taken in
what the "independence and integrity of the Ottoman
Empire" meant. They may not have seen how different a meaning is conveyed by the words " relations
between the Sultan and his subjects" from the meaning which those words bear when they are applied to
any European sovereign. They might not have taken
in the great distinction that, though the relations between any European sovereign and his subjects or part
of his subjects may happen to be bad and oppressive,
still the evil is incidental and may be reformed, but
that with regard to the Sultan and his subjects the
relation is essentially evil in itself and never can be
reformed. Diplomatists are so much governed by
words and names, they are so used to think so much of
sovereigns and courts, or at most of governments and
states, and so little of nations, that they may really
not have understood what it was to which they
were pledging themselves. But, whatever they meant
to pledge themselves to, what they did pledge

themselves to was this, that the Turk might do what he would with the nations of South-eastern Europe, and that the Christian powers would do nothing to hinder him.

The paper of false promises which was now put forth by Abd-ul-Medjid was not the first paper of the kind, neither was it the last. Sultan after Sultan has put forth paper after paper of the same kind. These papers have been full of promises which, if they had been carried out, would have made as good a system of government as a despotic government can be. Only they never have been carried out; they have never been meant to be carried out; they never can be carried out. The object of the Turk in making these promises is to go on working his wicked will on the subject nations, and at the same time to deceive the European powers who ought to step in and deliver them. The Turk promises anything, but he does nothing. His tyranny gets worse and worse, because it has become the tyranny, not so much of the Sultans themselves as of a gang of men about them. We have seen that in the time of the great Sultans the oppression of the subject people was not so great as it became afterwards. And when, in later times, the Pashas of the several provinces became hereditary and nearly independent, a Pasha would sometimes take a certain care and feel a certain pride in the well-being of his province, and would therefore not push oppression to the uttermost. It has been in the days of pretended reform that the last stage of oppression has been reached. Every chance, every hope, has passed away from the oppressed people since all power has come in our own day into the hands of a corrupt Ring—as the Americans call it—at Constantinople. These men have carried centralization to its extreme point, and with centralization, corruption, oppression, evil of every kind, have reached their height. A gang of men who in any other land would find their way to the gaol or the gallows rule the Ottoman Empire. It is worth while to see who these men are. A man who inherits power from his forefathers, if he has the faults, will also commonly have some of the virtues, of high birth ; he will understand the feelings which are expressed in the phrase "*noblesse oblige.*" A man who has risen from a low estate to a great one by his own merits is the noblest sight on earth. But the men who form the Ring at Constantinople belong to neither of these classes. The man who has risen from a low estate to a great one by vile means, the man who has bought his place by bribes, the slave who has risen by craft and cringing, the wretch who has risen by that viler path which Christian tongues are forbidden to speak of, but which is the Turk's surest path to power, in such men as these the lowest and basest form of human nature is reached. And such men as these rule at pleasure over South-eastern Europe. Barbarians at heart, false, cruel, foul, as any of the old Turks, but without any of the higher qualities of the old Turks, these men have picked up just enough of the outward show of civilization to deceive those who do not look below the surface. They meet the Ministers of civilized powers on equal terms ; they wear European clothes ; they talk an European tongue, and are spoken of as " Excellency" and " Highness." The wretched beings called Sultans are thrust aside as may be thought good at the moment ;

but the relations between the Sultan and his subjects, the relations with which at the treaty of Paris the Christian powers bound themselves not to interfere, go on everywhere in full force. There is no barbarian so dangerous as the barbarian who is cunning enough to pass himself off for a civilized man.

Under such a rule as this it naturally follows that sheer falsehood governs everything. Lying promises have been made over and over again, whenever it has been wished to make a fair show in the eyes of Europeans. But of course no promise is ever kept. The Turk professes to abolish slavery ; but slavery and the slave-trade go on. In truth the peculiar institutions of Turkish society could not go on without them. The Turk promises that Christians shall be allowed freely to own and buy land. But when the Christian buys land, his Mussulman neighbour comes and takes the fruits, or perhaps turns him out of the land altogether. The Turk promises that Christians shall have seats in local councils. That is to say, in a district where the Christians are a great majority, one or two Christians are admitted to the local council, simply to make a show. They are afraid to oppose their Mussulman colleagues, and their Mussulman colleagues are able to say that the Christian members have consented to the acts of the council. The Turk promises that men of all religions shall be equal before the law. But it is certain that in most parts of the Turkish dominions no redress can be had for any wrong done by a Mussulman to a Christian, except by bribing both judge and witnesses. Christians are put to death without trial simply for resisting Mussulmans in committing the foulest outrages. In short no Christian under the Turkish rule can feel that his life, his property, the honour of his wife and children, are safe for a moment. The land is ruined by heavy taxes, wrung from the people by every kind of cruelty, in order to keep up the luxuries and wickedness of their tyrants. Such, under the rule of the Ring, are the ordinary relations between the Sultan and his subjects. To keep on those relations untouched is one of those "sovereign rights" of the Sultan about which diplomatists are very tender. To meddle with his exercise of those rights—that is with the way in which the Ring exercises them for him—would be to touch his honour, his dignity, his susceptibility; it would be to interfere with the independence of the Ottoman Empire. To lessen the area within which those rights are exercised would be to interfere with its integrity. And the independence and integrity of the Ottoman Empire are, we all know, sacred things. They, and all that they imply, all that comes of them, are in some mysterious way essential to the welfare of Europe. They are cheaply purchased, we are bound to believe, by the desolation of wide and fertile kingdoms, and by the life-long wretchedness of their people.

One thing is always specially to be borne in mind, that oppression and wrong of every kind are not merely the occasional, but the constant, state of things under the rule of the Turk. We are apt to think of some sudden and special outburst, like the doings of the Turk in Bulgaria last year, as if it stood by itself. In truth those doings in no way stand by themselves. The kind of deeds which were done then, and at which all mankind shuddered, were nothing new, nothing rare, nothing strange. They were the ordinary relations between the Sultan and his subjects, the ordinary exercise of his sovereign rights. They were the necessary and immediate results of the independence and integrity of the Ottoman Empire. Deeds of the same kind which were done then are always doing wherever the Turk has power. The only difference between the "Bulgarian atrocities" and the ordinary state of things under the Turk is that certain deeds which are always being done now and then were done, in much greater numbers than usual, in particular places at a particular time. "Atrocities" were going on before ; they have been going on since ; the only difference is that in those particular places, at that particular time, they were thicker on the ground than usual. It is the same kind of difference as if a police magistrate, who is used to deal every day with some half-dozen charges of drunkenness, should some day find that he had to deal with hundreds or thousands of charges. In both cases, there is nothing new or strange in the thing itself ; only there is more of it than usual. This is a plain truth which must never pass out of mind. The ordinary state of things under Turkish rule, those relations between the Sultan and his subjects with which the powers of Europe pledged themselves not to meddle, are simply a lasting state of "Bulgarian atrocities." Only it is not often that so many are done at one time or in one place, as were done in particular times and places last year.

There is something very strange in the way in which the European powers, and England to our shame more than any other, have lent themselves to prop up this wicked dominion of the Turk. We have done for the Turk things that we do not do for any other power. We have treated him as if we had some special call to prop up his dominion, as if it was some special business of ours to persuade ourselves and to persuade others that bitter was sweet and that 'evil was good. Every thing that one power could do for another has been done for the Turk, although everything that is done for the Turk is done against the enslaved nations. It has been thought a great point to give the Turk every help in providing himself with a strong army and navy. The strong army and navy are of course among the means by which he holds the subject nations in bondage. Officers of Christian nations, Englishmen among them, have not been ashamed to take service under the barbarian and to help in his work of oppression. Christian governments have not been ashamed to lend officers to discipline the armies by which the oppressor holds down his victims. Christian men have not been ashamed to lend their money to the Turk, and Christian governments have not been ashamed to encourage them in lending it, well knowing that the money would be spent on the follies and cruelty of a barbarian court, and knowing that the interest on the money could be paid only by practising every form of oppression on the people of the subject nations. The subject nations themselves look meanwhile with somewhat different eyes on the sovereign rights of the Sultan and on the independence and integrity of the Ottoman Empire. To them those rights, that independence and integrity, simply mean subjection to strangers in their own land, subjection which involves every kind of wrong that one human being can do to another. In their eyes the Sultan who calls himself their sovereign is not their sovereign, nor do they hold that he has any rights over them. By them the foreign tyrant at whose bidding they are daily robbed, murdered, and dishonoured, is known, not as their sovereign, but as "the Blood-sucker." And to throw off the yoke of the Blood-sucker, they deem it their duty to strive in every way, and to strive with arms in their hands whenever they have the chance.

We have seen that by the treaty of 1856 the Turk promised to do this and that which he never did, and that the European powers declared that they had no right to interfere between him and those whom he called his subjects. Since that day the enslaved nations have had no hope but in their own swords. Servia and Greece had more or less of help from the European powers ; but in the later revolts against the Turk the Christians have never had any help from the European powers, and in most cases the influence of the European powers has been used against them and in favour of their masters.

Since 1856 there have been several revolts of the subject nations, and several wars have been waged by the Turks against the independent state of Montenegro. When the treaty of Paris was made, when there was so much care to guarantee the independence and integrity of the Turk, no one thought of guaranteeing the independence and integrity of Montenegro against the Turk. By the terms of the treaty it was lawful for the Turk to enslave any part of Montenegro ; it was not lawful for Montenegro to set free any part of Turkey. But in all struggles the free people of the Black Mountain have always helped their enslaved brethren, and their enslaved brethren have always helped them. And both have always been helped by the brave men of the *Bocche di Cattaro*, who themselves not so long back revolted against their Austrian rulers. But, though late events have led us to think more of the Slavonic nations than of the Greeks, we must remember that the Greeks have suffered equally, and that they have more than once revolted as well as the Slaves. And, when they have revolted, they have of course been helped by their free countrymen in the kingdom of Greece, just as the Slaves have been helped by their brethren in Montenegro and Dalmatia. To people who go wholly by words and names, it seems something strange and wicked that these free Greeks and Slaves should help their oppressed kinsfolk. They talk about "foreign aggression," "foreign intrigues," "secret societies," and every other kind of nonsense, sometimes of falsehood. Yet these men who help the oppressed are simply doing what brave and generous men would do and have done in every time and place. They are simply doing what every Englishman would do in the like case. If we could fancy a state of things in which one English county was free and the next county in Turkish bondage, it is quite certain that the men of the free county would help their enslaved neighbours when they revolted. It is quite certain that they would plan schemes of revolt with them, and would point out to them fitting times and places for revolt. To do this, which is simply what every good man would do everywhere, is, when it is done by Greeks or Slaves, called "foreign intrigue," "foreign agitation," and the like. So, if we could conceive Yorkshire being free and Lancashire being in bondage, and if the men of Yorkshire did anything to help the men of Lancashire, they

ought to be called "foreign intriguers" too. For there
is no greater difference between the men of Montenegro and the men of Herzegovina, between the
men of Aitolia and the men of Thessaly, than there
is between the men of Yorkshire and the men of
Lancashire. No reason can be given why one part of
either nation should be free and the other part in
bondage. At least, if there is any reason, it is a
reason that can be seen only by diplomatists or by
sentimental lovers of Turks. The reason is not seen
by those who are most concerned in the matter, and
it never will be seen by them.

Of the Greek revolts one was actually going on in
Epeiros at the time of the Crimean war. It was of
course thought very wrong both for the men of Epeiros
to try and set themselves free, and for the men of free
Greece to try and help them. They were said to be
stirred up by Russia and the like. If they were
stirred up by Russia, it is not easy to see what there
was to blame either on their part or on the part of
Russia. But another Greek revolt, ten years after the
treaty of Paris, is of more importance. The wisdom
of King Leopold, when he said that Crete ought to be
joined to the Greek kingdom, and the folly of those
who would not let it be joined, were now proved
indeed. In 1866 the people of Crete rose against
their tyrants, and they kept up a gallant struggle
till 1868.([7]) In this war the way in which the enslaved people were treated by the western powers,
and especially by England, comes out very strongly.
In many parts of the Turkish dominions English
consuls seem to be sent there only to cook reports
in favour of the Turk; but in Crete the English

consul, Mr. Dickson, was a humane man, who did all that he could to save women, children, and other helpless people from the cruelty of the Turks. Some of these poor people were carried off in safety to Greece in ships of several European nations, amongst others in the English ship Assurance under the command of Captain Pym. But the English Foreign Secretary, Lord Stanley, now Earl of Derby, forbad that any such act of humanity should be done again. It does not appear that the governments of any other European nation acted in the same way. England alone, or rather the minister of England—for few Englishmen knew much about it—must bear the shame of having in cold blood forbidden that old men and women and children and helpless persons of all kinds should be saved from the jaws of the barbarians. The thing is beyond doubt; it is written in a Blue Book; no man can deny the fact; no good man can justify it. No blacker page in the history of England, no blacker page in the history of human nature, can be found than the deed of the man who, for fear of being misconstrued in this way or that—for that seems to have been the real motive—could write letters forbidding any further help to be given to those who were simply seeking to save their lives from their destroyers. (⁸)   No doubt what was going on in Crete was the ordinary relation between the Sultan and his subjects ; no doubt the powers had pledged themselves not to interfere between the Sultan and his subjects ; still it is hard to believe that the treaty of Paris itself meant that no help should be given in such a case as this. But if it did, then the morality which can talk of the faith of treaties in such a case is the morality of Herod. If any one holds that Lord

Derby did right in deliberately ordering that the Cretan refugees should not be saved from their murderers, because of the treaty of Paris, he need only go one step further to hold that Herod did right in ordering John the Baptist to be beheaded, because his oath had bound him to do so. The faith of treaties and the sanctity of an oath are much the same in the two cases. No treaty, no oath, can bind a man himself to do a crime: nor can it bind him, when he has the power of hindering a crime, to allow it to be done.

Crete was in the end conquered; and, again to the shame of England, it was largely conquered by means of an Englishman. This was an English naval officer, Hobart by name, who was not ashamed to enter into the service of the barbarian, to take his pay, and to help him to bring Christian nations under his yoke. In the old days of the crusades, there was one Englishman, Robert the son of Godwine, who went to the holy war, who saved the life of King Baldwin in battle, who was at last taken prisoner by the Mussulmans, and who, rather than deny his faith, was shot to death with arrows in the market-place of Cairo. Somewhat later there was another Englishman, Robert of Saint Alban's, a knight of the Temple, who betrayed his order, his country, and his faith, who took service under Saladin, and mocked the last agonies of the Christians when Jerusalem was taken. We have had such men as both of these in our own day. The glory of Robert son of Godwine has its like in the glory of Hastings. The shame of Robert of Saint Alban's has its like in the shame of Hobart. Of all the deeds done in naval warfare surely the most glorious was

P

when Hastings went forth in his Kartería to free Greece from the barbarian. The basest was surely when Hobart abused English naval skill to bring back Greeks under the Turkish yoke. Crete was conquered; the Turk again, after his manner, made false promises, and set up a sham constitution. Under this constitution the island has of course been as much oppressed as ever, and it is now as ready as ever to seek deliverance from the yoke and union with its free brethren. So it always has been; so it always will be; men who feel the yoke on their own necks will always strive to cast it off. Men who see their brethren under the yoke will always come to help them to shake off the yoke. And they will do this, even though diplomatists tell them that, for some reason which they at least cannot see, the yoke must still be pressed upon them.

Among the other nations which are subject or tributary to the Turk, the Rouman lands north of the Danube have made great advances towards freedom since the treaty of Paris. By that treaty Wallachia and Moldavia were to remain distinct principalities under the supremacy of the Turk. The territory of Moldavia was somewhat increased by the cession of a small part of Bessarabia which Russia had by the treaty to give up, in order to keep her frontier away from the Danube. In 1858 the relations of these lands were more definitely settled. The two principalities were united for some purposes; but they were still to have separate native princes. The princes were to be chosen by the assemblies of each principality, and to be invested by the Sultan, to whom each principality was to pay a tribute. But the Rouman people were eager for a more perfect union. In 1859 the two principalities elected the same prince, Alexander Cusa. As the union of the two principalities made the Rouman nation stronger, the Turk and the friends of the Turk grumbled; but the Turk had to acknowledge the new state of things under protest. In 1866 Prince Alexander was deposed, and a prince of a reigning family, Charles of Hohenzollern-Sigmaringen, was chosen. The Turk again grumbled, and made show of fighting; but again he had to give way. And now Roumania, under a prince who is a kinsman of the German Emperor, may be looked on as practically independent of the Turk.

But the main interest of these later times gathers round the Slavonic subjects of the Turk and their free brethren in Montenegro. It will be seen at once by the map that the principalities of Servia and Montenegro come at one point very near to each other. They thus leave the lands of Herzegovina, Bosnia, and Turkish Croatia almost cut off from the mass of the Turkish dominion. These are the lands where oppression has been even worse than elsewhere. It has been so above all in Bosnia, where the Mussulmans are not Turks but descendants of renegade Slaves. And mark further that, while the oppression in these lands is even greater than elsewhere, their people have more to stir up hopes of freedom than in most other parts of the Turkish dominion. Enslaved Bosnia naturally envies free Servia; enslaved Herzegovina naturally envies free Montenegro. Add to this that a great part of these lands consists of wild mountains, where a few brave men can easily hold out against a much greater force. In these lands therefore revolts have been common. In Bosnia one might say that there is always some revolt of some kind going on, for in that land there is a treble discontent. The Christians are discontented, alike with their immediate oppressors, the Mussulmans of the country and with the Sultans who promise reforms and do not carry them out. The Mussulmans, on the other hand, who, though oppressors of Christians, are themselves for the most part very lax Mussulmans, are almost equally discontented with the Sultans, because, under the centralizing system at Constantinople, they have lost a good deal of their power. It seems strange that the part of the whole Turkish dominion which is in the worst bondage of all should be a land which is furthest away of any in Europe from the seat of the Turk's own power, a land which borders close on a Christian kingdom, to which part of it was actually joined by the peace of Passarowitz. But though there have always been disturbances of one kind or another in Bosnia, the great centre of real national revolt has rather been in Herzegovina. There men see the free heights of Montenegro rising above them, and they ask why they should not be as free as their brethren. It is no wonder then that the Turk has given his main efforts to subdue the valiant principality. A short sketch of its later history will therefore be needful in order fully to understand the relations between the Turks, the Montenegrins, and those neighbours of Montenegro who are, some under Turkish and some under Austrian rule.

Not very long before the Crimean war, the constitution of Montenegro was altogether changed. The line of prince-bishops came to an end. The bishopric, with the civil and military government attached to it, had been as nearly hereditary as a bishopric could be. That is, it commonly passed from uncle to nephew. In 1851 the last Vladika or Prince-Bishop, Peter the Second, died.(⁹) His nephew Daniel, who, according to rule, would have succeeded him, felt no call to become a Bishop; so it was agreed between him and the Senate that the spiritual and temporal powers should be separated, that Daniel should reign as an hereditary prince, and that the new Metropolitan should be simply Bishop without any temporal power. The Russian Emperor, the one protector of Montenegro, approved; but the Turk sought a ground of quarrel out of this change in the constitution of a perfectly independent state. The Prince and people of Montenegro had a clear right to make what changes in their own government they thought fit; but it must be remembered that the Sultans have always claimed a supremacy over Montenegro, which they have never been able to establish and which the Montenegrins have never acknowledged. In 1852 Sultan Abd-ul-Medjid sent the Slavonic renegade Omar to try to subdue the free Slavonic and Christian state. The people of Herzegovina, as usual, helped their free brethren, and the renegade was beaten in several fights. In 1853, by the intervention of Russia and Austria, the Turk suspended hostilities with Montenegro; the insurgents of Herzegovina had been already cajoled by the usual promises to lay down their arms.

During the Russian war Montenegro, as a state, took no share in the struggle. But, on the one hand,

Prince Daniel found it impossible wholly to keep his people from action against the Turk, and, on the other hand, his efforts to remain neutral only raised up disaffection and revolt in his own dominions. At the Congress of Paris, the Prince strove to get the assembled powers to acknowledge his independence, and to allow an extension of the Montenegrin frontier to the sea. But the powers were just then too busy providing for the interests of barbarian intruders to give any heed to the claims of the heroic people who had for so many ages formed the outpost of Christendom against them. He made the same appeal the next year, when part of the people of Herzegovina asked for annexation to Montenegro. But all that he got was a recommendation to acknowledge the supremacy of the Turk, on which condition some small increase of territory might be allowed to him. All this time war was going on, and in 1858 the Turks were utterly routed by the Montenegrins in the battle of Grahovo. Two years later Daniel was murdered. His rule had been harsh and stern; but he had done much to establish the reign of law and order in his principality. The same work has been carried on more peacefully and gently under the present Prince Nicolas, under whom the country has made perhaps greater advances than any other part of Europe has in the same short time. No land is now safer for the traveller, and the chief objects of the Prince have been peaceful objects enough, making roads and establishing schools. The death of Daniel raised the spirit of the Turks, and the spirit of the Turks shewed itself in the usual fashion by increased cruelties in Herzegovina. The land was given up to the rule of bashi-bazouks. Again the people rose against their tyrants, and, though the Prince did what he could to remain neutral, it was of course impossible to keep Montenegrin volunteers from going to help their brethren. The Turk then again attacked the principality. The renegade Omar was again sent to do a renegade's work against the faith and the nation which he had betrayed. Adorned by this time with the highest knighthood of an English order, our Grand Cross of the Bath went forth to do the errand of the barbarian to whom he had sold himself. This time unluckily he was more successful; Montenegro had now in 1862 to consent to an humiliating treaty. The claim of supremacy on the part of the Turk was not brought forward. But the Turk claimed to keep a road across the principality with Turkish garrisons and block-houses along it. The Turk also, with a mean spite, demanded the banishment of Mirko, the Prince's father, who had been the Montenegrin commander in the war. But neither of these conditions was carried out; the demand for them was simply a piece of Turkish brag, which did little real harm. In diplomatic language a concession was made to the honour, the dignity, the susceptibility, and all the other fine and delicate feelings of the Sublime Porte. The treaty was doubtless humiliating; but it was little more. The effects of Montenegrin victory in 1858 were far more deep and lasting than the effects of Montenegrin ill-success in 1862. Seven years later, the Prince had a yet more difficult part to play, when in 1869 a revolt arose, not against the Turk, but against the Austrian. The brave men of the *Bocche* rose against certain regulations which they deemed to be breaches of their privileges, and they stood their ground so manfully that at last they submitted only on very favourable

terms. Fourteen years of peace did much for the
principality; but, as was presently shewn, those
fourteen years of peace did nothing to weaken the
warlike strength of the unconquered race which had
kept its freedom for so many ages.

And now we have at last come to the great events
of the last two years, those events which all generous
hearts trust may be the beginning of the end, the
death-blow struck to the wicked dominion of the
Turk. The oppressed nations have risen over and
over again; they have been over and over again
cajoled or overcome. But this time they rose with
the full determination never to be again cajoled, but
either to win their freedom or to perish. And they
have kept their word. Wherever the Turk rules within
the lands which really rose against him, he rules only
over the wilderness that he has made. The people
of the land are either still holding their land in arms
against him, or else they have fled from his rage to
seek shelter in other lands where he cannot reach
them. The present movement has been the result of
a general stir through all the South-Slavonic lands.
The minds of the Slave people throughout the
peninsula were much moved on the occasion of a
visit made by Francis Joseph of Austria to his
Dalmatian kingdom. It was a visit of reconciliation,
and it suggested the thought that the King of
Dalmatia, Croatia, and Slavonia—such are among the
titles of the prince who is also King of Hungary and
Archduke of Austria—was likely to take up a policy
favourable to the Slavonic part of his subjects. A
vigorous hand at such a moment might perhaps have
gone far to carry out the dreams of Charles the Sixth.

A King of Slavonia who also ruled at Vienna might have done more than the work of Bulgarian Samuel or of Servian Stephen.

The revolt began in the summer of 1875. Like most of the great events of history, its causes and its immediate occasions must be distinguished. Its one abiding cause was the abiding oppression of the Turk. Men's minds were further stirred by the King's visit to Dalmatia, and some special outrages of the Turks caused the flame to burst forth. The immediate occasion was a specially brutal outrage of the barbarians towards two Christian women. Then the sword of the Lord was drawn, as it was drawn of old by Gideon against the tyrant of Midian, by the Maccabees against the tyrant of Syria. And from that day to this the sword of the Lord has not been sheathed. With the praises of God in their mouth and a two-edged sword in their hands, the champions of their faith and freedom have stood forth to be avenged of the heathen and to rebuke the people. On many a bleak hill-side the men of those rugged lands have waxed valiant in fight and turned to flight the armies of the aliens. Twice in the pass of Muratovizza have the hosts of the barbarian turned and fled, smitten down before a handful of patriots, as the Persian turned and fled at Marathôn, as the Austrian turned and fled at Morgarten. And the men who won those fights are still unconquered. Neither the arms nor the promises of the Turk have overcome them. The Bloodsucker sent his armies against them, and they cut his armies in pieces. He sent his emissaries with lying words to beguile them, and they cast his lying words back in his teeth.

As the first immediate occasion of the war was the visit of King Francis Joseph to Dalmatia, it seemet for a while as if the Austrian policy was not wholly unfavourable to the Christian cause. That the strong est sympathy for the revolt was felt through all the Slavonic lands under Austrian rule might be taker for granted. As many volunteers from Montenegre joined the insurgents, so did many—in some cases the full force of whole districts—of the fighting men from the *Bocche*. Under her governor, General Rodich, Dalmatia was a good neighbour to the kindred land cr Herzegovina. The insurgents practically got every help that they could have without what is called, in diplomatic language a breach of neutrality—that is without Austria openly taking the part of the patriots against the Turks. It was only much later, when the Magyar feeling in Hungary had shewn itself strongly against the Slaves, that the Austrian govern-ment took any strong steps the other way. The strongest step of all was the kidnapping and imprison-ment of the insurgent leader Ljubibratich, who was seized in May 1876 on Herzegovinian ground, and kept in ward till March 1877. The jealousy felt by the Magyars towards any thing like Slavonic inde-pendence has been one of the most striking things throughout the whole story. Their own land was delivered from the Turk by Slavonic swords; yet now they grudge any hope of deliverance to the Slavonic subjects of the Turk.

I need not here go in any detail through the his-tory, either military or diplomatic, of the year 1876. The leading facts are in everybody's memory; the time for them to be written in detail as a matter of past history has not yet come.([10]) I will only point

out some of those features of the story which have
been specially misunderstood, and which, by throwing
light on the real nature of Turkish rule, give us
practical lessons as to the course which Europe ought
to take at the present moment. The main facts of
the tale are easily told. The war had gone on for
nearly a year in Herzegovina and Bosnia, when an
attempt at a rising took place in Bulgaria also. The
Bulgarian people are a quiet, industrious, race, who
had been making advances in civilization which
seemed quite wonderful for people who had to bear
such a yoke as they had. There can be little doubt
that this advance of a subject nation aroused the envy
of the Turks, and that the Ring at Constantinople
worked with a deliberate policy to oppress and, if possible, to destroy the whole Bulgarian people. The
first means that they took to this end was to plant
colonies of savage Circassians in Bulgaria, who were
allowed to commit any kind of outrage against their
Christian neighbours. Thus Bulgaria had its own
special grievance. The ingenuity of the Highnesses
and Excellencies at Constantinople had lighted on a
new thing ; they had found out a third scourge, worse
than the Turk himself, worse than the renegade Slave
in Bosnia or the renegade Greek in Crete. Thus it
was no wonder that, when the Bulgarians saw the
success of their brethren to the North-west, they
tried to rise also. But Bulgaria is not a land fitted
for irregular fighting, nor are its people men of war
like the Slaves of the mountain lands. Thus the
Bulgarian revolt was a feeble revolt, compared with
revolts in the other two lands. While the Turks
could not put down the revolt in Bosnia and Herzegovina, they easily put it down in Bulgaria. How

they put it down all the world knows. They put it down in the usual Turkish fashion; the wild beast simply did according to his kind; only a great part of the world then learned for the first time what the kind of the wild beast really was. There can be no doubt that the massacre was deliberately ordered by the Ring at Constantinople, the Highnesses and Excellencies of polite diplomacy. This is proved by the facts that they honoured and decorated the chief doers of the massacre, while that they neglected, and sometimes punished, those Turkish officers who acted at all in a humane way. To this day, in defiance of all remonstrances from the European powers, the chief doers of the massacre remain unpunished, while we still hear of Bulgarians, sometimes being punished, sometimes being amnestied, for their share in the attempt to free their country. It is plain that the Ring do not dare to punish men who acted by their own orders, for fear lest their own share in what was done should come to light.([11]) Two things should be always borne in mind, first, that the doings of last May are still unpunished; secondly, that doings of the same kind, though doubtless not so thick on the ground, have been going on ever since.

By the time that the Bulgarian massacres happened, the patience of the two principalities of Servia and Montenegro was worn out. Volunteers had joined all along, but now the strain was too great; the governments could no longer keep in the national impulse, and both states declared war against the Turk. On the part of Montenegro, it must be borne in mind that that war has been thoroughly successful. The barbarians have been, as they have so often been before, utterly routed by the valiant men of the Black Mountain.   In negotiating with the Turk, the Prince of Montenegro has every right to negotiate as a conqueror with a conquered enemy.   With Servia the case has been different.   Its small force valiantly withstood the barbarians for a long while, but, even with the help of Russian volunteers, their strength was not equal to that of their enemies.   The Turk was thus able to occupy part of Servia, and in the part which he occupied he did after his wont ; he did as he had done in Bulgaria.   Then came an armistice; then came the European conference.   At the moment when I write Servia, has made peace, things being put much as they were before the war.   Victorious Montenegro is still negotiating, and of course demands the fruits of victory from the vanquished Turk.   In the greater part of Bosnia and Herzegovina the Turk rules over a wilderness.   In one corner of Bosnia the Christians still hold their own.   The barbarians have been utterly driven out; men are already beginning to speak of that corner of land as Free Bosnia.   May it ever remain so.([12])

Meanwhile, while both Christians and Turks alike have been acting in their several ways, the powers of Europe have been talking.   A great deal of paper and ink, a great deal of human breath, has been wasted on matters where paper and ink and talk of any kind were simply useless.   The note which was drawn up in December 1875 by the Austro-Hungarian minister Count Andrassy, and to which the other powers, England somewhat reluctantly, agreed, was a document such as has not often been presented to a power which calls itself independent.

It set forth in very strong words, flavoured in some parts with very strong sarcasm, the wickedness of Turkish rule and the constant breach of Turkish promises. As a sermon preached to the Turk to enlighten his conscience and to bring him to better ways, nothing could have been better. Only Europe ought by that time to have known that it is no use preaching sermons to the Turk, that no amount of preaching will ever enlighten his conscience or bring him to better ways. Five hundred years ago, when the Turk and his doings were something new, such a document would not have been out of place, and either the first or the second Amurath would have been more likely to listen to good advice than the corrupt Ring who now bear rule at Constantinople. To the Andrassy note, a good sermon and no more, England, so far as England is represented by Lord Derby, agreed. In May a stronger paper, called the Berlin Memorandum, was drawn up, which was somewhat more practical. It contained, among other things, proposals that the Christians should be allowed to be armed as well as the Mussulmans, and that the Turkish troops should be concentrated in certain particular places. Here was at least something definite, some approach towards doing something. It was indeed quite impossible that these proposals could be carried out without doing a great deal more; still it was a proposal to do something, as opposed to mere talk. But, as the Berlin Memorandum was a proposal to do something, England, as far as England is represented by Lord Derby, refused to join in it. Later in the year, when the heart of the people of England was thoroughly stirred up, Lord Derby himself wrote letters which also were very good sermons for the instruction of the Turk, but which served no practical purpose. Lastly, in December the Conference of the six great powers met at Constantinople. Strange to say, two Turks were allowed to sit along with the representatives of Europe, and one of them was allowed to be the President of the Conference. So to do was according to diplomatic traditions. That is to say, if the Conference had been held in London or Paris, an English or French minister would have had the presidency. But, putting diplomatic traditions aside, in the eye of common sense, to allow Turks to sit with European ministers was allowing the criminal to sit with his judge, and to settle the verdict and sentence upon himself. Of such a Conference nothing could come. The powers made certain proposals to the Turk, which, if they could have been carried out, would have been a real reform. The one fatal thing was that they never could have been carried out, as long as the Turk was allowed to remain in power. The Turks who were admitted to sit with the European ministers of course objected to every proposal which would have lessened their own power of doing evil. The European ministers yielded point after point, till the proposals were pared down to nothing, and then the Turks refused to accept even the wretched remnant that was left. Europe, in short, came together to see what was to be done with the Turk. The Turk snapped his fingers in the face of Europe, and Europe has up to this time sat down quietly under the insult.

While these greater matters have been going on, it might be easy to forget that the Sultan has been changed more than once. The truth is that now that the rule of the Turkish dominions has changed from a corrupt despotism to a more corrupt oligarchy, it matters very little who bears the title of Sultan. The Sultan, heir of Othman and Caliph of the Prophet as he is, is now set aside as suits the convenience of the governing Ring. The decay which has fallen upon the whole Ottoman power has specially fallen on Othman's own house. As no house once produced so many mighty men in succession, so now no house has fallen so low. The race of Mahomet and Suleiman, the race which produced men of energy so lately as the last Selim and the last Mahmoud, has sunk into a line of sots and idiots. This or that sot or idiot is set aside by the governing Ring, and another sot or idiot is drawn out of the harem in his stead as may be convenient. Abd-ul-Aziz was set aside, and presently died. Those who believe that Edward the Second of England and Peter the Third of Russia died of their own free will may perhaps believe the same of Abd-ul-Aziz. Then came Murad, and wonderful things were to be done in his reign; but presently the Ring set him aside too. Then wonderful things were to come of Abd-ul-Hamid. But as yet Abd-ul-Hamid has done no more than Murad. These modern Sultans at least gain one thing by their degradation. No one would think of blaming Murad or Abd-ul-Hamid personally for any of the crimes that have been done in their names.

For any purpose of practical politics, it is hardly worth mentioning that another way of relieving the Sultans from any responsibility for the deeds that are done in their names has been thought of within the last few months. Just as the Conference was meeting a Turk named Midhat, who was for the moment in power, but who has since, after the manner of Eastern ministers, fallen from power, put forth what he called a constitution for the Ottoman Empire. The Sultan was no longer to be a despot, but was to reign, like an European King, with a Ministry and a Parliament. The object of the trick was plain ; it was simply to throw more dust in the eyes of Europe, just at the time of the meeting of the Conference. The Turks who sat at the Conference were able to say, " We are going to make greater reforms out of our own heads than any that you bid us to make." Again they could say, " The Sultan is now a constitutional King, and cannot do this and that without consulting his Parliament." Any plain man could see through so transparent a trick ; yet some people in Western Europe have been so blind as to argue that time should be given to the Turk to work his new constitution and give his new reforms a chance. That is, the Turk is to be allowed so much time longer to go on doing his wickedness unchecked. For, as no Turkish promise has ever been kept, as none of the pretended Turkish reforms have ever been made, there is no reason to suppose that Midhat or any other Turk really meant any reform this time any more than any other time. And, supposing the constitution were to be carried out, it would, if it be possible, make things worse; it could not possibly make them better. For, first of all, the constitution is a mere sham. It is a copy of the sham constitution of France under the tyranny of Louis-Napoleon Buonaparte. It would leave all real power in the hands of the Sultan, or rather of the Ring, and the Ring would be able to carry on their oppression and

Q

corruption with some pretence of the approval of a constitutional assembly. And again, if the pretended Parliament had any real power, nothing would be gained. It would be simply the sham of admitting Christians to local councils done over again on a greater scale. Midhat took care that in his sham Parliament the Mussulmans should greatly outnumber the Christians. Again, the constitution would put the final stroke to the system of centralization, and would wipe out any traces that are still left of communities keeping any kind of separate being.

But a greater political truth than all this lies behind this pretence of a Turkish constitution. Setting aside the absurdity of putting the representatives of civilized European nations alongside of representatives of this or that barbarous Asiatic tribe, experience shows that a common Parliament is not a good form of government for several nations which have little in common, or which, from any cause, are strongly hostile to one another. A King who rules despotically over several nations will often rule them better than if he ruled with a common Parliament for all of them. For a well-disposed despot may deal equal justice to all the nations under his rule, and may not rule in the interest of any one nation in particular. But in a common Parliament of two or more nations which have no interests in common, or which have a mutual dislike, that nation which has the greatest numbers will outvote the others, and all legislation will be done in the interest of the dominant nation only. This is shown by several cases in our own time, even among civilized and kindred nations. To take one instance only, the Germans who were under the rule of the Danish Kings complained much less while the Danish Kings ruled despotically than they did after Denmark had a free constitution. And now that things are turned about, now that some Danes are under German rule, they have still less chance of being heard than the Germans had who were under Danish rule. Now, if nations like Danes and Germans, Christian, civilized, and kindred nations, cannot get on together with a common Parliament, how much less should Greeks, Slaves, Turks, and all manner of savages from Asia? The Parliament of the Turkish Empire, even if it really and freely represented all races and creeds in the Turkish dominions, would certainly vote every thing wholly in the interest of the Turks. All therefore that would come of it would be that the same oppression and corruption which now goes on in the name of the Sultan would go on with a fairer show in the name of the Parliament. Alongside of this, one might almost forget a piece of barbarian insolence on the part of Midhat, who decreed in his constitution that all subjects of the Sultan were to take the name of " Ottomans." Greeks and Slaves, sharers in the civilization of Europe, inheritors of the traditions of European history, were to be branded with the name of a gang of Asiatic robbers.[13]

The sham constitution was of a piece with another sham, that of trying to get the chiefs of the different Christian communities to join the Turks in a so-called "patriotic" declaration, that is, a declaration on behalf of the Turk. But this trick failed; for several of those who were summoned refused to betray their country in this way. And, so far as one can yet see, no real elections have been held under the sham constitution. In some places, naturally enough, no one seems to know what it means; in others the people, of whatever creed, refuse to elect at all; in others the Pasha names the members himself, or perhaps names the Mussulmans himself and orders the Bishop and the Rabbi to name the Christians and the Jews. We may be sure that those members of all three creeds will be named who will be the most ready to do the work of the Ring.

And now for some comments on those events of the last two years which we have thus so briefly run through. To those who had been watching these matters for many years, it seemed strange, and yet it did not seem strange, that, for a long time after the revolt began, it was the hardest thing in the world to get people in general to take any heed to it. People in the West really knew very little of the real state of things in the East. If they thought about them at all, they had a kind of notion that the Turk had been an ally both of England and of France, and that he had joined with England and France to win victories over Russia. Then too people had been brought up, so far as they thought about the Eastern Christians at all, in a kind of prejudice against them. It was a very old prejudice, a prejudice which dated from the times of the old disputes between the Eastern and Western Empires and between the Eastern and Western Churches. And this traditional prejudice has worked in the minds of many who have never heard of the disputes between the Empires or the Churches. Again, among those who knew a little more, there was a theological prejudice against the Orthodox Church in the minds both of Catholics and of Protestants. The Catholics have a feeling against the Orthodox, because they have never submitted to the Pope. On the other hand, Protestants are often taught to believe that the Orthodox are something worse than if they did believe in the Pope. Then there have been all kinds of foolish talk about the Turk being a "gentleman" and the like, and about his subjects being "degraded." Those who talked in this way did not stop to think who it was who had "degraded" them; they did not stop to think that it is very hard for men to improve so long as they are in bondage, and that the only way to make them improve is to set them free. Thus it came about that most people knew and cared very little about the matter, and that the prejudices of those who knew a little about the matter went largely the wrong way. Those who really knew what was going on, those who had looked at these matters all their lives, knew that a very great work had begun in South-eastern Europe. They knew in short that one of the great crises of the world's history had come. Of course those who could see were mocked at by those who could not see. It has always been so since the beginning of the world. Altogether it was very hard to make people really know or care anything about the great events that were going on, till the doings of the Turk in Bulgaria opened their eyes. Those who had been carefully watching the course of events saw nothing strange in those doings. But to the mass of people in England those doings seemed as strange as they were horrible. Till then they had never known what the Turk was. Now at last the Turk himself taught them what he was. He showed himself in his true colours, and when the English people saw him in his true colours, their natural feelings of right and wrong overcame all their traditional prejudices, and they declared that they would no more have anything to do with the doers of such deeds.

An opportunity was thus offered to the English Government to play a great and noble part, if they had known how to play it. Had the Government listened to the voice of the people, England might have done as great a work for right as she did fifty years before. But the English Government had no feeling for right, no understanding of the great events that were going on. And mere party men, men who thought it of more importance that this or that man should be for a year or two minister in England than that the wrongs of ages should be redressed, began to utter every kind of calumny against those who spoke for right, to misquote their words, to misrepresent their motives. It really seems that there are those who cannot understand that men do sometimes act from a feeling of right and wrong, and that everybody is not always thinking only about keeping this man in power or turning that man out of power. As the English Government refused to listen to the voice of the English people, the partizans of that Government set themselves to oppose the great and righteous national feeling. The noblest emotion that ever stirred any nation was checked by a paltry party-spirit. The truth is that political party ought to have had nothing to do with the matter. Conservatives and Liberals in England had sinned equally, they had often joined together in sinning, against the oppressed nations of the East. They might have joined together to repent, and to undo their misdeeds. The Liberal party repented; but it repented, not as a party, but as that part of the nation which thought right higher than party. The Conservative party did not repent, because the Conservative Government did not repent, and its followers did not know how to repent without orders from the heads of their party. Thus, what with mere political partizans, what with sentimental lovers of Turks, what with people whose whole notion of foreign politics is a foolish fear of Russia, England was hindered from doing as reason and the experience of the past would have led her to do. But reason and experience did something. The general feeling of the nation made it quite impossible for any minister, even the most reckless, to go to war with Russia on behalf of the Turk.

There is something which seems very strange in the utter blindness of the English Government and their partisans to the great events which were going on. The very day that I am writing this, I took up a newspaper dated in November 1875, and I there found it said that the insurrection in Herzegovina had been "unexpectedly prolonged" till the winter. In that word "unexpectedly" we see the key to the whole state of mind of Lord Derby and of men like Lord Derby. The things which are perfectly plain to men who use their eyes and their reason were "unexpected" to them. Any one who knew the nature of the country, the firm determination of the patriots, the utter corruption and demoralization of the barbarians, knew perfectly well that the revolt was not a thing that could be put down. But Lord Derby and people like Lord Derby were in the same state of mind in which such people commonly are at the beginning of

any of the great events of the world's history. To
men of this stamp the success of every great movement in every age has been "unexpected." They are
in the same frame of mind as the Persian King
when he asked who the Athenians were, or as Leo the
Tenth when he thought that nothing could come of
a movement begun by so small a person as Martin
Luther. Just in the same way, Lord Derby thought
that the revolt was something which could be very
easily suppressed, something which could be easily
put out of the way and got rid of, so as to give no
more trouble. He pooh-poohed the insurrection, because, like most great things, it looked little in its
beginning. He pooh-poohed it too, because it arose
from those great and generous feelings of men's
hearts which some men feel so little themselves that
they do not understand that other men can feel them.
Lord Derby, Foreign Minister of England in the
nineteenth century, pooh-poohed the movement in
Herzegovina, just as, if he had been Foreign Minister
of Rome or Persia in the seventh century, he would
have pooh-poohed the movement of the camel-
driver of Mecca and his first handful of followers.
He pooh-poohed it, as, if he had lived in the thirteenth century, he would have pooh-poohed the little
band which came to help the Seljuk Sultan against
the Mogul,—as, a few years later, he would have
pooh-poohed the rash resolve of the three little
lands among the mountains to match themselves with
the power of the Austrian Duke. All these things
seemed in their beginnings as if they might be easily
suppressed and got rid of. The Derbies of those
several ages doubtless thought that they might easily
be suppressed and got rid of. But in each case the

little cloud like a man's hand soon grew into a mighty storm. The small beginnings that men mocked at grew into powers which, for good or for evil, made their mark upon the history of the world.

But Lord Derby did something more than merely think that the revolt could be suppressed ; he did something more than merely wish it to be suppressed. He, a civilized man, a Christian, an Englishman, an English minister, was not ashamed to write letters urging the Turk to suppress the insurrection.([14])   He was not ashamed to write letters by which he hoped that the people of Dalmatia and Montenegro might be hindered from taking any part in the struggle.([15]) It is worth while to stop and think, though seemingly Lord Derby did not stop and think, what was the meaning of his own words when he spoke of the Turks suppressing the insurrection.   It is to be supposed that Lord Derby had learned something of the history of the century in which he lived, a century in whose history he was himself called on to be an actor. It is to be supposed that he had heard for instance of the massacre of Chios, of the massacre of Damascus, of any other of the doings of the Turks. He must surely have known the fate to which he had condemned his own victims in Crete.   What the Turkish suppression of an insurrection meant the world in general did not know till the doings in Bulgaria became known.   But it is to be supposed that a Foreign Minister, whose business it is to know something of the history and condition of foreign countries, must have known what every one knew who had given the matter a moment's serious thought. To advise the Turk to suppress the insurrection was in other words to advise

him to do as he had done in Chios and Damascus,
as he was to do in Bulgaria. It is not to be supposed
that any man calling himself an Englishman and a
Christian really wished such things to be done ; but
that was the plain meaning of the words of the despatch. The Turk was counselled to suppress the
insurrection ; the Turk would understand, and doubtless did understand, that England would stand by him
while he suppressed the insurrection in his usual way
of suppressing insurrections. The Turk did what he
could in Bosnia and Herzegovina to carry out the
advice which he had received from England. He
carried it out more fully in Bulgaria. There he did
thoroughly according to the advice contained in the
English despatch. He did suppress the insurrection
by his own forces. It is not to be thought that Lord
Derby really wished the Turk to do what he in effect
told him to do. But he told him none the less. A
dull man brought face to face with great events, great
movements, great stirrings of men's hearts which he
cannot understand, will be simply puzzled and frightened, and will hardly know what he says or writes.
But the fact that Lord Derby was puzzled and
frightened will not wipe the blood of Crete and
Bulgaria from his hands. The one notion of Lord
Derby, as of most of the professional diplomatists,
was to try to avoid trouble by getting rid of the thing
as soon as they could. Let it be suppressed out of
hand, never mind at what cost, so that it be suppressed and got rid of. But the thing could not be
got rid of. Lord Derby and the Turk and all the
diplomatists together could no more suppress that
mighty movement of men who had made up their
minds to win their rights or to perish than the king

in the legend could hinder the waves of the sea from flowing up to the foot of his throne.

The whole correspondence published in the Blue Book shews the same spirit.   There is no feeling of the greatness of the movement ; there is no sympathy with the righteousness of the movement.   One reads for instance of the news being more or less "satisfactory."   "Satisfactory" news, in the language of the Blue Book, means news by which it seems likely that the Turk will succeed in again bringing his victims into bondage.   The triumph of evil, the handing over of Christian nations to their oppressors, the doing of all the deeds which the Turk does when he gets back any piece of Christian soil into his power —this was what was called "satisfactory" in English consulates, in English embassies, in the English Foreign Office.   When Servia was about to strike her gallant blow for right, Sir Henry Elliot was not ashamed to tell the Servian agent that he hoped that Servia would be beaten.   The deeds of Bulgaria had then been done ; yet an Englishman, a representative of England, could tell the representative of a Christian people arming themselves for the freedom of their brethren, that he wished that they might be beaten by the Turk.   That is, he said that he wished that Servia might be dealt with as the Turk always deals with beaten nations, as the Turk had just before dealt with Bulgaria, as he presently did deal with so much of Servia as came within his clutches.   When Lord Derby called on the Turk to suppress the insurrection, he said in effect, Go and do your will ; slay, rob, burn, torture, ravish, force the flesh of the roasted child into his parent's mouth ; do all in short that you do when you suppress insurrections.   When

Sir Henry Elliot wished Servia to be beaten, he wished in effect that all these things should fall on Servia, or rather that they should fall on the whole of Servia, as they did fall on a part. No one believes that either Lord Derby or Sir Henry Elliot really wished for anything of the kind. But men who had either heads or hearts, men who were capable of understanding and facing the great events in which they found themselves actors, would have spoken in another way. There are no despatches of Canning exhorting Ibrahim to suppress the insurrection in Peloponnêsos.

One trick of the favourers of the Turk through the whole business has been, first to try to represent the insurrection as something quite insignificant, and when they found that this would not do, then, to represent it as wholly the work of foreign intriguers, foreign agitators, and the like. What is really meant by foreign intriguers and foreign agitators I have already shewn. They are foreign intriguers and foreign agitators in the same sense in which Sir Philip Sidney was a foreign intriguer when he died at Zutphen for the freedom of the Netherlands. As Englishmen then fought and died for the freedom of a kindred land, so now many men from Montenegro and from Russia, and from Italy too, fought and died the same glorious death for the freedom of the oppressed Slavonic lands. But the belief which was carefully spread abroad by the Turkish party in England, the belief that the revolt was no real revolt, that it was but a thing got up by men from other lands, is altogether false. It would seem as if those who talked in this way really could not understand that men could ever rise and fight for their own freedom.

That men should do so seemed so strange to them that they cast about for some other cause, and invented this talk about foreign intriguers. Montenegrins fought in Herzegovina; Russians fought in Servia; and in both cases, as was not wonderful, the people who knew less of the art of warfare were glad to accept commanders from the people who knew more. But it is a great mistake, if it is not something worse than a mistake, to say that the great mass, or even any considerable part, of the Herzegovinian army consisted of Montenegrins, or that the great mass, or any considerable part, of the Servian army consisted of Russians. In both cases the war was strictly national; volunteers came, volunteers were welcomed; but they were welcomed by men who had already risen to do the work for themselves. A moment's thought will shew how foolish this talk is about foreign intriguers and agitators. Men who are under the yoke of the Turk do not need to be told what oppressions they are suffering under; they do not need to be told that there is no way of getting rid of those oppressions but by drawing the sword for freedom. They know all that very well, without any foreign intriguers to tell them. If there are foreign intriguers, and if they get listened to, that of itself is proof enough that there is something which greatly needs redress in the land where they do get listened to. If foreign intriguers came into any well governed country and tried to persuade the people to revolt, no one would listen to them. If foreign intriguers stir up a people to revolt, and if that people listen to them, it is the surest of all signs that there is something to revolt about.

Perhaps the most daring case of all of saying "the

thing that is not," was that which was made by Lord
Beaconsfield at Aylesbury. He there—to be sure it
was after dinner—ventured to say that, when Servia
began the war, it was the "secret societies of
Europe which made war on Turkey." Now in truth
Servia did not make war on Turkey; Servia made
war on the Turk on behalf of Turkey. But of all the
untrue things that ever were said the most untrue was
that the Servian war was got up by secret societies. No
doubt much help has been given by societies in Russia
and in other Slavonic lands. But those societies are
no more secret than our Anti-Corn-Law League was,
or any other of our political or religious societies.
Lord Beaconsfield also ventured to talk about Servia
being "ungrateful" to the Turk. He called the Servian war an act of "treachery." All this was simply
using words without any meaning. Whatever an
open declaration of war may be, it is at least not
treacherous, and it would certainly be very hard to
find any reason that the Servians had to be grateful
to the Turk. Centuries of bondage, followed by
hideous breaches of faith, the impaling of their
grandfathers in 1815, the bombarding of their capital
in 1862, the violation of their frontier in 1876, would
seem to be the things for which, according to Lord
Beaconsfield, Servia ought to be thankful.

Another trick was to enlarge on and blacken to the
uttermost everything that was done, or said to be
done, on the patriot side which was not exactly
according to the laws of civilized warfare. The most
was made of anything amiss that was done, or said to
be done, by any insurgent, while anything that was
done by a Turk was slurred over or hushed up
altogether. Most of these stories were mere lies. For

instance, the Turks, Safvet and the rest of them,
tried to make the world believe that they were innocent lambs cruelly set upon by Bulgarian lions.([18])
There is no doubt that the mass of the stories which
were got up by the Turks and their friends against
the Christian insurgents were mere falsehoods. But
suppose, as is quite possible, that some of them were
true. Is it very wonderful if men who rise up to free
themselves from the most cruel yoke that man ever
was under, men who have been goaded to revolt by
every wrong that a human being could endure, should
not always behave like the soldiers of civilized armies,
whose nations or governments may have a dispute, but
who have no personal wrongs to embitter them against
one another ? In the most civilized and best disciplined
armies there will always be some men who do wrong
things. In an insurgent and irregular army the proportion of men who do such things will always be
greater. In strict morality, we must condemn men
who commit any kind of excess, even in avenging the
bitterest of wrongs. But we cannot wonder at them ;
we ought not harshly to condemn them. They are
doing as we ourselves should doubtless do in the same
case. In no case can the excesses of the insurgent
who is avenging his wrongs be put on the same level
of moral guilt as the excesses of the oppressor who is
wantonly inflicting wrongs. Men do not get better by
dealings either with barbarian masters or with barbarian
enemies. The way to make them better is, I must say
once more, to set them free from their bondage.

This is the fair way of looking at any particular
excesses which may have been here and there done by
the insurgents, whether in Herzegovina, Bulgaria, or
anywhere else. But most of the tales are simply false ;

and, in any case, what they may have done in revenge, was nothing compared with what the Turks did in wantonness. The same kind of falsehoods were told of the Servians. So they were of the Montenegrins. At a time when no Montenegrin prisoner was ever spared by the Turks, but when Turkish prisoners, a Pasha among them, were living quite comfortably in Montenegro, we were told of the horrible atrocities of the Montenegrins. The old custom, which the Montenegrins had learned of the Turks, was to bring home the heads of slain enemies as trophies. The Princes of Montenegro have long tried to stop this practice, and it is not now done by any troops who are under regular Montenegrin discipline. But the custom of cutting off the dead enemy's nose, as a kind of substitute for his head, has still been sometimes kept up both by the irregular insurgent bands and by the Albanians who have joined the Montenegrins. It seems that, in one or two cases, a man who was thought to be dead was wakened up by the loss of his nose. And this has been made the ground of tales of wholesale mutilation, torture, and the like. Nobody defends any such doings ; they simply come of the fact that men whose whole life has for so many ages been one long strife against a barbarous enemy have, as is not very wonderful, sometimes picked up a little of his barbarism. Take the Turk and his bad example away, and they will mend. And after all, though to cut off a dead man's nose is a brutal thing, it is hardly so brutal as roasting, torturing, and impaling living people ; it is not so brutal as the things which the Turks always do when they suppress insurrections, and sometimes when there are no insurrections to suppress.

So again, a great many falsehoods were told about
the Servians, how they mutilated themselves rather
than fight, how they shot Russian officers in the back,
how they refused to carry wounded men to the rear,
and the like.	Now it is certain that the Servians and
their Russian helpers did not always agree.	The
truth is this.	No men in any war ever behaved
more nobly in the way of risking and sacrificing
themselves than the Russian officers did in Servia.
But their habits in their own army did not fit them
to command a free citizen militia like that of Servia.
Disputes and ill will therefore arose in many cases.
Those who know the Servian army, and who know
other armies as well, say that in every army there
will always be found some black sheep who will now
and then do some of the things with which the Servian
army is charged.	But they add that to say that such
things were the rule, or that they were at all common,
in the Servian army is as great a slander as to say the
same of any other army.	Nor is it at all true to say
that the Servians are mere cowards.	It is true that their
militia, men who have come, one from his farm and
another from his merchandise, are not born fighters
like the men of the Black Mountain.	Neither would
an army of Englishmen be, if it was brought together
in the same way.	But no mere cowards would have
held out so long as the Servians did, with smaller
numbers than their enemies, and with inferior arms.([17])

Such are some of the mistakes and falsehoods which
have been going about ever since the beginning of
this great and righteous struggle.	And it may also
be well to notice that, while the diplomatists were
wondering and pottering and asking to have the

R

insurrection suppressed, the one rational way of dealing with the whole matter was many times set before them. Only they were too blind to see it. Experience shews that, wherever a land is set free from the direct rule of the Turk, it gains greatly by its deliverance. But experience also shews that the separation need not be complete and sudden; it shews that the tributary relation through which most of the nations passed on their road towards perfect bondage forms an useful intermediate stage on their road towards perfect freedom. So long as the Turk has no share in the internal government of the country, there is no great harm in the formal relation of tribute and vassalage. Indeed, as long as the Turk exists at all, the tributary relation to a common over-lord has one advantage. It helps to bind the several nations together; it helps to prepare the way for the time when the Turk can be got rid of altogether, and when the tributary relation may be exchanged for a federal relation. On the other hand, experience shews that the Turk's promises go for nothing, that his constitutions go for nothing. Experience shews that, wherever the Turk is allowed to keep troops or to have any share in the nomination of rulers of any kind, oppression goes on just the same as if no promises had ever been made. Experience further shews that Christians and Mahometans cannot live together—except as oppressor and oppressed—under a Mahometan government, but that they can live perfectly well together under a Christian government. From all this it follows that the only way to secure good government for the revolted lands is to put an end to the direct rule of the Turk over those lands. The only way is to establish some state of things in which, whatever

may be the form of government, the Turk shall have
no voice or authority in any internal matter. Nor
must he be allowed to keep garrisons in any of the
lands which are to be set free. Any form of government which compassed these two objects, will be so
far a real gain. One kind of government may be
better than another ; but by gaining these two points
the first essentials of good government will be secured.
Reason and experience taught this, and reason and
experience further taught that, if there was any
difficulty in creating absolutely independent states, any
difficulty in annexing the revolting lands to any of
the neighbouring states, there was the tributary relation to fall back upon. It had been tried, and it had
answered. The obvious immediate remedy therefore
was to enlarge the old tributary states or to make new
ones, in short to put the revolted lands in the same
position as Servia and Roumania. The lands would be
free, and the Sultan would still get all that he wants
out of them, some money, that is, to squander as
Sultans do squander money. But Lord Derby said
that the formation of tributary states lay, in a phrase
which has become a kind of proverb, out of the range
of practical politics. The truth is that it was the one
thing which did lie within the range of practical
politics, while everything that Lord Derby did lay
altogether without that range. Lord Derby's one idea
seemed to be a sentimental notion that the Turk
might be got to mend by preaching to him. And
just like the Andrassy note, so some of Lord Derby's
sermons, had they been preached to hearers·who were
the least likely to listen to them, were very good
sermons indeed. They got better still as soon as
Lord Derby found out that the people of England

were really in earnest about the matter. Still Lord Derby's whole course was sentimental and not practical. He refused the remedy which reason and experience had shewn would answer, and which lay within the range of practical politics. Instead of that, he tried the remedy which reason and experience had shewn would not answer, and which therefore lay without the range of practical politics. So of course nothing has been done. If, instead of Lord Derby's sentimental way of managing affairs, we had had Canning's practical way, things would have been very different.

Here then is the end of our history and of our comments upon it. In the last chapter we must see what the practical guides, reason and experience, tell us ought to be done to get us out of the difficulty into which we have been brought by a long and vigorous course of doing nothing.

NOTES.

(1, p. 167.) See Chapter XXVIII. of Jirecek, *Geschichte der Bulgaren*, headed *Pasvanoglu und die Krdžalijen*.

(2, p. 176.) Perhaps the rule of Sir Thomas Maitland, King Tom as he was called, may not have been much better than that of some Pashas. But he was hardly a specimen of English rulers in general. One Lord High Commissioner at all events, Lord Guildford, thoroughly deserved and won the thankfulness of the Greek people.

(3, p. 177.) There are several valuable narratives of the Greek War of Independence. The great work on the subject is the History of the Greek Revolution ('Ιστορία τῆς Ἑλληνικῆς Ἐπαναστάσεως), by Spyridôn Trikoupês, formerly Greek Minister in England. In German there is the *Geschichte des Aufstandes und der Wiedergeburt von Griechenland*, forming the fifth and sixth volumes of Gervinus' *Geschichte des neunzehnten Jahrhunderts seit den Wiener Vertragen*. In English we have the History by General Gordon, the plain narrative of an honest soldier, who played a distinguished part in the war. And we have the two volumes of the History of the Greek Revolution, which form the conclusion of Mr. Finlay's great series of mediæval and modern Greek History. This brings the history down to a much later stage than either of the others. It is the work of one of the keenest of observers, who knew the history of the country from the beginning to the end ; but the bitter and carping spirit in which it is written almost reminds one of Cato the Censor, and his epithet πανδακέτης. Plutarch, Cato Major, 1.

(4, p. 178.) See the account of the murder of the Mollah at Smyrna in Trikoupês, I. 289, Ed. 1 ; I. 251, Ed. 2. See also the story in Vol. II. p. 103, Ed. 1 ; II. p. 95, Ed. 2. Mahmoud himself disgraced his Grand Vizier, Beterli Ali, giving as his reason that he wished to spare the blood of the Greeks (ἠθέλησε νὰ φεισθῇ τῆς ζωῆς τῶν Ἑλλήνων, are the words of the official papers in Trikoupês, I. pp. 112, 374, Ed. 1. ; 90, 338, Ed. 2.) The Sheikh-ul-Islam was also deposed because he had refused his *fetva* for a general slaughter of the Greeks, i. 192, Ed. i. ; 163, Ed. ii.

(5, p. 192.) There was the Treaty of Unkiar-Skelessi in 1833, between Russia and the Porte, which concerns only the external relations between the two powers, and merely confirms the arrangements already made with regard to Greece. There were two Conventions of London in 1840, 1841 about the affairs of Syria ; and there was the Convention of Balta-Liman, between Russia and the Porte, in 1849, which settled the affairs of the Danubian Principalities, and which in fact sacrified their liberties both to Russia and to the Turk.

(6, p. 193.) See Annals of our Time, pp. 393, 401.

(7, p. 207.) Accounts of the Cretan war were written by Mr. Skinner, correspondent of the Daily News, in his book, "Roughing it in Crete," and by the then American Consul, Mr. Stillman, "The Cretan Insurrection of 1866-1868." The official papers are to be found in a Blue Book, "Correspondence respecting the Disturbances in Crete, 1866, 1867." In official language a patriotic war is a "disturbance." No doubt it is a "disturbance" to all the Foreign Offices.

(8, p. 208.) The despatch which contains Lord Stanley's order on this matter is No. 158, p. 140, of the Cretan Blue Book. The reasons given for refusing help stand thus :—

"Lord Stanley has received despatches from Greece which clearly show that the proceedings of her Majesty's ship, Assurance, in taking off from Crete a certain number of refugees, has been regarded in Greece, not in the light of a simple act of humanity, irrespective of political considerations ; but as an indication on the part of her Majesty's government that they sympathise with the cause of the insurgents, and Lord Stanley cannot doubt but that the same construction would be put on any similar proceedings on the part of her Majesty's ships of war, especially if taking place in consequence of express orders to that effect sent out from this country.

"Lord Stanley fears that the effect of any such step would be to hold out false hopes of assistance to the insurgents, and thereby in the end to create far more suffering by the protracting of the suffering than that which might be averted at the moment by the removal of these destitute persons.

"Her Majesty's government deeply lament the further ruin and misery in which a prolongation of the struggle cannot fail to involve the Christians in Crete, but it is their duty not to expose themselves to misconstruction, and not by an appearance of intervention, the moral effect of which might be very great, to depart from the position of strict neutrality which they have thought it their duty to assume."

In plain words Lord Stanley deliberately sacrificed these poor creatures to a cowardly dread of "misconstruction." It is to be noticed that he does not dare to condemn, though he very faintly approves, the conduct of Captain Pym and Mr. Dickson (see pp. 141, 150). Only, instead of doing right at all hazards, as they did, he was afraid of this and that ; he might be " misconstrued."

In noble contrast to Lord Stanley's despatch are the letters of Lord John Hay and Mr. Dickson in pp. 140, 141, 147, 151. That in 147 is a remonstrance from Mr. Dickson to a Turk called Ali Bey, who in p. 146 growls over the escape of his victims.

The crime of Lord Stanley was well rebuked by the Duke of Argyll in the House of Lords on March 8, 1867. Lords Kimberley and Grey, to their shame, defended the criminal, the former with some of the usual fallacious illustrations. There were other debates in the Commons on February 15, and the Lords on August 15. In that in the Commons the cause of evil found a characteristic supporter in Mr. Layard.

The moral aspect of the case, as of the whole of Lord Derby's dealings with Eastern Christendom, is instructive. We see that mere dulness, mere timidity and weakness of purpose, mere shrinking from obvious duty, may do just as much mischief as active cruelty. Canning wished, like Lord Derby, to put a stop to a wasting struggle. But he set about doing so in a different way from Lord Derby. In a word, Lord Derby was puzzled and frightened, and did not know what to do. Canning was neither puzzled nor frightened ; he saw the right thing to do, and he did it.

(9, p. 213.) This Peter is the Vladika of whom Sir Gardner Wilkinson has much to say in his book on Dalmatia and Montenegro. For the history of Montenegro, see *Le Monténégro Contemporain*, par G. Frilley et Jovan Wlahovitj, Paris, 1876.

(10, p. 218.) As yet there is not much to refer to besides Blue Books and newspapers. But there are already some pieces of history, as *Der Krieg in der Turkei. Zustande und Ereignisse auf der Balkanhalbinsel in den Jahren* 1875 *und* 1876, by Colonel Rüstow, Zürich, 1876. The story of the war in Herzegovina, down to the declaration of war by Servia and Montenegro, is told in Mr. Stillman's " Herzegovina and the late Uprising ; London, Longman, 1877. The writer here describes what he saw with his own eyes, eyes sharpened by his earlier experience of patriotic warfare in Crete.

(11, p. 220.) This point is strongly brought out in Mr. Gladstone's late pamphlet, Lessons in Massacre, and it is most forcibly argued in Sir George Campbell's Handybook on the Eastern Question, p. 133 et seqq. See also the very important letter of Consul Calvert in the Blue Book ; Correspondence respecting the Conference, pp. 170, 171.

(12, p. 221.) On the state of things in this corner, some most valuable letters have lately appeared in the *Manchester Guardian.* I hear from a private source that the insurgents in this quarter are largely Catholic. In another part the Catholic Mirdites are in arms, and in some parts the Mahometans themselves are rising. In short, there seems a hope that men of all creeds may join to shake off the yoke that presses on all.

(13, p. 227.) The same kind of talk was brought into the speech which, at the opening of the sham Parliament, was not spoken, or even read, by the Grand Turk himself, but read by somebody else at his side. Fancy Mahomet the Conqueror or Suleiman the Lawgiver having speeches read for them.

(14, p. 233.) In the despatch written by Lord Derby on August 12, 1875, in the Blue Book (Correspondence respecting Affairs in Bosnia and the Herzegovina, Turkey, No. 2, 1876), he writes thus to Sir Henry Elliot :—

" Her Majesty's Government are not aware whether your Excellency may have any opportunity of advising the Prince of Montenegro to restrain his subjects from aiding the Insurrection. Should such an opportunity offer, they do not doubt that you would avail yourself of it, and they wish you to direct her Majesty's agent at Belgrade to use his best efforts to counteract any dispositions which may be apparent in Servia to aid or foment the disturbances.

"At the same time her Majesty's government are of opinion that the Turkish government should rely on their own resources to *suppress the insurrection, and should deal with it as a local outbreak of disorder*, rather than give international importance to it by appealing for support to other powers.

" I have informed Musurus Pasha [the Greek who takes the pay of the Turk in London] of the substance of this despatch."

In the next letter we hear how " the Porte begged the Italian government to join the other powers in counselling the Princes of Servia and Montenegro to observe a prudent attitude." Perhaps by this time Lord Derby himself has found out that the victorious sovereign of the Black Mountain is more used to the "attitude" of Judas Maccabæus and of Rudolf Reding, than to any "attitude" that Lord Derby and the " Porte" might deem "prudent."

(15, p. 233.) See the letters of Lord Derby in the Blue Book (Correspondence respecting Affairs in Bosnia and the Herzegovina. Turkey No. 2, 1876, p. 6, p. 57)—where Lord Derby cherishes the vain hope of extinguishing the insurrection before the spring. So in Turkey No. 3, p. 18, where Lord Derby discusses the "great discouragement of the Turkish government " after a defeat of the Turks by the insurgents with Dalmatian help, and how " it is feared that the effect of it in Montenegro will be very mischievous." The letter in p. 115 to Mr. Adams is worth reading. It seems to have taken two or three Excellencies conferring together to find out that "by whateve measures Montenegro might be restrained, the result to Turkey of dissociating her from the insurrectionary cause would be a vital one." And so on, till on April 25, 1876, Sir Henry Elliot finds that the "last accounts from the north of Bosnia are entirely satisfactory," and adds how "Rashid Pasha says that, the Austrian frontier being now efficiently guarded, the bands of insurgents had been easily dispersed and tranquillity is restored in that district." What state of things is "entirely satisfactory" to Sir Henry Elliot, what kind of "tranquillity" is meant by Rashid Pasha, will be best studied in the letters of Miss Irby from the frontier of which he speaks.

(16, p. 239.) A curious illustration of the lengths to which Turkish power of lying may go will be seen in the speech of "his Excellency the President," otherwise Safvet Pasha, in the Blue Book of Correspondence respecting the Conference at Constantinople, pp. 217, 224. Lord Salisbury and General Ignatieff seem both to have answered as strongly as would be polite towards a fellow "Excellency."

(17, p. 241). These facts are known to every one who has really studied the course of the war, and has not been led away by slanderous words. I am happy to add from private sources the testimony of a highly distinguished Russian general, who distinctly asserts that the Servians are not inferior in military qualities to his own countrymen, and that in fact they shewed themselves capable of greater endurance.

CHAPTER VII.

THE PRACTICAL QUESTION.

AND now at last we come to the great practical question, What is to be done? What is the duty of England and of Europe in this great crisis of the world's history? I assume that England and Europe have a duty in the matter. I am old-fashioned enough to believe that there are such things as right and wrong, and to believe that right is to be followed, and that wrong is to be avoided, in the affairs of nations as well as in the affairs of private men. I assume that nations as well as individuals owe a duty alike to God above and to man below. It would seem that there are some who think otherwise. It would seem that there are some to whom any mention of right or wrong as having anything to do with the matter is ground enough for an outburst of wrath or of scorn. There are some who shamelessly put forth in the face of day the doctrine that interest alone is to be thought of, that it matters not what wrongs are done, what sufferings are borne, if some fancied interest of England is supposed to be jeoparded by doing right. I will quote, as an example of the spirit in which the affairs of the nation ought not to be carried on, the following passage from a letter in one of the published

Blue Books addressed by Sir Henry Elliot to the Earl of Derby, dated Therapia, September 4th, 1876 :—(¹)

" An insurrection or civil war is everywhere accompanied by cruelties and abominable excesses, and this being tenfold the case in oriental countries, where people are divided into antagonistic creeds and races, the responsibility and sin of those who incite a peaceful Province to rise becomes doubly heavy, and they now endeavour to throw them upon others.

" To the accusation of being a blind partisan of the Turks, I will only answer that my conduct here has never been guided by any sentimental affection for them but by a firm determination to uphold the interests of Great Britain to the utmost of my power, and that those interests are deeply engaged in preventing the disruption of the Turkish Empire is a conviction which I share in common with the most eminent statesmen who have directed our foreign policy, but which appears now to be abandoned by shallow politicians or persons who have allowed their feelings of revolted humanity to make them forget the capital interests involved in the question.

" We may, and must, feel indignant at the needless and monstrous severity with which the Bulgarian insurrection was put down, but the necessity which exists for England to prevent changes from occurring here which would be most detrimental to ourselves, is not affected by the question whether it was 10,000 or 20,000 persons who perished in the suppression.

" We have been upholding what we know to be a semi-civilized nation, liable under certain circumstances to be carried into fearful excesses ; but the fact of this having just now been strikingly brought home to us all cannot be a sufficient reason for abandoning a policy which is the only one that can be followed with due regard to our interests."

One's breath is taken away on reading such words as these. The only excuse or palliation for them can be that the writer, quartered so long among Turks, has caught some of the spirit of the Turk.

βεβαρβάρωσαι, χρόνιος ὢν ἐν βαρβάροις.(²)

Or perhaps so to speak is injustice to the Turk. When the Turk is suppressing an insurrection—I speak not of the Ring at Constantinople, but of the actual doers of the deeds—he may, in his fierce fanaticism, believe that he is doing good service to Allah and his Prophet. The motives confessed by Sir Henry Elliot are lower than this. Of right and wrong, of duty, there is not a word. The one avowed motive is interest, from one end to the other. It is not merely that the blind partizanship, the affection, whether sentimental or otherwise, which the writer shews for the Turk, comes out in the difference of tone between the first paragraph that I have quoted and the third. It is not merely that the devilish doings of the Turk are gently spoken of as "needless and monstrous severity," while the high moral tone about "responsibility" and "sin" is taken towards those who strove, however vainly, in the noble cause of Bulgarian freedom. This is not new. We can fancy Philip of Spain feeling the same holy indignation at the sin of William of Orange. We can fancy that there were milder moments when Philip himself deemed that the Fury at Antwerp was severity carried a little too far. But what is new, not perhaps altogether new, but characteristic of the dealings of the last generation or two with this particular subject, is the calm avowal that interest is to be the one guide of public action, and that to interest humanity and every other nobler feeling must give way.(3) Whether the disruption of the Turkish Empire would be good or bad for the nations that live under it is not even thought of. All that matters is that the interests of Great Britain are deeply engaged in preventing that disruption. We are graciously allowed to be indignant at Turkish severity ; but even revolted humanity must not allow us to forget the higher claims of "capital interest."

It matters not who may perish, 10,000 or 20,000, if their perishing will hinder changes that will be "most detrimental to ourselves." We must prevent those changes. We uphold a semi-civilized nation, and the nature of the power that we uphold has just now been strikingly brought home to us. But if the upholding of that power is the only policy which can be followed with a due regard to our own interests, nothing that that semi-civilized power may do can be a sufficient reason for abandoning it. Such is the morality, such is the doctrine, such, it seems, is the practice, of a representative of England in the nineteenth century. One feels, in reading Sir Henry Elliot's words, as Chatham felt when he burst forth in that strain of righteous eloquence which would hardly sound parliamentary in the delicate ears of a modern House of Lords. He called on Judges and Bishops to "interpose the purity of their ermine and of their lawn" to "save his country from pollution." He could not rest his head on his pillow till he had poured forth "his eternal abhorrence" of "principles preposterous and enormous," "equally unconstitutional, inhuman, and unchristian." In his day to profess humanity and Christianity as motives for public conduct had not yet become matter for scorn. In the moral code of Sir Henry Elliot Christianity seems to have no place. Humanity appears only as an offering of small account, which may be wisely offered up at the shrine of all-ruling interest.

I take this passage merely as a specimen. Coming as it does from an official person, couched in all the calmness of official language, it proves more than the wild outpourings which are sent forth daily and weekly by a certain section of the English press, a section for which the name "Mahometan press" is far too honourable. Their sneers, their revilings, are in truth the most honourable tribute which can be paid to the "shallow politicians" of Sir Henry Elliot's attempted sarcasm. With men to whom every noble sentiment, every generous feeling, seems simply matter of mockery, with men who by their sneers at "humanity" and "philanthropism" seem to proclaim their hatred of their own species, it is in vain to argue. One's labour would not be more utterly lost, if one argued with a tiger or a Turk. It is indeed sad and shameful that such men are ; but the only thought that we need give to them is the thought that their jeers and slander make the noblest wreath of honour that an honest man can twine around his brow.

I assume then the opposite doctrine. I assume, in opposition to Sir Henry Elliot, but in company with the Chatham of one age and the Gladstone of another, that there is such a thing as right and wrong in public affairs, and that nations have their duty before God and man as well as individuals. Sir Henry Elliot himself would perhaps allow the existence of duty in the case of private men. I cannot believe that he conducts his private affairs on the principles on which he would have us conduct the affairs of the nation. I cannot believe that, in his everyday dealings with his fellow-men, he would look on his own interest as plea enough for any breach of the laws of justice and humanity. Yet, if interest is not to be every thing, if right and wrong are to count for something, in the dealings of this and that man with his fellow, it is hard to see why interest is to be every thing and right and wrong to go for nothing, in the dealings of those aggregates of men which we call powers and nations.

For it must not be forgotten that powers and nations are simply aggregates of men, that every act of national right or wrong doing is really an act of personal right or wrong doing on the part of those men, few or many, whose will determines the national action. And, if interest is to be the only rule in national affairs, if it is to be a rule to which humanity is to give way, it is hard to see what acts of national perfidy and national cruelty may not be justified. A morality which holds that Bulgarian massacres are no ground for ceasing to uphold the power which is guilty of Bulgarian massacres, has little right to blame that power for " needless and monstrous severity " in the Bulgarian massacres themselves. If the Turk deemed the Bulgarian massacres to be for his interest, he did right, in Sir Henry Elliot's morality, in not allowing feelings of humanity to hinder him in following the course which interest dictated. If he was mistaken in thinking that the massacres were for his interest, that would be, in Sir Henry Elliot's morality, at most an error of judgement, and not a moral crime.

I make then one assumption. I make it as the geometer makes those few assumptions with which he starts, assumptions which he cannot prove, but which he deems can abundantly prove themselves. With those who deny that things which are equal to the same are equal to one another the geometer does not argue. With such an one he has no common ground for argument. So neither can the moralist argue with one who says either that there is no right and wrong, or that right or wrong concern private conduct only. With such an one he has no common ground for argument. I must make my assumption, as the geometer makes his. But having made the assumption at starting, I trust that I may, like the geometer, go on for the future, not with assumption, but with argument. I trust to shew, not indeed by geometrical proof, but by such proof as the nature of the subject allows, first that England has a duty in this matter, and secondly, that, in this matter interest and duty do not clash.

The duty of England and Europe towards the nations which are under the Turk is simply the duty of redressing a wrong which England and Europe have themselves done. Neither a man nor a nation is at all called upon to go all over the world seeking for wrongs to redress. If either a man or a nation undertook so to do, that man or that nation would soon find that there was very little time left to do anything else. Neither man nor nation is called upon to practise such mere knight-errantry as this. Nor does it necessarily follow that either a man or a nation is bound to go forth to redress wrongs, even when those who are suffering the wrongs call upon him to do so. It would be very hard to settle beforehand in what cases either a man or a nation is bound to give help to those who call upon him to give it. The duty of either man or nation in such matters must greatly depend on the circumstances of each particular case. But one thing no one will deny to be the duty of each particular man. If he has himself done a wrong, then it is his duty to redress that wrong. This will be denied by no one who professes any moral principle at all, by no one who believes that there are such things as right and wrong in the common dealings between man and man.

And—to make our one assumption once for all—if there be such a thing as right and wrong in public affairs, if nations are to be guided in their dealings with one another by the same moral rules by which private men ought to be guided in their dealings with one another, then it follows that, when a nation has done a wrong, it is the duty of that nation to redress that wrong. For a nation to say that it will not discharge this duty, because it is not for its interest to do so, is exactly as base as it would be for a private man to refuse to redress any wrong that he had done, because it would be against his interest to do so. Every kind of law, the law of honour, the law of the land, the law of morals, the law of religion, all say that a man who has done a wrong must redress that wrong. They all say he must redress it, even if it be against his interest to redress it. And the higher forms of teaching would go on to tell him that it was in any case his real interest to redress it. They would tell him that the approbation of his own conscience, the esteem of other men—the law of religion would add the approval of his Maker—are worth more than any sacrifice that he might make by doing right. So, if we believe that right and wrong are to be thought of in public affairs, if we do not think that a nation may do any cruelty, any perfidy, that it may fancy to be for its immediate interest, it follows that a nation is as much bound as a private man to redress any wrong that it has done. It must do right, even to the prejudice of its own interests. It may, if it pleases, comfort itself by thinking that, according to the true saying that honesty is the best policy, its interests will not suffer in the long run by doing its duty.

S

Now that England, and Europe in general, but England in a more marked way than any other nation of Europe, have done wrong to the subject nations of South-eastern Europe hardly needs proof. We need go no further than the passage which I quoted a few pages back from Sir Henry Elliot's letter to Lord Derby. Sir Henry Elliot there says, in so many words, "We have been upholding what we know to be a semi-civilized nation, liable under certain circumstances to be carried into fearful excesses." In other words, we have been upholding the Turk in his wicked dominion over Bulgaria, Thessaly, Crete, and the other subject lands. It is not merely that we have left things in those lands to take their own course; it is not merely that we have not helped the oppressed; we have actively helped the oppressor. This Sir Henry Elliot confesses. We have upheld him, upheld him, knowing, as Sir Henry Elliot goes on to say, what manner of thing it was that we were upholding. Knowing that the rule of the Turk was a rule of the foulest oppression, we have not merely done nothing to put an end to that oppression, we have actively upheld the oppressor in his oppression. All the powers that signed the treaty of Paris have been more or less guilty on this score. England has been more constantly and glaringly guilty than any other. We have throughout, for more than forty years, upheld the Turk, because we thought that it was for our own interest. That is, we have done as a nation towards other nations in a way which any man among us, Sir Henry Elliot I doubt not as well as any other man, would blush to do in common every day dealings between one man and another.

Our great crime of all, the general crime of
Europe, the great sin against the oppressed nations of
the East, was the signing of the treaty of Paris. By
that treaty, as I have before shewn, England and the
other powers bound themselves to let the Turk do
what he would with his Christian victims, and to do
nothing to hinder him. This was a very different
matter from merely not doing anything to help them,
or even from refusing to help them when they asked
us. It was not a mere negative omission; it was a
positive wrong. Before the Crimean war the
Christians under the rule of the Turk had a protector,
at least a power that claimed to be their protector, in
Russia. It is no use here to dispute either how far the
protectorate of Russia was formally acknowledged, or
how far the protection of Russia was either sincere
or effectual. Russia was at least a nominal and professed protector. Now it would have been perfectly
fair to argue that it was not well that the protection
of those nations should be left to Russia alone, but
that it would be better that all the other powers, or
some of them, should join with Russia in protecting
them. It might have been argued that such a joint
protectorate would be better for the general interests
of Europe, better even for the interests of the subject
nations themselves. To substitute such a protectorate
as this for the sole protectorate of Russia might have
been a wise and just measure. It might have been a
step towards getting rid of the Turk altogether. But
this was not what the treaty of Paris did. The treaty
of Paris took away from the subject nations what
little chance of protection they had, and it gave them
nothing instead. It took away the protectorate of
Russia, whatever that might be worth, and it put

S 2

nothing in its place. The powers pledged themselves
not to interfere with the relations between the Sultan
and his subjects, knowing what those relations were,
what they always must be. They handed over the
subject nations to the power of the Turk, with no
better guaranty than the Turk's paper of lying
promises. That is, they left the lamb in the jaws of
the wolf, with no safeguard except the wolf's promise
not to bite the lamb.

The fault in the matter of the treaty of Paris was no
special fault of England. It was shared by England
with the other powers which signed the treaty. But
there is no other power which has so steadily shewn
itself the friend of the Turk and the enemy of the
subjects of the Turk as England has done. There is
no other power which has so steadily, in the happy
phrase of Sir Henry Elliot, *upheld* the Turk. The
best proof of this is to be found in the feelings of the
Turks themselves. Through the whole of the doings
of the last two years, the Turks have always taken for
granted that England was their friend. It has been
hard to persuade them that England was not ready to
stand by them in any cause and against any enemy.
One instance will do among many. At one point of
the doings of last year, the English fleet was, as all
the world knows, sent to Besika Bay. Why it was
sent there was at the time not perfectly clear. As
happened more than once in the events of last year,
Lord Beaconsfield gave one reason and Lord Derby
another. It matters little what the real reason was.
The instructive point of the business is the way in
which it was looked upon by every man, Turk or
Christian, in the lands which were most concerned.
Every man, in those lands, Turk or Christian,

believed, rightly or wrongly, that the fleet was sent to encourage the Turks and to discourage the Christians. That such a belief could be general speaks more than any long argument as to the conduct of England in that part of the world, as to the reputation which the conduct of England has won for her in that part of the world. Turk and Christian, oppressor and oppressed, agreed in taking for granted that an English fleet could have come for no end except to carry on the usual work of England in upholding the oppressor. Nor was anything done to undeceive either Turk or Christian. Though it was known what Turk and Christian alike believed to be the reason of the fleet's coming, the fleet was still left there. That is, England, so far as England is represented by those who then and now rule England, was not unwilling that England should be looked upon by Turk and Christian alike as the friend of the Turk and the enemy of the Christian.

It is hardly needful to pile together instances to shew how truly Sir Henry Elliot speaks when he says that we have upheld the Turk. Our loans of money, our loans of men, our honours bestowed on the barbarian and the renegade, the Grand Cross of Omar, the Garter of Abd-ul-Medjid and Abd-ul-Aziz — the reception given to the last-named tyrant at the very moment when his hands were reeking with the blood of Crete — the hideous crime of refusing the shelter of English vessels to the Cretan refugees—that dark day of shame and sorrow when other nations did the work of humanity and Englishmen were forbidden to share in it—all the black doings of last year—the letters hounding the Turk on the patriots of Herzegovina—the other letters written to and fro to stir up Austria to depart from her wise and righteous policy during the first days of the war—the refusal of every note, of every proposition, from every other power which seemed likely to do any thing to lessen the sufferings of the oppressed nations—all these things, done by our rulers, uncensured by our Parliament, but branded in the movement of last autumn by the righteous and repentant voice of the English people—all these things form a black catalogue of wrong, a catalogue of deeds done to uphold the oppressor and to snatch away any shadow of hope that might arise in the breasts of his victims. The England of Canning and Codrington, the England of Byron and Hastings, has come to this, that the world knows us as the nation which upholds oppression for the sake of its own interests. We have indeed a national sin to redress and to atone for. We are verily guilty concerning our brother, in that we saw the anguish of his soul when he besought us and we would not hear. Nay, our guilt is deeper still. We have not only refused to listen to our brother's cry for help ; we have not merely looked on and passed by on the other side ; we have given our active help to the oppressors of our brother. We have "upheld" the foulest fabric of wrong that earth ever saw, because it was deemed that the interests of England were involved in "upholding" the wrong and trampling down the right.

Such a list as this might be made much longer. Perhaps one fact alone is a more speaking comment than all of the way in which England has "upheld" the Turk. The tale has often been told in full(⁴) ; all that I need do is to call it to remembrance. When Sir Henry Bulwer was British Ambassador at

Constantinople, a circular was sent to the British
consuls in the Turkish dominions, bidding them send
in an account of the state of the country. Another
letter went with the circular, bidding them make their
report as favourable as they could to the Turks.
One consul received the circular without the letter ;
he sat down and wrote a true account, a vivid picture of the horrors of Turkish rule. Then came the
Ambassador's letter, and the consul sat down and
wrote a humble apology for having spoken the truth.
No means then, not even deliberate falsehood, are
deemed too base, if they can anyhow help to "uphold"
the Turk. We may believe that Sir Henry Bulwer
would not have been guilty of falsehood, or of encouragement of falsehood, in any transaction between
man and man. But in his public character, the great
duty of upholding the Turk was held to override the
dull rules of every-day morality. In his character as
Ambassador, he was to carry out the old definition
of an Ambassador ; he was to act as "an honest man
sent to *lie* abroad for the good of his country."

Our national crime then is that we have upheld the
Turk for our own supposed interests. That is, for the
sake of our own supposed interests, we have doomed
the struggling nations to abide in their bondage. We
have doomed them to stay under a rule under which
the life and property of the Christian, the honour of
his wife, the honour of his children of both sexes alike,
are at every moment at the mercy of the savages
whom our august and cherished ally honours and
promotes in proportion to the blackness of their
deeds. We have, for our own interest, upheld the
power which has done its foul and bloody work in
Chios, at Damascus, and in Bulgaria, which is still

doing the same foul and bloody work wherever a victim is to be found. And, if we listen to Sir Henry Elliot, though we know all this, though we know it better than we ever did before, we are still to go on upholding the doers. We uphold the power whose daily work is massacre and worse than massacre. It matters not whether ten thousand or twenty thousand perish. We are still to uphold the slaughterer, for it is to our interest that he should not be shorn of his power of slaughtering.

Now, if there be any such thing as right and wrong in public affairs, if moral considerations are ever to come in to determine the actions of nations, it is hard to see how there can be deeper national guilt than this. Unjust wars, aggressions, conquests, are bad enough ; but they are hardly so bad as the calm, unblushing, upholding of wrong for our own interests. Men may be led into wars and aggressions by passion and excitement, by the fantasies of national honour and glory, even by generous feelings led astray. But here there is nothing to cloak the cold wickedness of a base and selfish policy. We look on, we count the cost, we see how the wrong-doer deals with his victim, and we determine to uphold the wrong-doer, because we think that to uphold him will suit some interest of our own. There is no question of national glory, no question of national honour, nothing which can stir up even a false enthusiasm. It is a calm mercantile calculation that the wrongs of millions of men will pay. This is the case as stated by Sir Henry Elliot ; this is the case as it is set forth by Lord Derby, and by all who follow him in the ostentatious setting forth of interest as the one motive of national action. I do not believe that so base a code of

national conduct will be approved by any large body
of thinking Englishmen.   It may indeed be approved
by those who glory in their shame, who make their
boast of putting justice and humanity out of sight,
whose pride is that they never feel, or that, if they
feel, they succeed in speedily stifling, all the higher
and more generous feelings of man's nature.   But
I would fain believe that, beyond such circles as
these, no deliberate approval would be given to the
base doctrine of making interest our only rule.   Some
may be misled by mere party-blindness.   Some may
be misled by the mere traditional repetition of meaningless formulæ.   But I do not believe that the bulk
of the English people are ready to affirm that the
conduct of the nation is to be systematically guided
by principles on which any honest man would shrink
from acting in the common affairs of daily life.

I assume then that wrong has been done, that we
are, as a nation, guilty of the sufferings of our Eastern
brethren.   I assume that, by upholding the Turk, we
have made ourselves, as a nation, partakers in his
crimes.   From this I infer that, where wrong has been
done, redress must be made.   I infer that we must not
merely fold our hands and let events take their course,
but that we must, as a nation, stand forth to undo the
wrong which, as a nation, we have done.   We must
do as we did fifty years ago, in those brighter days
when the policy of England was guided by an
Englishman with an English heart.   We must do as
Canning did.   We must stand forth, in common, if it
can be, with the other powers of Europe, or with so
many of them as will join us, or if all fail, alone in the
strength of a righteous cause, to undo the wrong that

we have done, to wipe away the tears that we have made to flow, to burst asunder the chains that we ourselves have riveted.   We must do it by peaceable means, if peaceable means can be made to serve our turn.   But, if peaceable means will not serve our turn, then, we must do it by force.   If we have to fight, we never can fight in a worthier cause.   We have fought for this and that dream of national glory—we have fought for this and that doctrine of the balance of power— we have fought to maintain the rights of this and that claimant of foreign crowns—we have even fought to maintain the Turk in his dominion ; let us now fight, if we must fight, as we fought fifty years back, for righteousness.   No army could ever march forth with so sure a certainty that every blow that it dealt would count among the good works of him that dealt it, as the army that should go forth to free the Greek and Slavonic lands from Turkish bondage.   Our thoughts go back to the days when crusades were still crusades, before the warriors of the cross had turned aside from their work to storm Zara and Constantinople, or to become the tools of papal vengeance either on Emperors or on so-called heretics. We should go forth with the pure zeal of the great assembly of Clermont ; we should put the cross upon our shoulders with the cry of " God wills it " on our lips and in our hearts.

For force then, for coercion in the euphemistic language of our times, that is, in plain words, for war, if war be needful—that is, not war on behalf of the oppressor, but on behalf of the oppressed—not war for the Turk as in 1854, but war against the Turk as in 1827—we must stand ready.   But the readier we are for war, the more fully we have made up our mind for

war if war be needed, the less likely it will be that war
will be needed. A real union of the powers of Europe,
a real and frank union between England and Russia,
can do all that is needed without war. If England
can once make up her mind to act cordially with
other powers, if she will cease to reject every proposal,
to put stones in every path, to put spokes in every
wheel, the thing may be done. The one thing to be
fully understood must be that, though it may be done
without fighting, it cannot be done by mere talking.
Those who know the Turk know how to deal with the
Turk.   They know how little his brag really goes
for, if it is met as it ought to be met.   The bully is at
heart a coward.   He will yield, if he once fully under-
stands that nothing will be yielded to him.   With
the Turk it is as easy to gain a great point as a small
one ; it is as easy to take the ell as to take the inch.
To mere talk he will never yield the inch ; to real
firmness he will at once yield the ell.   All who have
had practical dealings with the barbarians know this.
When they have gained any point, they have gained
it, not by talk, not by empty courtesy, but by strong
words and strong deeds, by bringing to bear on the
barbarian mind the one argument which the barbarian
mind can understand, by cowing the wild beast by
sheer fear.   By a resolute mien and resolute words,
unarmed Europeans have made parties of armed
Turks tremble before them, and turn about and do
their bidding like humble slaves.   It is exactly so in
dealings on a greater scale.   The Turk brags as long
as he thinks that there is anything to be gained by
bragging.   As soon as he finds that nothing can be
gained by bragging, he knocks under to the power
which he knows to be stronger than his own.

The whole mistake lies in dealing with the Turk as the civilized nations of Europe deal with one another. He should be dealt with as we deal with any other barbarian. We have already seen that certain Turks have learned to talk European languages, and to dress themselves up in European clothes. It must always be remembered that this makes no difference. The men who ordered the massacres in Bulgaria wear tight coats and jabber French, and expect to be called Highnesses and Excellencies. But they ordered the massacres in Bulgaria all the same. They ought to be dealt with, not as Highnesses and Excellencies, but as the men who ordered the massacres in Bulgaria. Their tight coats and French ought not to save them from being treated as what they are, as wild beasts who have put themselves out of the pale of human fellowship. Above all, the Turk should be made to understand that his word goes for nothing. He has lied too often to be believed. Reason and experience tell us that, when a man has lied nine hundred and ninety-nine times, it is foolish to believe in the thousandth time. It is only the foolish sentimentalists, the people who talk about the Turk being a "gentleman," the people who think it proves something that he does not shake hands (⁵), who would have us trust the convicted liar once again. The Turk should be made to feel that his most solemn assertions, his most solemn promises, the pledges of this and that Excellency, of this and that Highness, or of his Imperial Majesty himself, are simply words without meaning. He should be told that his Irades and his Tanzimats, his Hatti-sheriffs and his Hatti-humayouns, are all so many names which the copiousness of the Turkish language has devised to express the single idea of waste paper. He must be told that his Midhat constitution is simply a mockery, a delusion, and a snare, a net spread in the sight of the birds who ought to be too wise to be caught by it. When the Turk feels that Europe knows what he is, and has made up its mind to treat him as what he is, there will be an end of his brag, an end of his lying. He will most likely crouch humbly and accept his fate at the hand of his masters. If he chooses to rush upon his doom, Europe is surely strong enough to do execution on the convicted criminal.

This is the way which reason and experience teach us to deal with the Turk. Any other way of dealing with him lies without the range of practical politics. To put trust in him, to accept his promises as going for anything, springs either from silly sentimentalism, which still puts faith in the "gentleman," murderer and liar as he has shewn himself, or else it springs from a guilty shrinking from the discharge of duty, or indeed from doing anything at all. Perhaps the very height of blindness, the highest point that could be reached in the art of doing nothing, the art of cowardly shrinking from duty, is to be found in a short letter from Lord Derby to Lord Salisbury dated December 22, 1876.([6]) Lord Derby there says "that Her Majesty's Government have decided that England will not assent to or assist in coercive measures, military or naval, against the Porte." He adds, "the Porte must on the other hand be made to understand, as it has from the first been informed, that it can expect no assistance from England in the event of war." That is to say, the Conference was to do nothing. It was settled beforehand that nothing was to come of it. It was absolutely certain, in any but the blinded eyes of a Foreign Secretary, that the Turk would do nothing except under coercion. Yet it is laid down as a rule that England will not join in coercion. Even if other powers do, England will not The European concert is to be broken, the arm of justice is to be stayed, because Lord Derby either has a sentimental belief in the power of talk, or else because he is afraid to do anything at all. To do something for the Turk, to do something against the Turk, are courses of which one is wrong and the other right, but both of which come within the range of practical politics. To expect that the Turk will yield anything to talk, when he knows that it will be all talk and that no coercion will be used, is the very height of silly sentimentalism. The simplicity of what follows is indeed charming. "In the event of the Porte persisting in refusing and the Conference failing, your Excellency will of course come away." What would the Porte do except persist in refusing when the Porte knew that it would gain everything by refusing and nothing by yielding? How could the Conference do otherwise than fail, when it was agreed beforehand that nothing was to come of it? The Conference failed, because it was doomed to failure before it met. It was doomed to failure, because the representatives of Europe, instead of calling up the convicted criminal to hear his sentence, admitted two of the Ring, two of the Highnesses and Excellencies who had ordered the Bulgarian massacres, to sit with them as equals, and one of them to take his place as president of an assembly of civilized men. We have already seen that the falsehoods with which Safvet opened the Conference were contradicted by both the English and the Russian ministers. But something more was needed than a contradiction. The liar should have been taught his place ; he should have been made to understand that his talk went for nothing. He should have been told that Europe had come together, not to hear him talk, but to pronounce sentence upon him. Instead of this, point after point was yielded. When the first point was yielded, all was over. Indeed all was over before anything began ; all was over when the barbarian criminal was allowed to take his place among his European judges.

The Conference then failed. It could not but fail. And, now that it has failed, one might appeal to a feeling which once was strong in the hearts of Englishmen, a feeling not so high as the sense of duty, but at least higher than the mere base reckoning of interest. Is the honour of England dead ? Does no man among the rulers or the people of England feel his cheeks tingle at the insult that England and all Europe has received at barbarian hands ? There were times when English swords would have leaped from their scabbards at far lighter ignominy than that which England and Europe bore then. Surely they never bore greater shame than when their representatives were brought together simply to hear that a barbarian power which lingers on only by their sufferance would have none of their counsels and none of their reproof. The Turk snapped his fingers in the face of England and of Europe ; he shewed England and Europe the way to the door ; and England and Europe have walked out quietly. There is, at least there was, such a feeling as national self-respect. In the Government, in the people, which can tamely endure such treatment as this from a power which needs our upholding, that feeling of self-respect would seem to be wholly dead. In the new code of conduct we are taught that right and humanity are to be offered up to the Moloch of interest. It would seem that the honest sense of shame, to say nothing of the feeling of knightly honour, are to be cast into the fire along with them.

We see then that, in the name of morality, there is something to be done, and that, in the name of common sense, it must set about being done in some other quite different way than what was done at the late Conference. The proposals made at that Conference all lay out of the range of practical politics. They were all sentimental proposals, proposals which could never be carried out, because they all went on the supposition that the Turk might possibly do something without being forced to do it. Such a supposition is belied by all experience ; it is therefore wholly unpractical. I must here insist more fully on a doctrine which I have already laid down, that in settling the affairs of the South-eastern lands, two points must be laid down as principles, without which no lasting or satisfactory settlement can be made. In any land on which it is proposed to bestow freedom—I use the plain word freedom, not the silly word "autonomy," invented by diplomatists, because it may mean anything or nothing—in any such land no Turkish soldier must be allowed to tread, and the Turk must have no voice in the appointment of its rulers, magistrates, or officers, high or low. Every proposal which does not embody these principles lies without the range of practical politics. Any proposal which does not embody them can never lead to any lasting reform, because it leaves with the Turk the power of undoing whatever is done the moment the back of Europe is turned. There was talk of confining Turkish troops to particular spots, and of giving the Turk a voice along with the European powers in the choice of Governors. It is curious to read how this very moderate form of restraint was met by a Turk, as shown in a letter of Sir Henry Elliot to Lord Derby, dated December 30, 1876.([7]) He there describes a conversation which he had had with Midhat Pasha. Midhat, it should be remembered, besides being one of the Ring who ordered the great Bulgarian massacre, had already been Governor of Bulgaria. He had there undoubtedly made some improvements in the way of roads and the like, improvements of that kind which might be useful for the ruling powers. But his personal cruelties and excesses of other kinds are already written in the pages of Bulgarian history.([8]) With this man Sir Henry Elliot had "long been intimate." The proposals of the European powers were thus commented on by the Turk talking to his "intimate" English friend.

"The project, as it now stood, would be a step towards the certain realization of the Russian dream of creating small autonomic states in European Turkey.

"We had only to look back to what had occurred fifty years ago in Servia to become convinced that the compulsory confinement of the Ottoman troops to the fortresses and principal towns would shortly lead to the expulsion of the Turks from the Province, and the establishment of *quasi* independence."

It would seem from this confession that the blessings of Ottoman rule, as set forth by Safvet at the opening of the Conference, even the special blessings of the personal rule of Midhat, were not fully appreciated

T

in Bulgaria. Bulgaria, like Servia, sought for independence. It had no love for the presence of Ottoman troops. But Midhat must have given his English "intimate" credit for a large amount of ignorance of Servian history. "What occurred fifty years ago in Servia," to which this Turk ventures to appeal, was the brutal breach of faith on the part of the Turks, when they impaled men to whom their lives had been promised. Midhat feared that even the mild proposals of the Conference would hinder himself or any other Turk in Bulgaria from doing the same again. He feared that the presence of foreign commissioners, of foreign troops, of foreign *gendarmerie*, would hinder him or any other Turk from bombarding any Christian city which they fancied to bombard, as they bombarded Belgrade only fifteen years back. The barbarian is wise in his generation. He will admit of no restraint on his power of doing evil. He will not endure that the barbarian troops should be confined to particular places, least of all to places like large towns, where numbers, and in some cases the presence of Europeans, may be some slight check. He and his fellows must have the whole land to range through unrestrained, and to do their pleasure on all whom they find in the land. Servia is free; the Turk has left her soil; life, property, family honour, are safe within her boundaries. Such an example is not lost upon Midhat. He will allow no step which shall look at all in the direction of extending these blessings to Bulgaria. One land has escaped from his clutches; he has learned to be all the more careful lest another land should escape from them also.

The example of Servia to which Midhat appeals in this conversation is indeed an instructive one. It

proves the whole point. Servia is free, Servia flou-
rishes, because the direct power of the Turk has
wholly ceased within its borders. It is tributary and
no more. Turkish soldiers are no longer quartered
on any spot of the emancipated land. The Turk has
no voice in the choice of prince or minister or magistrate for any spot on Servian soil. As long as Servia
was under Turkish rule, the land was as wretched as
Bosnia or Bulgaria. The extinction of Turkish rule
has made the change. Only ten years ago, while
there were still Turkish garrisons in certain places,
those places were still exposed to the crimes and
outrages which are implied in the presence of Turkish
garrisons. The Turkish garrisons are gone, and the
people of Belgrade and the other towns which are
delivered from their presence are as safe as any inhabitants of other Christian towns elsewhere. In the
eyes of Midhat this state of things naturally seems
like the loss of a victim. For that very reason, Europe
should the more strongly insist on the deliverance of
the other victims of Midhat and his fellows. Midhat's
objection to confining the garrisons to certain points
proves that the confining them to certain points would
be a gain. His fears that such confinement would
lead to total expulsion may be read as a hope that it
will lead to total expulsion. But the experience of
Servia proves that the confining the enemy to certain
spots is not enough. As long as there is a Turkish
garrison in any Bulgarian town, that town may at any
moment be dealt with as Belgrade was in 1862. Therefore no Turkish soldier must be allowed to set foot
in any land which is supposed to be set free. The
usual law comes in. It is as easy to get much out of
the Turk as to get little. It will cost no more trouble

to compel the Turk to take away his garrisons altogether than it will cost to compel him to confine them to certain places. The Turk will never submit to restriction without coercion ; under coercion he will submit as easily to the greater restriction as to the less.

One practical lesson then is learned by the example of Servia; Turkish troops must be shut out of every land which it is designed to set free. The other great principle is that the Turk shall have no voice in the appointment of any one who is to bear rule or office in the liberated lands, be he a prince or be he a beadle. It is vain to stipulate that the governors or other officers to be appointed shall be natives, or that they shall be Christians. The Turk can always find Christians as ready to do his work as any Mussulman. He finds Greeks ready to do his work of falsehood at European courts ; he has found at least one Englishman ready to do his work of blood in Crete. The native who sells himself and his country for the pay of a foreign master will always be a worse ruler than the foreign master himself. In truth, one would rather be ruled by those worthy Mussulmans who refused to do the work of blood in Bulgaria than by any Christian who would take the pay of the Turk. Nor is it anything to say that these governors shall be appointed with the approval of European powers. Of all the proposals in the world this is one which is most sure to lead to what diplomatists so greatly fear by the names of "difficulties" and "complications." Such a proposal is a very seed-plot of difficulties and complications. The Turk is cunning, and he will be sure to find some way of setting the powers together by the ears, and of getting his own way by the help of some of them. Once more, the appeal is to experience. Look at Roumania under the rule of princes who, though Christians, were nominees of the Turk. Look at Roumania now under the rule of an independent prince. Doubtless there are things to amend in the state of Roumania, as there are in the state of other lands. But it is perfectly certain that, whatever Roumania has still to mend, she has gained much since she attained a practical freedom, and that whatever still needs mending in her will not be mended any the quicker by giving the Turk a voice in her affairs.

Two principles then are to be laid down, two principles which are taught us by the witness of experience. Wherever it is meant to give any degree of freedom, to work any degree of reform, within those borders the presence of Turkish troops must be forbidden, and the Turk must be shut out from any voice in the internal affairs of those lands. These are the only guaranties which are really any guaranties at all. They are the only securities against a continuance or a revival of all the horrors of Turkish rule. Any proposals which do not start from those two principles lie without the range of practical politics. They may be dictated by a sentimental regard for the honour, the dignity, or the susceptibility of the Turk. They may be dictated by a desire to escape for the moment from the hard necessity of doing something. They are not dictated by a rational regard for the welfare of the lands that are to be benefited, or for the permanence of the reforms which it is sought to make. Lord Derby once sneeringly spoke of "the eternal Eastern Question." He forgot perhaps that it was his own do-nothing policy which has done more than anything else to make the Eastern Question eternal. For, as long as attempts at settlement are made which are not founded on these two principles, the Eastern Question will remain eternal. It will always be cropping up again, because nothing practical will have been done to settle it. But these two provisions will secure, at least negatively, the freedom and good government of any land to which they are applied. That is, they will take away the great hindrance to freedom and good government, namely the power of the Turk. They may not settle the Eastern Question for ever, but they will settle one stage of it ; they will make the way ready for a full and final settlement.

These two points, the shutting out of Turkish garrisons and the denial to the Turk of any voice in the appointment of governors, are matters of principle, matters of absolute necessity. Everything else is matter of detail, in settling which all manner of particular circumstances may rightly be taken into account. I felt no call here to bring forward any cut and dried scheme. To draw up any minute scheme would be impossible without going into minute inquiries as to the condition and prospects of every province, almost of every district. It is necessary alike for Bosnia and for Thessaly that both those lands should be set free from Turkish soldiers and from rulers appointed by the Turk. It does not follow that the political state which would be best for Bosnia would be best for Thessaly. Shall the liberated lands become wholly independent states ? Shall they be united by any federal tie ? Shall they, or any of them, remain in an external vassalage to the Turk ? Shall any of them be annexed to existing states, tributary or independent ? Shall their

constitutions be monarchic or republican? Shall
their princes be hereditary or elective? All these
are important, and some of them difficult, questions,
questions which are not to be answered off hand,
questions to which no single answer can be given, but
which must be answered one by one, according to
the particular circumstances of each district. The
point is that, under any of these systems or forms of
government, freedom and good government are at
least possible ; under the direct rule of the Turk they
are impossible. Let the liberated lands be as Greece,
let them be as Montenegro, let them be as Servia, let
them be as Dalmatia. In any of these cases, they
will be better off than they can be if they remain as
Bosnia and Bulgaria are now. In any of these cases,
it is possible—it is enough to say "possible," without going on to "probable" or "certain"—that the
essentials of good government and civilized order
may be had. Where the Turk either sends troops
or appoints rulers, they never can be had.

The question will now naturally come, to what
lands are these advantages to be granted? The
answer doubtless is to as many lands as possible.
The greater the number of human beings that are set
free from the yoke of the Turk, the greater the gain
for mankind. But the Turk grew by degrees, and
something may be said for letting him die out by
degrees. The Roman world was once, in Gibbon's
words, confined to a corner of Thrace ; and it may be
no unnatural stage in the course of events if for a
while the Turkish world, as far as Europe is concerned,
should be confined to the same corner of Thrace also.
As a matter of feeling, as a matter of historic

memory, the recovery of the Imperial City would be the foremost object of all. Before thoughts of Bosnia and Bulgaria, before thoughts of Thessaly and Crete, would come the cleansing of the New Rome, the chasing of the barbarian from the throne of the Cæsars, the driving out of the misbeliever from the mighty temple of Justinian. But, in a calmer view, if the essential freedom of the Greek and Slavonic lands can be purchased by letting the barbarian still linger on a little while within the bounds of Constantinople, let that sacrifice be made. In Constantinople the Turk is less mischievous than he is anywhere else. He cannot, in the great city, under the eyes of Europeans, indulge the same frantic excesses of tyranny which form his daily sport in Bosnia and Bulgaria. Again, till Greek and Bulgarian have settled their differences and drawn their boundary line, till it is settled whether the next Cæsar of the East shall be a successor of Basil or a successor of Samuel, it may be as well to keep the glittering prize out of the hands of either claimant. If then Bulgaria and Bosnia and Herzegovina, Albania, Epeiros, and Thessaly, Crete and every island of the Ægæan, are set free from the direct rule of the Turk, let him, if such is to be the price, still tarry for a while in New Rome. If it pleases Turkish susceptibility, or rather if it would better win the good will of any European power, let the Sultan still be over-lord ; let him still take tribute from the lands which are freed from his yoke; let him exercise a Sultan's right of squandering that tribute as he will. The Highnesses and the Excellencies may lose ; but the Imperial Majesty will not lose. The Highnesses and Excellencies will lose their power of mischief ; the Imperial Majesty may still wallow in a marble sty and gorge itself out of a gilded trough. The lands would be set free ; their people might be flourishing and happy. The sum of human happiness would be increased ; the nations would be happier; the Sultan would not be less happy; the nations might again live the life of nations ; the Sultan might go on living the life of a Sultan ; it is only the Ring and its tools, the Highnesses and the Excellencies, who would lose by such an arrangement, and all that they would lose would be the power of doing evil.

The plan of tributary states thus seems to be the least violent form of change, and yet to be change enough to secure all immediate practical objects. That plan is the one practical course, the course which experience dictates ; there are none but sentimental objections to it. But there is one of those sentimental objections which takes a somewhat plausible shape. To those who have studied these questions all their lives it is amusing to see how certain writers in the weekly and daily press, who have just found out for the first time that there are such beings as Slavonic-speaking Mussulmans, are suddenly kindled with a burning zeal for the welfare of these same Slavonic-speaking Mussulmans. The same men who think the slaughter and outrage of any number of Christians a mere joke, who sneer at humanity and philanthropy when Christians are their objects, who put "atrocity" in inverted commas when it is a Christian who suffers the atrocity, who put "insurrection" in inverted commas when it is a Christian who rises against his oppressor—these men are very eager, sometimes in sentences of wild screaming, sometimes in sentences of lumbering solemnity, to set forth the possible wrongs of the Bosnian Mahometans, in case Bosnia should ever be put under a Christian government. Those who sneer at philanthropy on behalf of a Christian victim can become wonderfully philanthropic on behalf of a Mussulman oppressor. Those who will not allow the "atrocity" of evil deeds when the Christian is the sufferer, shriek with horror at the "atrocity" the moment the Christian is the possible doer. Those who will hardly bring themselves to believe that the Turk is other than a suffering lamb clutch at the faintest shadow of rumour to paint the revolted patriot as a wolf. Let this kind of folly pass. We might indeed answer that no great wrong would be done in the long run, if the oppressing minority and the oppressed majority were to change places for a season. But a worthier answer may be given. The abolition of the direct rule of the Turk is as much needed in the interest of the peaceable and orderly Mussulman, who conscientiously follows his own law and is ready to leave his Christian neighbour to follow his, as it is in the interest of the Christian himself. Such Mussulmans no one wishes to injure ; no one wishes to make them the subjects or inferiors of the Christians, or to put them under any disability as compared with the Christians. To them the rule of the Sultan, that is in truth the rule of the corrupt and bloody gang at Constantinople, is almost as oppressive, though not quite in the same way, as it is to the Christian himself. The disabilities of the Christian often wrong the peaceful Mussulman as well as the Christian. A wanton murder of Mussulman by Mussulman has been known to go unpunished when Christian witnesses only could prove the fact.([9]) Peaceable Mussulmans, who keep those virtues which are said to distinguish the private Turk from the official Turk, would have a far more favourable field for the practice of those virtues under a Christian government. Such a government could give equal justice to all its subjects, and to them among the rest. Such equal justice they cannot find under a government which corrupts part of its subjects by giving them a power of oppressing the rest.

While the notion of good government for the Christian under Mussulman rule is purely dreamy and sentimental, to secure good government for the peaceable Mussulman by putting him under Christian rule is in every way practical. Those who know the Mussulman character best believe that the peaceable Mahometan population, where there is any, would sit down in perfect contentment under a government of any kind which would relieve them from the oppression of their present masters at Constantinople, and would respect their religion and customs. The Bulgarian beys with whom Mr. Calvert talked invited of their own accord the help of an European in the administration of the province. They complained of the ruling powers at Constantinople almost as strongly as the Christians did. On two points only would they support the powers at Constantinople; they would not be annexed by Russia; they would not "have the Bulgarians put over their heads."([10]) Most certainly no one wishes to annex them to Russia; no one wishes to put the Bulgarians " over their heads," in the sense in which they have hitherto been put over the heads of the Bulgarians. Even in the land where oppression has been worst of all, the Bosnian beys, the descendants of renegades, still keeping up the old spite of the

renegade, are described none the less as very lax
votaries of Islam, as remembering their Christian
descent, as treasuring up the patents of nobility which
their forefathers received from the ancient Christian
kings. Those who know them well think that, if
they were put under a Christian government, their
reconversion would not be hard ; the bey would
easily slide back into the baron. At this very moment some of them are crying out for an Austrian
occupation of their country ; in other parts the native
Mussulmans are rising against the corrupt rule of the
Ring, against a constitution which is as great a
mockery for them as it is for the Christians. In short,
we have again only to make our old appeal to experience. Both Greek and Slavonic experience teach that
under a Mussulman government Mussulmans and men
of other religions cannot live together on equal terms.
English and Russian experience teaches that under a
Christian government Mussulmans and men of other
religions can live together on equal terms. In truth
Greek and Slavonic experience proves the same also.
There is a mosque at Chalkis and there is a mosque
at Belgrade. In this war even Mussulman refugees
have found a hospitable shelter in Montenegro. The few
Mahometans at Chalkis suffer no wrong or disability.
At Belgrade the case is still more instructive. When
the Turkish garrison left Belgrade, the settled Mussulman population went also. But why did they go ?
Not by their own free will; not by the will of the Servians, who wished them to stay. They went by orders
from Constantinople, where the ruling powers wished to
make a case again Servia, as if Servia had driven them
out. But the mosque is there still; and its minister
is paid by the Servian state for his services towards

any Mussulman remnant that may be left, or towards any Mussulman travellers that may pass by. Here surely there can be no charge of intolerance ; there may be some ground for disestablishment.

In the particular case of Bosnia, if any special safeguard is needed, the safeguard is plain. I believe that either the Servian government in case of annexation, or a native Bosnian government in case of the foundation of a separate state, would be both able and willing to do justice to its Mussulman subjects. But, if it be thought otherwise, there is a neighbouring power which is quite able to do all that is needed. Let the King of Slavonia, Croatia, and Dalmatia become King of Bosnia also.([11])

Another question may be raised, Are our thoughts in this matter to be directed only to Europe ? Is Asia to go for nothing ? It is undoubtedly a fact that Turkish rule has done its work yet more thoroughly in Asia than in Europe. It has been even more utterly desolating and blighting. It has more thoroughly turned the garden into a wilderness. We ask for the seats of Greek colonization, of Macedonian and Roman rule, for the cities famous in the early days of ecclesiastical lore and ecclesiastical controversy. A far greater proportion of them than in Europe have utterly perished; a far greater proportion, if they have not utterly perished, have ceased to be the abodes of Christian and civilized men. The territory of ancient commonwealths and kingdoms has become the pasture of a few wandering herdsmen. To win those lands back again to civilized rule would indeed be a noble work. It would be a noble work too to free Syria, all its races, all its creeds, united in nothing else, but united in hatred towards the

Ottoman master, from the yoke which equally weighs down all the representatives of all the older inhabitants of the land. Yet it is in Asia, in the Anatolian peninsula and in the Anatolian peninsula only, that the Turk is really at home. The Ottoman is hardly at home even there; but the Turk, the representative of the earlier and better Turkish races, is at home. There alone can we speak of a really Turkish nation or people, as distinguished from a mere Turkish army of occupation. Europe and Asia then stand on different grounds, and at all events the settlement of Europe is the nearer and the more pressing claim. In Europe the rule of the Turk must be wholly got rid of; in Asia the Turk may be left alone in those parts where he really forms the people of the land, provided full room for freedom and developement is given to that fringe of civilization which still, as of old, cleaves to the Euxine and Ægæan coasts. The line of Othman is worn out; but a Seljuk Sultan at Ikonion need be the object of no more dislike or jealousy than a Shah of Persia.

Our argument then seems perfect. Granting our one assumption to start with, the stages follow on one another almost like a demonstration in Euclid. If there be such a thing as right and wrong in national affairs, then a nation which has done wrong to another nation is bound to make redress to that nation. England has done deep wrong to those nations of Europe which are under the rule of the Turk. Therefore England is bound to make redress to those nations. But no real redress can be made to them as long as they are left under the direct rule of the Turk. Therefore they must be set free from the direct rule of the Turk, and put in a relation at least not worse than the present relation of Roumania and Servia. And this can be done, most likely without fighting, if only the powers of Europe, or some of them, will agree to deal with the Turk in the only way in which it is any use trying to deal with him.   And such an agreement with other powers may be made, if only England will leave off making objections to every scheme which seems likely to do the least good to the oppressed nations.   In a word our duty is plain, our duty is easy ; we have nothing to do but to do it.

And it must be done at once.   The tales which come day by day from every corner of the lands which still groan under Turkish tyranny might move the heart of a Turk ; they have moved the hearts of some Turks, of those good Turks whom the Ring punished for their goodness.   One might almost think that they were enough to move the heart of an Ambassador or a Foreign Secretary.   Every day we hear the same tales of murder and robbery and burning, of insult and outrage of every kind, which show that those relations between the Sultan and his subjects of which the treaty of Paris was so tender have at least not changed for the better since the treaty of Paris. So it is, so it ever has been ; so it ever will be, as long as an inch of Christian soil is left under the wasting rule of the barbarian.   There must be no delay, no shilly-shallying, no cowardly or sentimental chatter about a year of grace.   It is enough to tell us what the year of grace means, that it was proposed by the Turk himself through the voice of Midhat.[12]   It means that the Turk wants a little longer time to work his wicked will on Eastern Christendom, and that for that end, he wants a little more time to throw dust in the eyes of Western Christendom.   A year's grace is asked to carry out reforms.   What reason is there to

think that these reforms would be any more carried
out than the reforms which have been promised a
hundred times before ?   What reason is there to think
that, if they were carried out, they would do the
slightest good to the oppressed nations ?   For they
would not take away the rule of the Turk, and where
the rule of the Turk is there can be no reform.   The
year of grace will be spent in putting on a little
varnish and veneer in places where European eyes
are likely to see it, while the back parts of the
fabric of rottenness will remain untouched.   It will
be spent in whitening the sepulchre which will
still be full within of dead men's bones and of all
uncleanness.   It will be spent in setting things so as
to make a fair show at Constantinople and Thessalonica and a few other places where deluded Europeans
will see the show, while the relations between the
Sultan and his subjects, the relations from which
Midhat complains that Servia is set free, will go on
as ever in the dark places of Bosnia and Bulgaria, of
Thessaly and Crete.   Yet it would seem that there
are Englishmen, that there are English statesmen,
who cannot or will not see through such a flimsy
cheat as this.   The net is set in vain in the sight of
any bird, but it may be set openly enough in the eyes
of an English Foreign Secretary.   Or is it merely
the shrinking from doing anything, the cowardly hope
that, in the space of a year, something may happen
to save the sad necessity of action and decision ?
" The King may die, or the ass may die, or I may die
myself."   And this hand-to-mouth way of doing
things, this helpless waiting on something—hardly on
Providence—is what nowadays is called statesmanship.
A statesman now is not the man who strives by the

lessons of the present and the past to shape his course for the future; it is the man who can devise some petty momentary shift to save himself from the trouble and responsibility of taking any course at all. Rather than face the responsibility of making up his mind to do anything, the modern statesman will face the responsibility of condemning suffering nations to go on bearing their sufferings unhelped and unpitied. To such a statesman as this the notion of a year of grace, a year in which he may save himself from acting or thinking, is a Godsend indeed. Those who do not wilfully shut their eyes, those who walk by the light of reason and experience, would be inclined, instead of talking of a year of grace, to echo the cry, Now or never, now and for ever. Of all the schemes which lie beyond the range of practical politics, surely official weakness and cowardice never lighted on a scheme which lay further beyond that range than the scheme of giving the Turk a year of grace to work his sham reforms.

The main argument then stands thus; but there are one or two by-points to which it may be well to give a word or two. We are told over and over again that, after all, the Turks are no worse than other people, that Christian governments and Christian nations have done things just as bad, that the Turks and the Christians in the South-eastern lands are both very bad, that there is nothing to choose between them, and that we shall do best to leave them to themselves. Now most of these statements are quite false, and the arguments which are founded on them are the merest fallacies. Still there is just enough truth mixed with the falsehood to make the

U

falsehood more dangerous. It may be therefore worth while to point out where the falsehood and fallacy lies.

One argument on behalf of the Turk, that which is drawn from the fact that Christians are said to have done things equally bad, has spread to the Turks themselves. At the Conference, when the Turks Safvet and Edhem were trying to deceive the European ministers by quibbles about the meaning of the word "Bulgaria," they had the further impudence to speak of certain doings in France in past times, as the massacre of Saint Bartholomew and the *dragonnades*, as parallels to the doings which they had themselves ordered. The French ministers were naturally angry.([13]) The Turks doubtless thought that they were saying something clever, arid showing their knowledge of European history. But what they said was very little to the purpose. If Turks do evil now, it does not make that evil any the less to say that Frenchmen do evil even now, much less to say that Frenchmen did evil a long time ago. Let it be proved that Charles the Ninth or Lewis the Fourteenth was as bad as Safvet himself, that does not make Safvet any the better. Comparisons of this kind prove nothing. But, if it can be proved that the government of Marshal MacMahon, even that the government of Louis-Napoleon Buonaparte, is much better than that of Charles the Ninth, but that the government of Midhat, Edhem, and Safvet is much worse than that of Suleiman the Lawgiver, something is proved the other way. When we see that all the European governments, whatever faults they may still have, have changed greatly for the better during the last three hundred years, while the rule of the Turk has simply got worse and worse, we are brought back to the distinctions which we drew in an earlier chapter. The worst form of misgovernment in an European state is after all only the corruption or perversion of a thing which is in itself good and which therefore may be reformed. The rule of the Turk is in itself evil, and cannot be reformed. It is perfectly true that European governments, therefore that Christian governments, have in past times done particular acts which were as bad, or nearly as bad, as the doings of the Turk. But the worst doings of Christian governments have been in a manner incidental. They have been the crimes of particular men or of particular ages. They are not the necessary consequence of any form of the Christian religion, or of any form of government, from despotism to democracy, which has ever existed in any European state. Therefore European governments have left off doing such things. All European governments have mended ; some have mended more than others, but all have mended more or less. The very worst have mended so far as to be a great deal better than the rule of the Turk. Take the country which we commonly think has mended least of any in Western Europe. Take Spain. A Spanish Protestant a hundred years back was liable and likely to be burned alive. He would have been better off as a Christian subject of the Turk. But now, though the Spanish Protestant complains with good reason of vexatious restrictions on the public practice of his religion, yet his life and property are as safe as those of the Catholic. He would not now be better off by becoming a Christian subject of the Turk. Christian governments have done particular acts as bad as those of the Turk. But no Christian government has been evil in its very nature in the way in which the rule of the Turk is evil. No Christian government has gone on ruling so badly for so long a time as the Turk has done. For any European government is, in its idea, a government of men by rulers of their own nation, established for the general good of the nation. It may carry out that idea more or less perfectly; but the idea is in itself a good one, and, when it is departed from in practice, reforms may bring things nearer to what they ought to be. But the idea of the Turkish rule in Europe is a thing which is bad in itself. It is always and essentially, not now and then and incidentally, the rule of men of one religion over men of another religion, carried on in the interest of the men of the ruling religion only. Its very nature involves the subjugation and degradation of the mass of the people of the land; and subjugation and degradation are sure to grow into direct oppression and outrage of every kind. Therefore the worst European government is only misgovernment, the abuse of a good thing which may be reformed. The rule of the Turk is not government at all. It is a thing evil in itself, which cannot be reformed, but which, like other evil things, is sure to get worse and worse.

Let us take the things which, if they are true, are worst of all. Let us take the worst stories which have been told of the doings of Russia in Poland and in Turkestan. I need not enter into the truth of either; for argument's sake, let us take them at the worst.([14]) If the worst stories are true, nay, even if we take off a good deal from the worst stories, no right-minded man will defend them. Still they are quite different

from the doings of the Turk. The worst stories from
Turkestan are after all not so bad as the doings in
Bulgaria. The element of brutal outrage and mockery,
for the sake of outrage and mockery, is wanting. And
in any case all these things are incidental. They
are done towards enemies or revolters. The particular doings in Bulgaria might also be said to be
done to enemies and revolters. But then something
of the same kind, though not so much of it at,
once, is always going on in the Turkish dominions,
whether there are any revolts or not. The worst
things that have been said, truly or falsely, of any
Russian in Poland or Turkestan are incidental evils
which might be reformed. They are not always
going on in all times and in all places under the
Russian dominion. But doings of the same kind are
always going on in all times and in all places under
the Turkish dominion. For they are the direct consequence of the nature of the rule of the Turk, and
therefore they cannot be reformed.

Perhaps the most striking way of shewing the
difference between governments which can improve
and governments which can only get worse is to look
at the signatures to the treaty of 1856, and to compare
the history of the powers which signed it during the
twenty-one years that have passed. That treaty was
signed by England, France, Russia, Sardinia, and the
Turk. In 1856 England still kept up traces of the
days when the people of Ireland were bondmen on
their own soil, as the people of Thessaly and Bulgaria
are still. In 1877 the dominion of the alien Church
has passed away, and the soil of Ireland has been
set free. In 1856 France was under a blood-stained
tyranny, and her troops held Rome in bondage. In

1877 France is a commonwealth ; Rome is the head of free Italy, and he who figures in that treaty as King of Sardinia is King of the whole ransomed land. In 1856 Nicolas of Russia reigned óver a people of whom all but an exclusive class were bondmen. In 1877 Alexander the Liberator reigns over a people who are not yet politically free, but among whom every man's personal chains are broken. He reigns over a land where the voice of a nation, strong in its renewed life, is heard for the first time as it bids its sovereign march forth to the relief of the oppressed. In all these lands reforms may be wrought and have been wrought. But all the change that one and twenty years have wrought for the lands under Turkish rule is that in 1877 the scorpions of Safvet and Midhat and Edhem, of Selim and Chefvet and Achmet, are felt to be yet harder to bear than the whips of Abd-ul-Medjid were in 1856.

As for the feeble cry that the Christians in those lands are as bad as the Turks, that I have dealt with already in more places than one. All that need be said here is one parting word of wonder and pity at the moral state of those who can rake up and gloat over every fault which long ages of wrong may have caused to stain the glorious uprising of our suffering brethren, while they catch with desperate zeal at every straw which they deem may be twisted to make out a case for their oppressors.(15)

But now comes the last point which we have to argue. Is there after all any clashing in this matter between the duty of England and her interests ? Those who truly love their country, those to whom her honour is dear, those to whom her real well-being is dear, will say that, if duty and interest clash, it is interest that must give way. But it is only the feeblest and shallowest and most short-sighted view of English interests which can persuade men that any English interest will be jeoparded by England doing right. If we can conceive a man from some distant land, able to understand and judge, but knowing nothing of the actual facts of European politics—if we can conceive such an one being told that it was for the interest of an island at one end of Europe that the people at the other end of Europe should go on bearing unutterable wrongs—if he were told that the people of that island had strained every nerve, that they had poured forth their treasure and their blood, to prolong the bondage of those nations —if he were told that it was handed down as the traditional policy of that island that the oppressors of those nations should at all hazards be upheld in their power of oppression—one is tempted to apply the words of the apostle ; Would he not say that ye are mad ? To such an one it would seem the paradox of paradoxes to be told that the wrongs of Bosnia and Crete could in any way promote the interest of England. And the paradox would seem greater still when he heard the way in which the dark saying was explained, when he was told in what way it was that England was supposed to find her interest in the plundered and outraged homes of South-eastern Europe. He would be told that there was another power, another nation, a nation which had never wronged us, but to which we had done deadly wrong, a nation whose advance we thought good to dread and which we thought ourselves specially called on for the sake of our own interest to keep back from winning influence over those lands. He would be told that these lands were struggling for freedom—that in every struggle for freedom they had first looked for help to the home of freedom—that, when they needed protection, it was English protection which they first sought—that, when they had a crown to bestow, it was to an English prince that they first offered it—but that England steadily refused help, steadily refused protection, for fear of increasing the strength of the rival power, and so drove those nations, against their will, to seek at the hands of that rival power for that help and protection which England refused to them.

This is in truth what we have been doing for many years. And to our supposed impartial observer it would indeed seem a strange way of strengthening ourselves and of checking the advance of that rival power. If the man from the distant land spoke his thoughts out openly, he would say, " O fools and blind, you are working in the cause of the power which you wish to weaken. You are doing all that you can to tarnish your own fame, and to brighten the fame of the rival power. You are throwing away the allies who offer themselves to swell your strength, and driving them against their will to swell the strength of your rival." He would perhaps even be tempted to go on and say, " Is this your own counsel ? Is it not rather some device of the very power which you dread ? You tell me that that power is a dark, subtle, intriguing power, a power which has its spies and emissaries everywhere, prying and thrusting themselves into every corner, and everywhere doing the work of that power in secret. Are you sure that you have no traitor in the camp ? are you sure that the policy of which you boast your-selves is not in truth a suggestion of some spy or

emissary of your rival ? Has no such emissary cun-
ningly found out the way to lure you into the path
where your interests will be sacrificed to the interests
of your rival, where your honour will be tarnished and
his honour made to shine brighter ? "

If we look the case fairly in the face, without
troubling ourselves with oft repeated formulæ, it does
indeed seem like madness when we profess to dread
the advance of Russia in South-eastern Europe, and
then by way of checking that advance, do all that we
can to make the nations of South-eastern Europe the
friends of Russia, the enemies of England. We profess
to fear that Russia may add the European dominions
of the Turk to the empire which she has already.
Our way to keep her from adding those lands to her
empire is to drive those lands to seek for annexation
to her empire, as the lesser evil in a choice of evils.
Those lands have not the faintest wish for annexation
to Russia. They are glad of the friendship of Russia,
as they would be still more glad of the friendship of
England. But there is not a man from the border of
Croatia to the border of liberated Greece who wishes
of his own free will to become a Russian subject.
We drive them to wish for it ; we bring about a state
of things which leaves them no choice except the
Russian or the Turk ; and then we turn about, and
wonder and cry out and deem ourselves wronged, and
look on those nations as monsters of wickedness, if,
in the sad choice which we ourselves have forced upon
them, they choose the lesser evil rather than the
greater. If a day ever comes when those lands are
formally annexed to Russia, if a day ever comes
when, without being formally annexed to Russia, they
are brought under such exclusive Russian influence

as to become practically subjects of Russia, the men who have brought all this about will be the men who have held up the Russian hobgoblin before the eyes of England. Foremost among the truest friends of Russia is the man who, when the people of England and the people of Russia were stirred at the same moment by the same high and generous feelings, when the sovereign of Russia was offering us the right hand of fellowship in the noblest of works, had no answer to give in the name of England but brags of insolent defiance, sent forth, not from the council-chamber, but from the banquet. And a trusty, though unwitting, yoke-fellow he has found in the colleague who surpasses all men in stirring heaven and earth to find the means of doing nothing. If a Russian Emperor ever mounts the throne of the New Rome, the men who will have done most to guide him thither will be Benjamin Earl of Beaconsfield and Edward Henry Earl of Derby.

It does indeed seem to be a matter of simple common sense that, if we are afraid of Russian encroachment, of Russian influence in those lands, we ought at once to seize every opportunity of making the people of those lands our friends, every opportunity of teaching them to look to us and not to Russia for help and for counsel in their need. Except during the short moment when the counsels of England were swayed by wisdom and generosity under the rule of Canning, we have done everything that we could to drive the people of those lands to look to Russia as their helper. This strange course is supposed in some mysterious way to be likely to check the advance of Russia and to lessen her influence. There is really some reason to suspect that we have here a result of a confusion which was spoken of in an earlier chapter. It really looks as if this kind of traditional policy largely sprang out of sheer inability to distinguish between Turkey and the Turks. Lord Palmerston, in words worthy to rank with the passage which I before quoted from Sir Henry Elliot, says: " We support Turkey for our own sake and for our own interests. (¹⁶) " The truth is that we do not support Turkey at all; we support the enemy of Turkey, namely the Turk. To support Turkey would be not only a generous policy ; for those who deem it a matter of paramount importance to check the advance of Russia, it would be also a wise policy. To support Turkey ought to mean to support the people of Turkey, to support the nations which inhabit Turkey, to encourage every movement which can give them more strength and more freedom, and thereby to make them a stronger barrier against Russian encroachment, if Russian encroachment is dreaded. But to make Turkey free, strong, national, able to hold her own, able to withstand encroachments from Russia or anywhere else, the only way is to free Turkey from the Turk. In supporting Turkey in this sense, we should be upholding a moral power. In upholding the Turk at the expense of Turkey, we are upholding a power of simple brute force. The power of the Turk can never get beyond brute force ; it hás no moral basis, no moral strength, and the lack of moral strength weakens its physical strength also. The Turk can never bring against Russia or against any other power the full resources of the lands over which he rules. The ruler of any other land can call into the field the full strength of the nation which inhabits the land. But the Turk can never call into the field the full strength of the nations which inhabit Turkey. At the outside, all that he can bring is the strength of the army of occupation which keeps the nations of Turkey down. But he cannot even bring the full strength of the army of occupation; for part of that army of occupation must be employed in keeping down, or rather in fighting against, the subject nations. Its full force therefore can never be brought to act against the invader from without.

We are thus brought again to one of the distinctions which we drew at the beginning. We here see the difference between a land which has a national government and a land which is held down by strangers. The national government is essentially strong; the domination of strangers is essentially weak. When France and Germany were at war, each side had to dread the efforts of the enemy abroad; neither side had any reason to dread the efforts of any enemy at home. Every man in France was ready to fight for France; every man in Germany was ready to fight for Germany. But if Russia went to war with the Turk, the vast majority of the people of European Turkey would at once spring to arms. not to fight for the Turk but to fight against him. The Turk would have to wage war in every corner, not only against the invading army, but against the people of the land which he calls his own. In trying then to support the Turk, we are supporting a thing which is not only wicked, but is in its own nature weak. If we hold that our interest leads us to support Turkey, as a check on Russia, or for any other reason, we must get rid of that which makes Turkey weak, namely the rule of the Turk. In short, duty and interest, if there be any interest in the matter,

do not clash, but both lead us the same way. Duty
bids us set free those suffering nations as an atone-
ment for the wrongs which we have done to them.
Interest, if there be any interest in the matter, leads
us to set them free, in order that South-eastern
Europe may become strong, and may be mistress of
the whole of her own resources, which she never can
be while she is under the foreign yoke of the Turk.

In saying this, I do not put out of sight the inherent difficulties of the case. We cannot call up at
a moment any single power which may at once take
the place of the Turk. We shall have to face the
difficulties which arise from the fact that so many
separate nations dwell in those lands, and that some
of them are unhappily divided by grudges against
one another. In such a case, it would be impossible
to call into being any power which should have the
full national unity and national strength as is pos-
sessed by such a power, for instance, as France.
Such a power has never been in those lands, and it
never can be. That is the natural result of that
permanent distinction of races in those lands which
were spoken of in an earlier chapter. The utmost
that can be thought of, at all events for a long time
to come, would be a number of states united by a
close federal tie. And no one can hope that such
a federation of states would have the strength of
a single national power. But it would be stronger
than the Turk. Jealousies between the several states
would be likely enough, and they would undoubtedly
be a source of weakness. But they would not be
the source of such utter weakness as the necessity
under which the Turk lies of fighting at once against
his enemy without and against the great mass of those

whom he calls his subjects within. But more important still would be the moral power which such an union of states would have, as compared with the wicked rule of the Turk. If Russia, as those who call themselves her enemies say, cloaks all manner of evil designs under the pretext of helping the oppressed, that pretext would be at once taken from her. She has always—I am again speaking the language of her professed enemies—a plausible excuse for interfering in those lands as long as the Turk rules over them. She will have no longer any such pretext as soon as the rule of the Turk comes to an end. Any Russian attack on the Turk can now be coloured so as to have a fair show in the eyes of men; no such fair show could ever be given to an attack on the freedom of any Greek or Rouman or Slavonic land. One favourite fallacy is that, because tributary Roumania and Servia and independent Montenegro have now to look to Russia, and largely to direct their policy by that of Russia, the whole of European Turkey, if it were set free, would in the same way look to Russia. But why are those states now driven to look to Russia? Simply because they have a dangerous neighbour in the Turk, and no helper but Russia offers himself. Take away the Turk, and there would be no longer any necessity for looking exclusively to Russia. Those lands might well look to Russia with a traditional friendship; but they would be released from all necessity of practical dependence upon her.

Again it does seem blindness indeed when those who take up the cause of the Turk strive to serve his cause by drawing the blackest picture of Russian rule that can be drawn, by heaping together every tale, true

or false, that can be found to the disparagement of
Russia. Of the real fallacy of some of these pictures I
have spoken already. But take the doings of Russia
in Poland and Turkestan at the very worst, Russia
would not, for her own interest's sake, deal in the
same way with the people of Bosnia or Bulgaria. She
would not deal with those whose affections it was her
interest to win in the same way in which she deals,
or at least is said to deal, with enemies and revolters.
But set this aside; take the very blackest picture
of Russia that can be drawn. We then ask, whose
concern is it? It is the concern of those who are
playing the game of Russia by letting Russia win
moral influence. It is the concern of those who, by
refusing all other help to the subject nations, are
driving them to seek help from Russia. We who
assert the rights of the subject nations have no wish
to see them annexed by Russia. We have no wish
to see them brought under exclusive Russian influence. They do not themselves wish for such
annexation or for such exclusive influence. Without
believing all that is said against Russia, fully taking
in the difference between Russia now and Russia
twenty years back, neither we nor the people of those
lands themselves believe that Russian annexation or
exclusive Russian influence would be any gain for
those lands. We therefore wish to strengthen those
lands, to strengthen them, if needs be, against Russia,
by freeing them from the Turk. But those who
believe in the extreme blackness of Russia, those who
make no distinction between the comparatively free
Russia of to-day and the enslaved Russia of past
times, are yet more called on to pause than we are
before they give Russia the moral advantage of repre-

senting herself as the one refuge of the oppressed. All that we on the other hand say, all that the nations themselves say, is this. Let us have neither Turk nor Russian; but, if we must choose between Turk and Russian, then let us have Russian. It will be wholly the fault of those who cut off those nations from the hope of anything better than. either, those whose blind policy first drives those nations into the arms of Russia, those who thus do the very work that Russia would have done, and who then turn round and tell us how very black a power it is for whose objects they are themselves steadily working.

If then Russian advance in the South-eastern lands is a thing to be dreaded, it is the party that is always crying out against Russia which is really playing the game of Russia. Our traditional policy, the policy of upholding the Turk against the people of Turkey, gives Russia even physical, and still more moral, advantages which otherwise she could not have. This strange notion of adapting means to ends is of a piece with the glaring inconsistency of many of those who now raise the cry of " Poland." That cry is raised by many who never thought of Poland, whose sympathies were all with Russia against Poland, till they suddenly found out that Poland might be turned into a convenient cry on behalf of the Turk or the Turk's friends. *We* have a right to talk of Poland, if we choose ; and we have a right to talk also of something nearer than Poland. If the Russian hobgoblin ever appears to me as a hobgoblin, it is when I look on the map and see how very closely Russian guns are pointed towards the capital of a people of our own race, our own faith, almost our own language. It is not on behalf of the Turk, not even on behalf of the Pole, but on behalf

of the noble kingdoms of Sweden and Norway, that
Russia is really to be feared, if she is to be feared at
all. We talk about Sebastopol and the Black Sea, about
the danger of Russian fortresses on her own shore,
about the danger of a Russian ship of war being seen
in the Mediterranean. It would have been a worthier
object of European policy to insist that Russia should
withdraw from the isles of Åland. But the two glorious
kingdoms of the North were never thought of till, in
the days of the Crimean war, it was found for a
moment that they too might be turned into a means
for upholding the Turk.([17]) We who speak up for the
victims of the Turk, as we have no special hatred for
Russia, so we have no special love for her. All that
we ask is that Russia may be dealt with on the same
terms as any other European power. We ask that
she may be treated as neither better nor worse than
any other of the powers which make up the European
concert. We do not ask that she should be treated
with greater confidence than any other power; we do
ask that she may not be suspected, thwarted, insulted,
in a way in which we should not suspect, thwart, and
insult any other power. We believe that Russians,
like Englishmen, Germans, Frenchmen, or any other
nation, are neither angels nor devils, but men, capable
alike of good and of evil. We have no great faith in
governments, least of all in despotic governments.
But we have a faith in nations; and we see in the
great uprising of the Russian nation on behalf of its
oppressed brethren one of the noblest movements of
generous sympathy that the world ever saw. And
though we have little faith in governments, we may
now and then have faith in personal rulers. We
cannot look wholly askance at the prince who has
given freedom to his people. We have no love for

X

despots; yet we can reverence a Marcus and an Akbar. And along with the names of Marcus and of Akbar the voice of truthful history will one day place the name of the second Alexander.

After all, when we come to shake off mere vague traditionary fears, it is not easy to see where the real danger to England from Russia lies. No one believes that Russia has any notion of annexing or invading the British Islands. The fear is always for India. Now in those vast lands of Asia the mission of Russia and the mission of England is really very much the same. Russia and England are the two European powers on whom the duty has fallen of carrying European rule into two different parts of the great Eastern continent. England is far more favoured in the lot which has fallen to her share; but the duty which is laid on both the powers is the same. I say the duty; for neither for England nor for Russia can Asiatic empire be thought either a gain or a glory, while for both it is a fearful responsibility. No right-minded man will justify all the acts either of Russia or of England in their Asiatic dominions; but both have the same general mission, the mission of keeping nations at peace which cannot be kept at peace, except under the rule of some power stronger than themselves. And both alike seem to be carried on by a kind of irresistible destiny, which makes each annexation lead to some further annexation. The dominions of the two powers may some day meet; and, when they do meet, it will be of the highest moment for the world that they should meet as friendly neighbours, and not as enemies. To be always stirring up ill blood between the two powers before that time comes is as foolish as it is wicked.

As for the notion that a Russian occupation of Constantinople would interfere with our road to India, a glance at the map is enough to lay that hobgoblin. It is in Egypt, not at Constantinople, that our interest in that matter lies.

A more plausible ground of alarm is sought in the alleged danger from the Mahometans of India, or at least the Sonnite part of them, if we deal otherwise than very respectfully with their supposed spiritual head at Constantinople. But those who know the Indian Mussulmans best say that they really care very little for their supposed Caliph, that they most certainly will not revolt on his behalf. And one would really think that a devout Mussulman would have very little respect for the Ring which deals with Caliphs so lightly, and by whom the Successor of the Prophet may any morning be set aside. From the point of view of Mussulman orthodoxy, one would rather expect to see a non-juring schism arise on behalf of Murad, or to hear of miracles wrought at the tomb of the martyred Abd-ul-Aziz. One thing is certain, namely that, if the Indian Mahometans are likely to revolt on behalf of their Caliph, the way to show them that revolt is useless will be to show that their Caliph is no object of fear to us. Firm dealing with the Turks will have a good moral effect through the whole of Islam. Many Mussulmans believe that the Sultan is really the lord of all European powers. It is time to undeceive them.

But, after all, it is only a very shallow way of looking at things which really believes that Russia has any thought of annexing Constantinople. To gain exclusive influence in the South-eastern lands, even to place a Russian prince on the throne of Constantinople, are

X 2

possible and rational objects of Russian policy. Not so
the annexation of the Imperial city. Russian statesmen are wise enough to know, if English statesmen
are not, that the New Rome cannot change her nature.
The Queen of Nations, seated at the junction of two
worlds, can never give up her Imperial calling. Her
empire may be shut up within her own walls; but
she can never be subject. In the last agony of her
Latin Emperor, in the last agony of her restored
Greek Emperors, she was still the seat of rule, ready
again to become the seat of wider rule under stronger
masters. Constantinople cannot be ruled from Saint
Petersburg, neither can Saint Petersburg be ruled
from Constantinople. The Romanoff may reign in
New Rome; the Russian cannot. For the Romanoff
on the throne of New Rome would cease to be
Russian. A cautious student of politics not long
ago proposed to place on that throne a prince who
might be said to be English, German, and Russian
all at once Once on that throne, he would not long
remain either English, German, or Russian. The
magic of the spot would assert its right. That magic
has touched the Turk himself. What Abd-ul-Hamid
may deem himself to be it is hardly worth while to
ask; but Mahomet the Conqueror deemed himself
to be Cæsar as well as Sultan. An European prince
on the throne of all the Constantines could not remain
merely English, merely Russian; he would again be
the Cæsar of the Eastern Rome, and nothing less.

One word more. It may be doubted whether there
is much to be said, from the point of view either of
morals or of politics, for these excessively long-sighted
views of things. The interests of England and the

interests of Russia may possibly clash at some far
distant day. Therefore, in order to make matters
worse when that day does come, we are to spend all
the time till it comes in making a sore and rubbing at
it, in doing everything to stir up jealousy and ill will
between the two countries. We are to suspect and
thwart Russia in every way that we can think, to force
her to become an enemy by treating her in all things
as an enemy. This is an over-wisdom which is nearly
allied to folly. It is really only because Russia is so far
off that we can venture on such a course. We should
soon feel the effect if we dealt with a nearer power,
say France or Germany, in the same way. Diplomatists themselves cannot tell the future for certain.
On the eve of a great war or revolution they generally
tell us that things are remarkably tranquil. When
they do come face to face with a great movement, all
that they can think of is to suppress it. In all this
there is an odd mixture of a longsightedness which
lays plans for generations to come, and a short-
sightedness which cannot see the clearest facts of
to-day and to-morrow. These very elaborate calcu-
lations leave out two important elements in the
reckoning ; they leave out the will of God and the
will of man. A single man, great whether for good
or for evil, a Mahomet, a Buonaparte, a Garibaldi, is
enough to upset all their reckonings. A really great
man, one who is righteous as well as great, has a
higher wisdom. Such an one knows that the truest
prudence is to do the immediate duty of the moment,
believing that so doing will clear the way for the duty
of the next moment, whatever that duty may prove
to be. We are sometimes twitted with proposing to
drive out the Turk without having drawn out any

exact schemes as to what is to take the place of the
Turk.   The answer is that, by taking the first steps,
the steps which are our manifest duty, we shall learn
what are to be the next steps.   The greatest deeds
that have ever been done, never would have been
done, if their doers had waited till they had drawn out
their journals beforehand for seventy or for seven
years to come.   If William the Silent had waited to
strike for the freedom of the Netherlands till he had
the Articles of Union of the Seven Provinces ready
in his pocket, he would have waited for ever.   If
Washington had waited to strike for the freedom of
the American colonies till the Federal Constitution
had settled exactly what form of government was to
be put in the place of King George the Third, he too
would have waited for ever.   But one thing we may
foretell beforehand.   In one case we may write our
journals beforehand.   If we make up our minds to
bring no real force to bear upon the Turk, if we give
him Midhat's year of grace, or any kind of grace at
all, then we may write our journals beforehand, and
we may fill them beforehand with difficulties and
complications, with atrocities and insurrections, with
commissions and conferences, with notes and proto-
cols, with all things which arise out of the Sultan's
relations with his subjects, and out of the feebleness
and blindness which refuses at once to strike the blow
which shall put those relations to an end.   To do
nothing, to give a year of grace, may be a noble diplomatic triumph ; in the eye of common sense it simply
means to leave every thing to be done over again.

We have thus seen what the Turk is, what he has
done, how he has grown, how he has decayed, how

his victims have risen up against him, and how we
have dealt between him and his victims. We have
seen what is our duty to the brethren whom we have
wronged ; we have seen that our interest and our
duty do not clash. The policy of 1827 should be the
policy of 1877. " Pax in terris hominibus bonæ
voluntatis." Peace and friendship, frank and cordial
union, among all powers that will join to cleanse
Europe from its foulest wrong, its blackest shame.
But not peace where there is no peace—no partnership, no paltering, with evil—no year of grace which
will only be another year of broken promises—but
united action in the noblest of causes, united action
to free the East from bondage, and to clear the West
from dishonour. Let us once more remember what the
enemy is. It is the common enemy of mankind. If
he no longer sacks Otranto or bombards Vienna, it
is not because he lacks the will, but merely because
he lacks the power. Where he still holds power, his
power is in no way better, it is rather in all things
worse, than it was when he sacked Otranto and bombarded Vienna. What the Turk, his Sultan and his
Sultan's following, then were, that they still abide,
in all except the dazzling greatness which half leads us
to forget that their greatness was wholly a greatness
of evil. The Turk came into Europe as a stranger
and an oppressor, and after five hundred years he
is a stranger and an oppressor still. He has hindered the progress of every land where he has set his
foot. He has brought down independent nations to
bondage ; by bringing them down to bondage, he has
taught them the vices of bondmen. He has turned
fertile lands into a wilderness, he has turned
fenced cities into ruinous heaps because under his

rule no man can dwell in safety. Wherever his rule has spread, the inhabitants have dwindled away, and the land has day by day gone out of cultivation. While other conquerors, even other Mahometan conquerors, have done something for the lands which they conquered, the Ottoman Turk has done nothing for the lands which he has conquered; he has done everything against them. His dominion is perhaps the only case in history of a lasting and settled dominion, as distinguished from mere passing inroads, which has been purely evil, without any one redeeming feature. The Saracen in South-western Europe has left behind him the memorials of a cultivation different from that of Europe, but still a real cultivation, which for a while surpassed the cultivation of most European nations at the same time. But the Turk in South-eastern Europe can shew no memorials of cultivation; he can show only memorials of destruction. His history for the five hundred years during which he has been encamped on European soil is best summed up in the proverbial saying, "Where the Sultan's horse-hoof treads, grass never grows again."

NOTES.

(1, p. 251.) Correspondence respecting the affairs of Turkey p. 197.

(2, p. 251.) Euripides, Orestes, 479.

(3, p. 252.) The most open profession of the doctrine that right goes for nothing is to be found in a book of scraps, called "England's Policy in the East" by a "Baron Henry de Worms." The Baron is constantly speaking of *we* and *us*, as if he were speaking of some nation. but he does not tell us on behalf of what nation he is entitled to speak. In p. 15 a little knowledge of the Hebrew Scriptures might have stood the Baron in good stead.

(4, p. 262.) The story will be found in full in Mr. Denton's Christians in Turkey, 17-22.

(5. p. 268.) This singular argument will be found in a pamphlet called "The Turks, Their Character, Manners and Institutions, as bearing on the Eastern Question, by H. A. Munro-Butler-Johnstone, M.P." It comes in the very first page.

(6, p. 269.) Correspondence respecting the Conference at Constantinople p. 56.

(7, p. 273.) Correspondence respecting the Conference at Constantinople, p. 243.

(8, p. 273.) See Jireček, *Geschichte der Bulgaren*, 556, 558. Midhat seems to have had a special fancy for hanging children.

(9, p. 282.) See Denton, Christians in Turkey, p. 131.

(10, p. 283.) Correspondence respecting the Conference, p. 170.

(11, p. 285.) I argued in favour of the annexation of Bosnia by the Austro-Hungarian Monarchy in the Fortnightly Review as long ago as December 1875, on the very ground which the friends of the Turks did not think of till some months later.

(12, p. 287.)   Correspondence respecting the Conference, p. 243. "Let a fixed time, say a year, be granted to the Porte for carrying out the reforms now being *inaugurated*, and at the end of that period let the Ambassadors report whether they were being fairly executed or not."

(13, p. 290.)   See Lord Salisbury's letter in p. 271 of the Correspondence respecting the Conference, where this scene is described as I have said in the text.   But nothing like it can be found in the protocol of the Meeting, p. 341.   How are these things edited ?

(14, p. 292.)   Perhaps the worst will be found in the book of the Baron Henry de Worms mentioned already.   I know not on what evidence the Polish stories rest ; but, even if we believe the worst, the remarks in the text still apply.

(15, p. 294.)   On the subject of mutual "atrocities," to use the word which has become technical, Trikoupês remarks candidly and reasonably, i. 305. Ed. i., p. 286. Ed. ii.   "Τοιουτοτρόπως Χριστιανοὶ καὶ Τοῦρκοι ἐφάνησαν ἐπὶ τῆς ἐπαναστάσεως πολλάκις μαθηταὶ ἑνὸς καὶ τοῦ αὐτοῦ σχυλείου, ἀλλὰ σχολείου Τουρκικοῦ διδάσκοντος νὰ παιδεύωνται διὰ πταίσματα, ἄλλων οἱ μὴ πταίσαντες."

(16, p. 299.)   Lord Palmerston says, in a letter to Lord Aberdeen, Life of Lord Palmerston, in September 1853, ii. 44, "It would be easy to shew that strong reasons political and commercial make it especially the interest of England that the integrity and independence of the Ottoman Empire should be maintained." At p. 46 he says, "We support Turkey for our own sake and for our own interests ; and to withdraw our support, or to cripple it, so as to render it ineffectual, merely because the Turkish government did not show as much deference to our advice as our advice deserved, would be to place our national interests at the mercy of other persons." This is the doctrine of Sir Henry Elliot put forth somewhat less unblushingly.   Right and humanity are put out of sight ; they are not, as with Sir Henry Elliot, brought in to be insulted. It is curious, in reading Lord Palmerston's letters, to see how little, with all his sharpness, he understood the real facts of South-eastern Europe.   There is a curious letter in Vol. ii. p. 212, in which he seems to be just getting a little glimmering of the real state of things at the time of the accession of Abd-ul-Aziz.   Earlier in September 1853 (see Vol. ii. p. 37) he seems really to have believed in Turkish reforms. The Russian troops were then in the Principalities.   "Let him [the Russian Emperor] be satisfied, as we all are, with the progressive liberal system of Turkey, and let him keep his remonstrances till some case and occasion arises and calls for them.   At present he has not been able even to allege any oppression of the Christians, except that which he himself practises in the Principalities."   In a letter, so late as 1853, addressed to Baron Brunow, Vol. ii. p. 230, we get the usual talk about Russia stirring up insurrections and the like, especially in Bosnia. Did Lord Palmerston really fancy that it needed Russians or anybody else to stir up insurrection there, among either Christians or Mussulmans?

(17, p. 305.) It is a speaking illustration of this real danger, if it be true, as has just been stated in the papers, that the King of Sweden and Norway is seeking an alliance with the Turk.

THE END.

LONDON: R. CLAY, SONS, AND TAYLOR, PRINTERS, BREAD STREET HILL, QUEEN VICTORIA STREET.

WORKS BY EDWARD A. FREEMAN, D.C.L., LL.D.

THIRD EDITION, WITH NEW PREFACE.

HISTORY AND CONQUESTS OF THE SARACENS.
Six Lectures. Crown 8vo. 3s. 6d

HISTORICAL AND ARCHITECTURAL SKETCHES;
CHIEFLY ITALIAN. With Illustrations from Drawings by the Author.
Crown 8vo. 10s. 6d.

HISTORICAL ESSAYS. Third Edition. 8vo. 10s. 6d.

HISTORICAL ESSAYS. Second Series. 8vo. 10s. 6d.

THE GROWTH OF THE ENGLISH CONSTITU
TION FROM THE EARLIEST TIMES. Third Edition. Crown 8vo. 5s.

GENERAL SKETCH OF EUROPEAN HISTORY.
Fifth Edition, enlarged, with Maps, &c 18mo. 3s. 6d.

COMPARATIVE POLITICS. Lectures at the Royal
Institution. To which is added, THE UNITY OF HISTORY. The Rede
Lecture at Cambridge in 1872 8vo 14s

DISESTABLISHMENT AND DISENDOWMENT:
WHAT ARE THEY? Crown 8vo. 2s. 6d.

HISTORY OF THE CATHEDRAL CHURCH OF
WELLS, AS ILLUSTRATING THE HISTORY OF THE CATHEDRAL
CHURCHES OF THE OLD FOUNDATION Crown 8vo. 3s. 6d.

OLD ENGLISH HISTORY. With Five Coloured Maps.
Fourth Edition, Revised. Extra fcap. 8vo 6s.

HISTORY OF FEDERAL GOVERNMENT, FROM
THE FOUNDATION OF THE ACHAIAN LEAGUE TO THE
DISRUPTION OF THE UNITED STATES. Vol. I. GENERAL INTRO
DUCTION—HISTORY OF THE GREEK FEDERATIONS. 8vo. 21s.

MACMILLAN AND CO. LONDON.

In Five Vols. 8vo price £4 19s.

MR. EDWARD A. FREEMAN'S HISTORY OF THE
NORMAN CONQUEST OF ENGLAND: ITS CAUSES AND ITS
RESULTS.

Vols I, II. THE PRELIMINARY HISTORY AND THE REIGN OF
EADWARD THE CONFESSOR Second Edition. 8vo. Price 36s

Vol. III.—THE REIGN OF HAROLD AND THE INTERREGNUM
Second Edition 8vo. Price 21s.

Vol. IV.—THE REIGN OF WILLIAM THE CONQUEROR. Second
Edition. 8vo. Price 21s.

Vol. V.—THE EFFECTS OF THE CONQUEST. 8vo. Price 21s.

"A history in which vast and varied learning is combined with indomitable
patience, scrupulous accuracy, great literary skill, a fine historical style, and a fire of
eloquent enthusiasm, which abundantly justify our estimate of the first volume, that
it is by far the greatest history of our day."—*British Quarterly Review*

"These volumes bear witness to his patient and vast research, and to an accuracy
which has very seldom been surpassed or equalled, a history at once vivid, accurate,
and from its own point of view exhaustive."—*Fortnightly Review.*

Oxford : Printed at the Clarendon Press, and
PUBLISHED BY MACMILLAN AND CO. LONDON,
Publishers to the University.

794521

Printed in Great Britain by
Amazon.co.uk, Ltd.,
Marston Gate.